PICTURING THE PAGE

Illustrated Children's Literature and Reading under Lenin and Stalin

Based on sources from rare book libraries in Russia and around the world, *Picturing the Page* offers a vivid exploration of illustrated children's literature and reading under Lenin and Stalin – a period when mass publishing for children and universal public education became available for the first time in Russia. By analysing the illustrations in fairy tales, classic "adult" literature reformatted for children, and wartime picture books, Megan Swift elucidates the vital and multifaceted function of illustrated children's literature in repurposing the past.

Picturing the Page demonstrates that while the texts of the past remained fixed, illustrations could slip between the pages to mediate and annotate that past, as well as connect with anti-religious, patriotic, and other campaigns that were central to Soviet children's culture after the 1917 Revolution.

MEGAN SWIFT is an associate professor of Russian Studies at the University of Victoria.

Picturing the Page

Illustrated Children's Literature and Reading under Lenin and Stalin

MEGAN SWIFT

UNIVERSITY OF TORONTO PRESS
Toronto Buffalo London

ISBN 978-1-4426-4715-2 (cloth)   ISBN 978-1-4426-6742-6 (EPUB)
ISBN 978-1-4426-1531-1 (paper)   ISBN 978-1-4426-6741-9 (PDF)

Library and Archives Canada Cataloguing in Publication

Title: Picturing the page: Illustrated children's literature and
reading under Lenin and Stalin / Megan Swift.
Names: Swift, Megan, 1971– author.
Description: Includes bibliographical references and index.
Identifiers: Canadiana (print) 20200176307 | Canadiana (ebook) 20200176315 |
ISBN 9781442647152 (cloth) | ISBN 9781442615311 (paper) |
ISBN 9781442667426 (EPUB) | ISBN 9781442667419 (PDF)
Subjects: LCSH: Children's literature, Soviet – Illustrations. |
LCSH: Illustrated children's books – Soviet Union – History. |
LCSH: Illustration of books – Soviet Union – History. | LCSH: Children's
literature, Soviet – History and criticism. | LCSH: Children – Books and
reading – Soviet Union – History.
Classification: LCC NC985.S95 2020 | DDC 741.6/4209470904 – dc23

This book has been published with the help of a grant from the Federation
for the Humanities and Social Sciences, through the Awards to Scholarly
Publications Program, using funds provided by the Social Sciences and
Humanities Research Council of Canada.

University of Toronto Press acknowledges the financial assistance to its
publishing program of the Canada Council for the Arts and the Ontario
Arts Council, an agency of the Government of Ontario.

 **Canada Council Conseil des Arts
for the Arts du Canada**

 ONTARIO ARTS COUNCIL
CONSEIL DES ARTS DE L'ONTARIO
an Ontario government agency
un organisme du gouvernement de l'Ontario

Funded by the   Financé par le
Government   gouvernement
of Canada   du Canada   **Canadä**

 MIX
Paper from
responsible sources
FSC   FSC® C016245
www.fsc.org

Contents

Contents

Illustrations

Figures

Colour plates (section follows page 104)

Acknowledgments

Frank Swift (1944–2012), my father, planted the seed of my lifelong fascination with Russia when I was ten years old, and he would have been extremely proud to see this book come to fruition. My mother, Nancy Swift, has also been a big supporter of my studies and my work, including looking after my children so I could travel to do research, and offering well-timed snacks to revive me after long flights back from Russia.

At the University of Victoria, British Columbia, I have been fortunate to have a wonderfully gifted colleague and office neighbour, Serhy Yekelchyk, who has helped and advised me at various important junctures in my life and on this book. The university supported the research and writing of this book through multiple internal research grants and two faculty fellowships at the Centre for Study in Religion and Society – both of which facilitated conference papers and articles that grew into chapters. I would also like to thank the University of New Brunswick and the Eileen Wallace Fellowship in Children's Literature for their generous support of this work in 2012–13 and 2013–14.

A number of librarians have gone above and beyond the call of duty in tracking down rare editions of books that I desperately wanted to study. Dave Pretty in the Interlibrary Loan office at the University of Victoria, Slavic librarian Jan Adamczyk at the University of Illinois (Urbana-Champaign), and Slavic librarian Thomas Keenan at the Princeton Fireside Library deserve special mention.

My colleague Alison Rowley has been a steadfast advocate of this work from the beginning and not only encouraged me when I needed it the most but also made valuable comments at conferences, generously sent me rare materials from her collection, and read and commented on the entire manuscript. I would also like to thank Mark Lipovetsky, who read and commented on parts of this manuscript with his usual intelligence and kindness, and Annie Gérin, who offered both intellectual and human guidance.

I was lucky to work with wonderful student research assistants like Milya Zakirova in Saint Petersburg and Moscow, and Morgan Pulsifer and Kate Ehle in Victoria, who helped me with manuscript preparation.

I am grateful to the two editors with whom I worked at University of Toronto Press, Richard Ratzlaff and more recently Stephen Shapiro, for their professionalism and pep talks.

This book has been published with the help of a grant from the Federation for the Humanities and Social Sciences, through the Awards to Scholarly Publications Program, using funds provided by the Social Sciences and Humanities Research Council of Canada.

Finally and closest to home, I am thankful every day for the love and encouragement of my husband, Jay. I dedicate this book to our daughters, Bella and Lola.

Abbreviations

BGTO	Be Ready for Labour and Defence
Dal'stroi	Main Administration for Construction in the Far North
Detgiz	Children's Section of the State Publishing House
Gosizdat	State Publishing House
GTO	Ready for Labour and Defence
Komsomol	Young Communist League
LEF	Left Front of Arts
Narkompros	People's Commissariat of Enlightenment

PICTURING THE PAGE

Illustrated Children's Literature and Reading under Lenin and Stalin

Introduction: Picturing a New Childhood

"And what is the use of a book," thought Alice, "without pictures?"
— Lewis Carroll, *Alice's Adventures in Wonderland* (1865)

Alice tumbled down the rabbit hole in part because her older sister's book could not hold her attention: it contained no illustrations. After the 1917 Russian Revolution, illustrations to a newly emerging Soviet children's literature, new book art produced to accompany the works of the past, and repurposed illustrations from the pre-revolutionary period became powerful mediums because of their immediate impact on young readers and their ability to convey critical messages about the values and world-view of the Soviet state to the upcoming genera-tion. The extraordinary book art for young readers that emerged in the first three and a half decades of Soviet power filled a deficiency that was noted by scholars of pre-revolutionary children's literature, like Petr Dul'skii who wrote in 1916: "Contemporary Russian illustrations in publications for children are richly represented in books exclusively for the very youngest age; books for the intermediate age are less illus-trated with good images, and books for the senior age, with few excep-tions, *mostly do not have decent graphics.*"[1]

Post-revolutionary book illustrations, with their bold and vibrant images, corrected this shortcoming, and by the 1920s Soviet book art for children was inspiring and was guiding Western artists via Soviet book exhibitions in Europe and America.[2] An early expert wrote in 1927 that Soviet literature for children and adolescents had become as impor-tant from the "depictive [*izobrazitel'nyi*] side" as from the literary side.[3] Elena Danko, a critic and children's author, went even further in the early 1930s, writing that "the artist of the word in general has clearly lagged behind the artist of the image."[4] As it was vital to the state that

Soviet values be carried forward by the new generation, children's literature was a well-resourced state priority from the 1920s to the early 1950s, under Lenin and Stalin, the first two Soviet leaders, and garnered the talent of its best designers and artists.[5] Cultural policy in this period, however, powerful and far-reaching as it was, was anything but monolithic. The cultural campaigns of the 1920s, 1930s, 1940s, and early 1950s, as they touched upon the past, classics, fairy tales, magic, religious belief, and a host of other compelling themes and images, were dramatic, rapid, and above all inconsistent. Furthermore, from 1917 until the inception of the Children's Section of the State Publishing House in 1924, and even after this date, there was considerable overlap in the consumption of illustrated literature by adult, adolescent, and child readers. Illustrated versions of fairy tales, for example, may have been consumed by all three. Therefore, the careful reconstruction of the interconnections between reading and literature for children, book illustrations more broadly, the cultural contexts that produced them, and their relationship to the literature curriculum in public schools, which is presented in this book, forms necessarily a story of dramatic evolution, flux, and change.[6]

Importance of the Study and the Approach

The story of this book began in one of the reading rooms of the St Petersburg Public Library, where I was researching Alexander Benois's illustrations to one of the most eerie and chilling works of Russian literature, Alexander Pushkin's *The Bronze Horseman*.[7] Suddenly I noticed that Stalin-era editors had carefully abridged Benois's illustrations and republished these officially repudiated modernist images for an unexpected audience – the young adolescent reader. Puzzled, I ordered every illustrated version of *The Bronze Horseman* held by the library. I discovered that this classic work had made its first appearance as *children's* reading under Stalin, but the four other Stalin-era illustrated versions of *The Bronze Horseman* led to new questions. Why had illustrated editions been commissioned from three different artists in the same year, 1949? And what could possibly explain the optimistic depictions of St Petersburg, a city beset by calamity and tragedy in Pushkin's work, by the artist Mikhail Grigor'ev? The answers led to the Stalin-era Pushkin anniversaries, to siege commemoration and its suppression, and to the placement of *The Bronze Horseman* at the grade-eight level of the public school curriculum, which are described in chapter 3.[8] Clearly children's illustrations were not on the periphery of mass political culture; they were positioned at the very heart of it. This discovery was the first seed of a book about illustrated children's literature from the Russian Revolution of 1917 to the death of Stalin in 1953, or, specifically, a book that looks at the multifaceted function of illustrations: as the visual articulation of new book art, but also as an important agent in repurposing the works of the past, reorienting them towards the child reader, mediating the past to signal and connect with political and cultural themes of the day.

A number of excellent studies of illustrated children's literature exist, both in English and in Russian, and are dealt with in the literature review found at the end of this introduction. My book distinguishes itself from them because, in addition to exploring the picture book (*knizhka-kartinka*), I also investigate lesser-known illustrated works for the child and adolescent reader: many of the illustrations found in this study have not been reproduced since the 1920s, 1930s, or 1940s. The book is also set apart by its method, which traces a single work in multiple illustrated versions rather than making a chronological study of the major artists or artistic schools of the period. *Picturing the Page* has been invigorated by the voice of the writers, critics, pedagogues, and state representatives from the 1920s to the 1950s. It is grounded in primary sources from libraries and rare book collections, including the public school textbook *Russian Literature* for the years 1936–53 and children's journals and newspapers, but most importantly the period illustrations themselves. I offer close readings of texts, analysis of book art, and commentary on cultural history, and I show how each illuminates and complicates the other. To my knowledge, this is the only study of children's illustrations that includes the illustrations and literature curriculum found in the public school textbook of the Stalinist period. The images and texts from the 1920s to the 1950s are the bedrock of my study, joined by a rich analysis that places them in the context of their production. In order to create a comprehensive snapshot of the period, I have taken into account a variety of source material, including prominent public debates, the diverging opinions of powerful bureaucrats, and textbooks and teachers' manuals.

This book is aimed at specialists in the field – cultural historians, literary scholars, art historians, folklorists, and curators and librarians of children's collections – but it has been written to be enjoyed by the educated non-specialist as well.

The New Lexicon

The extent to which childhood represented a crucial Soviet state interest is expressed in one of the most striking mottos of the 1930s: "Thank

Figure 0.1 "Thank You, Dear Stalin, for a Happy Childhood!," the 1936
poster by Viktor Govorkov (see also colour plate 1). Photograph ©
Fine Art Images / Heritage Images.

You, Dear Stalin, for a Happy Childhood!"[9] The Viktor Govorkov poster emblazoned with this motto, which featured smiling schoolchildren
offering gifts and embraces to Stalin, was created in 1936 (fig. 0.1).[10]
Redolent of Stalin-era hyperbolic excess, the principle at the heart of a
motto expressing a fundamental state commitment to education and
upbringing, and an attentiveness to children as a crucial demographic,
is nonetheless shared by both the Lenin and the Stalin eras. The point
was not just that a Soviet childhood should be happy but that it should
be an entirely new kind of childhood, supported by cultural products
that reinforced new values through themes like collectivism, labour,
modernization, and internationalism. Book illustrations were fundamental to the creation of a visual language that was expected to convey
such complex and abstract themes to a young audience. The creation of
this language, however, was formidably difficult and remained a work
in progress until at least the mid-1930s.[11] It had to be created out of a
turbulent polyphony of official state messages, public campaigns, and
responses by book artists. Furthermore, the creators of this visual language emerged from radically different dialect groups. These included

illustrators originating in avant-garde groups like the suprematists (El Lissitzky), futurists (Vladimir Mayakovsky), and constructivists (Olga and Galina Chichagova, Vladimir Lebedev, Alexander Rodchenko); book artists who had been associated with the pre-revolutionary, neo-romantic, retrospectivist World of Art group but then began to work in the increasingly realist Soviet publishing industry for children (Yury Annenkov, Vladimir Konashevich, Aleksei Kravchenko); the neo-folklorists of the 1930s (Dmitry Butorin, Yury Vasnetsov); and the artists working in the children's book in the late 1930s, when socialist realism was fully consolidated, and through the war years (Adrian Ermolaev, Aleksei Pakhomov, Nikolai Tyrsa).[12] As Sergei Oushakine has recently argued, the visual language of the Soviet children's book was fashioned in a piecemeal process of selection, assemblage, fabrication, and creation of secret codes.[13] This book is neither a study of the attempts to circumvent state authority by artists nor a study of the positive or negative reception of this art; rather, it follows the modulations of that turbulent conversation between state and cultural agents that resulted in a new graphic language and a new way of depicting the world. If, as Oushakine has shown, a new visual lexicon was eventually created for the children's book by reducing the revolution and its Marxist idiom to a limited set of schemes like good and bad, and yesterday and today, thus homogenizing the radicalism of the revolution, then this occurred principally in the newly created book art of the Soviet period, and specifically in picture books for the youngest readers.[14] Scholarship has not yet dealt with the emerging visual language of another extensive section of children's reading and literature – works from the past for an older, usually adolescent audience that had been newly illustrated by Soviet artists. Here the visual language had different modulations. It may have been schematized according to prescriptive state priorities about "what is good and what is bad" (to quote the title of a children's book by Mayakovsky from 1925); however, these evaluative criteria were constantly shifting. As I show in the following pages, the magical fairy tale was "bad" in the 1920s but "good" in the 1930s, while classic authors like Dostoevsky were "good" and then "bad." Furthermore, the posterization that Oushakine identifies as a guiding artistic element in the Soviet picture book, a reference to artist and illustrator El Lissitzky's theory that the revolution had torn, enlarged, intensified, and vivified book art, took place to a much lesser extent when illustrations were required to interact with texts from the past.[15] Therefore, I posit that there were actually multiple visual languages at play in illustrated children's reading and literature. This study deals not with the abstract themes of Soviet children's literature (like heroism of labour or the war with nature) but, at a more essential level, with the concrete images (like worker, peasant, or mother) that made up the "words" of this evolving new lexicon.

Illustrated Children's Literature and Children's Reading

It is important to distinguish between illustrated children's literature, which is designed for and consumed by the child reader, and the more amorphous category of illustrated children's reading. The picture book, for instance, with its large ratio of colourful illustrations and small proportion of text easily comprehensible by the pre-schooler and the early reader, is unequivocally the domain of illustrated children's literature.[16] The picture book was certainly a revolutionary medium under Lenin and Stalin, as well as a venue for some of the most innovative and attractive graphic art of the period. Oushakine argues that the art of the picture book created a new visual language that spoke in the idiom of the revolutionary poster and represented a kind of "intra-cultural translation" that mixed codes in an attempt to assemble and convey Marxist ideas to the child reader.[17] While the art of the picture book – from the much less-examined war-time period – forms approximately one-third of my study and is the focus of part III, this book also deals with a more ambiguous subject: works like Pushkin's *The Bronze Horseman* that were targeted beyond an audience of adult readers to *become* illustrated children's literature, usually for the first time, in the Soviet era and hence are more properly termed "illustrated children's reading." "Children's reading" is a term that has an important connection to both pre-revolutionary children's publishing and one of the earliest proponents of Soviet children's literature. *Detskoe chtenie* (Children's reading) was a journal published from 1869 to 1906, a childhood favourite of both Lenin and his wife, Nadezhda Krupskaia.[18] The term re-emerged in the Institute of Children's Reading (Institut detskogo chteniia), established by children's librarian, scholar, and activist Anna Pokrovskaia in 1920, which placed an emphasis on the child's reaction to works presented in storytelling circles. In this context "children's reading" was understood as both the activity of the child and the study of the interrelationship of the child and the book, a process in which the child was to be consulted about favourite works and deferred to as an arbiter of taste.[19] A more recent use of the term, in this case pluralized as "Children's readings" (*Detskie chteniia*), comes from the present-day journal dedicated to Russian children's literature and suggests the totality of texts consumed by the child reader as well as the academic study of those texts.

Organization of the Book

In the first part of the book, "Fairy-Tale Nation," I look at the prominent debate over the fairy tale in the 1920s and trace its outcome in the 1930s. I then explore the visual text of two pre-revolutionary fairy tales that were radically updated, reoriented to the child reader, and brought into line with the contemporary Soviet cultural agenda through their illustrations. The second part of the book, "The Afterlife of Russian Classics," deals with the task of what Maurice Friedberg memorably called putting "Russian classics in[to] Soviet jackets," and examines how illustrations facilitated that process.[20] Republished "classics," which are defined narrowly here as the great works of nineteenth-century Russian literature, were a notable area of contention for the state or, specifically, how to position the great works of the past for an upcoming generation of little comrades. As with fairy tales, there was a shift in policy between the 1920s and the 1930s, but how the state attitude shifted depended on which great author was under question. I have chosen to look at illustrations to two of the greatest classics of Russian literature – Pushkin and Tolstoy, each of whom was handled quite differently in his Soviet incarnation. Finally, the third part of the book is dedicated to an exceptional chapter in the history of Soviet children's literature – the war-time period from 1941 to 1945 – and here I turn from children's reading to children's literature, specifically picture books for the youngest reader. While full-length studies exist of the Soviet picture books of the 1920s and 1930s, much less scholarly attention has been given to the war-time picture book. I introduce two of the first illustrated books for readers under five years of age, published after the German invasion, and then look at how war-time picture books connected not only with child readers but also with their parents, the first generation of Soviet readers and the generation now called upon to defend the nation.

Distinguishing illustrated children's reading from children's literature is an important starting point for contextualizing the first two sections of this book, which deal with pre-revolutionary fairy tales and classics. Illustrated literary fairy tales and classics originating from the imperial era were often not intended primarily for child audiences; they were multi-audience and multi-purpose works.[21] In the Soviet period these works were directed to the child reader *specifically*, though not exclusively, for the first time. Partly this was a matter of timing: a mass publishing industry for children came into existence only in 1924 with the Children's Section of the State Publishing House and when the public school curriculum, in which classics were made to play an important role, became universally available to Soviet students in 1930. Many of the illustrated works treated in parts I and II of this book – Ershov's *Little Humpbacked Horse* (1834), Pushkin's *The Bronze Horseman* (1833), and Tolstoy's *Anna Karenina* (1873) – were issued by children's publishing houses for the first time under Lenin or under Stalin. Illustrated children's reading, then, is a broad category that encompasses the distinct category of illustrated children's literature and includes those texts that are extended beyond the borders of their original, usually adult, readership. But the reorientation to a child audience and the importance of conveying a Soviet world-view to young readers required a new way of perceiving works of the past, and illustrations often came to serve as the means by which a transformative shift took place.

This striking shift becomes clear in the case studies of children's reading presented in chapters 1–4, which look at a single work and how it was successively illustrated over three and a half decades, through often contradictory waves of cultural policy. Reading and viewing a single story in multiple illustrated versions is an unusual way to experience a work of literature, and for that reason it freshens our perception of the sea-changes taking place in key images like the peasant, the priest, the countryside, the tsar, mothers, children, and the nation. These represented a new lexicon from which a Soviet visual language of children's culture was constructed. I selected illustrated works by canonical authors that contained powerful and controversial images and connected to the campaigns that were central to children's and often adults' culture in this period. A satirical fairy tale like *The Tale of the Priest and His Worker Balda* reached a new importance in the 1920s and 1930s. Thanks to a virulent anti-religious campaign and the onset of collectivization in 1928, the status of the tale's villain and hero, the priest and the peasant, was under constant renegotiation. Chapter 1 shows the astonishing transformation, in illustrations, of the worker Balda from underdog to hero and traces how he became younger, stronger, blonder, and more vengeful at the same time that the state was attempting to project a message of plenitude and calm about a collectivized countryside plunged into turmoil.[22] In chapter 2, I explore how the repurposing of a deformed fairy-tale horse into an attractive sidekick linked the pre-revolutionary little humpbacked horse to Stalin's heroic era of flight and the hobby known as *stranovedenie* (studies of the country). The great author Pushkin himself, as well as the city of St Petersburg, came under renegotiation in illustrated editions of the Russian classic *The Bronze Horseman* that were aimed at adolescent readers of the Stalin era, and is addressed in chapter 3. In chapter 4 the changing role and expectations for mothers is explored through Soviet illustrations to Tolstoy's *Anna Karenina*. I place the study of how classics were republished alongside their treatment in the textbook published after 1936 for public schools called *Russian Literature* and the textbook of the same name produced for teacher's training colleges. The result is a fascinating reconstruction of the editing and pruning process that took place when the classics were presented to young adolescents through the school system.

In part III the focus shifts from illustrated children's reading to illustrated children's literature and the war-time picture book. While Steiner, Blinov, and other scholars of children's book art choose to close their historiography at the end of the 1930s, arguing that state suppression of children's writers and artists and the strictures of socialist realism compromised the once startling and original voice (and vision) of Soviet children's illustrations, I decided to include illustrations from the war-time period 1941–5 *because* they represent a break and a turning point in the story of children's illustrated literature.[23] Mayakovsky's *Let Us Take the New Rifles*, a children's poem first published in 1927 but repurposed during the war in mass illustrated editions that harked back to the preparations for national defence under Lenin, is dealt with in chapter 5. The issue of war-time sequels to favourite illustrated works of the 1920s is addressed in chapter 6, which focuses on Samuil Marshak's *Mail* (1927) and *War-Time Mail* (1944).

In part III and the conclusion I return to the emergent theme of the first two parts: the importance that illustrated literature and reading had in positioning the past for the child reader. I argue that in war time an important turning point was reached in the sense that children's literature was finally able to close the circle and address its own (Soviet) past, refer to its *own* created canon, and connect with its own first readers. Again, this was partly a matter of timing: twenty-four years had passed between the 1917 revolution and the onset of the war. The first generation of Soviet child readers who had consumed the picture books of the 1920s were now reading those books to their own children. The war-time period was important because it actualized the canon of Soviet children's literature and in this sense moved beyond the problem of how to mediate the imperial past and into a period where children's literature could link to a created past of its own.

Negotiating the Past

Illustrations played an important role in bridging the gap between yesterday and today, in patrolling and annotating the past while highlighting the achievements brought about by the advent of Soviet power. The literature of the past was a territory at once objectionable and obligatory

for the early framers of Soviet children's literature. While the creation
of new works for little comrades was at the top of the agenda, the process of adapting and conveying communism to children, as Oushakine
has argued, was a process that was "far from simple, straightforward,
or quick. There was no available legacy to build on, or even a clear
narrative to express."[24] If the picture-book art of the 1920s was eventually able to create a vivid ideological language in which to express
the values of the state, its output was still not sufficient to meet the
growing needs of a new mass market of child readers whose education
and upbringing were deemed of fundamental importance to the state.
As Anatoly Lunacharsky, the influential first commissar of education
put it, "every citizen of our Union" should understand the "enormous
societal importance of the problem of bringing our children up to be
new people."[25] Although some campaigners in the state and the literary
avant-garde advocated jettisoning the literature of the past altogether,
in practice the fairy tales and classics of the imperial period entered
Soviet life as a necessary, if ideologically flawed, supplement to newly emerging children's literature. The place and correct proportion of
works from the past on Soviet reading lists was the subject of vitriolic
debate in the 1920s. The role of Lenin's wife, Nadezhda Krupskaia, in
the campaign for the exclusion of the magical fairy tale from children's
bookshelves is dealt with in part I. The past provided both a sounding-
board and a corrective for new works, prompting Pokrovskaia to con-
clude in 1927 that "post-revolutionary children's literature arose, first
and foremost, as a contrast to the old, pre-revolutionary literature."[26]
She also noted that, ten years after the revolution, successful novelistic
models for young adolescent readers were far from plentiful. The issue
of children and contemporaneity was at the forefront of debates among
critics, pedagogues, and state representatives in the first decade of
Soviet power. Viktor Shul'gin expressed the state's sense of the hostile,
uneasy relationship between yesterday and today when he claimed, in
the foreword to a 1928 mass poll on the attitude of children towards
the revolution, that "the child lives by the present, the child is part
of the present, this is why it worries, torments and cheers him, why he
is interested in it. The past is incomprehensible to him, difficult. He can
understand the past only by proceeding from the present."[27]

In fact, Soviet illustrations to carefully selected fairy tales and classics
of the past, published for child readers by children's publishing houses
for the first time, emerged as an expedient way to proceed from the
present into the past. The texts themselves were fixed, but illustrations
proved to be a malleable medium that could begin to imbue works with
new meanings, make ideologically appropriate shifts and adjustments,

and connect to the values of the present. Illustrations could be the voice of today sounding from the pages of yesterday.

Parameters of the Study

Any study of illustrated children's literature needs to define what is understood by "childhood," although this definition will necessarily be an approximate one since childhood is a culturally determined category that shifts in different time periods and with the prioritization of different cultural values. Still, it is possible to say how the Soviets delimited childhood, and its commensurate stages, because we have the evidence provided by their own categorizations, although amorphous borders still remain. Under Stalin the publishing industry produced children's books for "preschoolers" (up to five years of age; sometimes one to five), "children of the youngest age [deti mladshego vozrasta]" (five to ten), "children of the intermediate age [deti srednego vozrasta]" (ten to fifteen), and "children of the senior age [deti starshego vozrasta]" (fifteen to eighteen), suggesting that after age eighteen one was no longer a child. The mass Soviet youth group Pioneers was for children aged ten to fifteen years, suggesting that after age fifteen one became an adolescent or youth. The mass youth group Komsomol (Young Communist League), which began at age fourteen, ran all the way up to age twenty-eight, suggesting that one was still a youth in one's mid-twenties. For purposes of military enlistment, childhood ended at age eighteen, but during the war the upper limit was lowered to fourteen, in practice if not officially.[28] This study uses the term "childhood" to denote a broad category of pre-adulthood stretching from about age three to approximately age eighteen; within this general frame, adolescence is defined as stretching from the age of about fourteen to the age of eighteen. This book addresses the reading and illustration-viewing practices of both child and adolescent readers, and to some extent of parents who read books to preschoolers and children of the "youngest age" and were directed to make appropriate reading selections through published lists called "What to Read to Children" or "What I Should Read" (fig. 0.2).[29] The period under study encompasses 1917 through to 1953, under the first two Soviet leaders, Vladimir Lenin and Joseph Stalin. In the 1920s, Soviet culture focused on breaking free of the past, and this was reflected in the flourishing of avant-garde literature and art and in a censorious if somewhat contradictory attitude towards traditional forms like the fairy tale. In the 1930s, that same past was reclaimed and elevated, leading to a revival of both the fairy tale and the classics. Beginning with Soviet Russia's entry into the Great Patriotic War in

Figure 0.2 "What I Should Read" poster with list of recommended children's literature, produced by the State Publishing House in 1928 (see also colour plate 2). Reproduced with permission of Willamette University's Hatfield Library Archives.

1941, children's literature responded to a new and stark reality by dealing with the theme of invasion in books for very young readers and by creating a pantheon of child martyrs for adolescent readers.

The 1920s to the 1950s was a crucial period of formation and consolidation of Soviet power, as well as unprecedented strengthening of the cultural institutions responsible for children's upbringing and education. A *Pravda* article by L. Kormchii of February 1918 announced that "the children's book as a major weapon for education must receive the widest possible distribution."[30] The Lenin era saw the birth of a state publishing industry for children with the establishment of the Children's Section of the State Publishing House (Detgiz in 1924), later transformed into Detskaia literatura (Children's Literature), the monolithic publishing house, in 1932. In 1936, leading children's writer Samuil Marshak noted that the circulation of children's books had skyrocketed from the tens of thousands to the millions and now penetrated "into the very depths of the country, to those places where the children's book has never been before."[31] Indeed, the 1930s saw accomplished what had only been a dream of the 1920s: a mass state system of education and communication with children. Under Stalin, universal public school education was created, in 1930, and the first public school textbooks for Russian literature were produced regularly beginning in 1936. This book deals with the period from the 1920s to the 1950s because of its seminal importance to the birth and flourishing of Soviet children's reading.

Soviet Children's Literature, Culture, and Book Art in Review

Russian and Soviet children's literature has fairly recently become the object of serious scholarly attention, but a number of new publications and projects suggest the emergence of a fertile field. The editors of the journal *Detskie chteniia* (Children's readings) noted in their foreword to its first issue in 2012 that as late as the 1990s research into children's literature, although a crucially important area of literary studies, remained largely undeveloped.[32] Despite the publication in 2003 of *The Children's Collection: Articles on Children's Literature and the Anthropology of Childhood* (*Detskii sbornik: Stat'i po detskoi literatura i antropologii detstva*), which represented a landmark "first special edition about children's literature created by philologists" and dealt with the history and reception of the children's book, pedagogy, and the representation of children in literature, its editorial collective called for work addressing important areas that still remained to be studied, including the state and social institutions that directed children's literature in the Soviet period, the history of censorship in children's literature, and the evolution of pedagogical ideas from the imperial to the Soviet and post-Soviet periods.[33] As late as the 1970s and 1980s, children's literature and culture rarely appeared as the main subject of a monograph in the West. Those infrequent publications include Elena Sokol's *Russian Poetry for Children* in 1984 and Felicity Ann O'Dell's *Socialisation through Children's Literature: The Soviet Example* in 1978, which looked at the importance of *vospitanie*, a concept encompassing upbringing, moral education, and character development. New contributions to the field emerged in the collection *Russian Children's Literature and Culture* edited by Marina Balina and Larissa Rudova in 2008, which included essays that explore Soviet children's literature, theatre, comics, and film in the period 1917–91.

Catriona Kelly's *Children's World: Growing Up in Russia, 1890–1991* (2007) represents a monumental study of childhood and adolescence,

its public institutions and private family side. Kelly's contribution
retrieves children's culture from the sidelines and reassimilates it into
the grand narrative of Soviet cultural history. Two more recent works,
which focus on war-time children's culture, similarly advocate for the
recuperation of children's culture into a central narrative of Soviet
political culture. Olga Kucherenko's *Little Soldiers: How Soviet Children
Went to War, 1941–1945* (2011) and Julie K. deGraffenreid's *Sacrificing
Childhood: Children and the Soviet State in the Great Patriotic War* (2014)
both argue for the profound assimilation of children's culture into the
war effort and war-time consciousness. Ben Hellman's 2013 *Fairy Tales
and True Stories: The History of Russian Literature for Children and Young
People (1574–2010)* makes a comprehensive study of children's publishing, in both books and journals, over five centuries. Sara Pankenier
Weld shows in her 2014 monograph *Voiceless Vanguard: The Infantilist Aesthetic of the Russian Avant-Garde* that children's culture played a
significant role for the avant-garde of the early Soviet period in that
primitivists, futurists, formalists, and other artistic groups appropriated the child's perception and voice in their own ground-breaking art.
The approach of my study shares much common ground with Weld's
2018 book *An Ecology of the Russian Avant-Garde Picturebook*. This "eco-
logical" approach focuses upon the "complex interactions" of Soviet
children's books with their "literary, artistic, historical and political
environment."[34]

The study of children's book illustrations was recently reinvigo-
rated by Sergei Oushakine's 2016 article "Translating Communism
for Children: Fables and Posters of the Revolution," which uses the
methodology of contemporary translation studies to analyse the situation evolving in early Soviet children's book art. Oushakine argues
that the process of adapting communism for children involved the
selection and assemblage of various codes capable of conveying dia-
lectical materialism to a mass audience that was only provisionally
literate. As mentioned, the new language that was developed "tore"
up the traditional book and "posterized" it into a graphic language
that, through its "gaze-appeal" (*nagliadnost'*) could boldly and directly
transmit revolutionary ideas to child audiences.[35] The book art of the
Lenin and Stalin period itself has recently been displayed in several
vibrant art-catalogue-style studies. An excellent one is Valerii Blinov's
2005 *Russkaia detskaia knizhka-kartinka, 1900–41* (The Russian children's
picture-book, 1900–41), which includes the work of the major book artists from the birth of the genre until Russia's entry into the war. The
recent, lavish publication of Vladimir Semenikhin's two-volume study,
Kniga dlia detei 1881–1939: Detskaia illiustrirovannaia kniga v istorii Rossii

1881–1939; Iz kollektsii Aleksandra Lur'e (2009, The book for children: Illustrated children's books in the history of Russia, 1881–1939) brings to light fascinating period and avant-garde children's illustrations from the private collection of Russian emigré Alexander (Sasha) Lurye. Another valuable recent publication that, like Semenikhin's work, puts a greater emphasis on showcasing period illustrations than subjecting them to scholarly analysis, is *Inside the Rainbow: Russian Children's Literature, 1920–1935; Beautiful Books, Terrible Times* (2013), edited by Julian Rothenstein and Olga Budashevskaya, which looks at the illustrated books put out by the influential but short-lived Raduga (Rainbow) Publishing House. Lovers of children's book art should also be directed to *Schili-byli=shili-byli: Russische kinderbücher, 1920–1940* (2004), edited by Peter Noever, and *Adventures in the Soviet Imaginary: Children's Books and Graphic Art* (2011), edited by Robert Bird. Any admirer of book art will be impressed by the rich and colourful array of illustrations reproduced in these studies.

In spirit, this book is closest to Evgeny Steiner's *Stories for Little Comrades: Revolutionary Artists and the Making of Early Soviet Children's Books* (trans. 1999), an excellent study of children's illustrations that combines cultural and historical context with analysis of art and graphic design. Regrettably, Steiner's study is limited only to constructivist illustrations and breaks off with the demise of that movement, in the 1930s. My work continues a vibrant conversation among specialists that was begun with, and owes a debt to, the Soviet scholars Andrei Chegodaev and Ella Gankina, who produced the first, important but now dated, works on Soviet illustrated children's literature. Chegodaev's *Puti razvitiia russkoi sovetskoi knizhnoi grafiki* (1955, The path of development of Russian Soviet book graphics) and Gankina's *Khudozhnik v sovremennoi detskoi knige* (1977, The artist of the contemporary children's book) and *Russkie khudozhniki detskoi knigi* (1963, Russian artists of the children's book) are tributes to the gifted book artists who were their friends and colleagues.

I hope that *Picturing the Page*, with its large selection of vibrant images from the period, will be enjoyed by specialists, enthusiasts, and students alike.

PART I

Fairy-Tale Nation

The fairy tale became a highly contested genre under Lenin and Stalin, undergoing a dramatic reversal of fortune over the course of the 1920s and 1930s.[1] Vilified in the 1920s for romanticizing the tsarist era, the fairy tale was restored in the 1930s in the interests of glorifying a heroic national past. This cultural volte-face created an intensity and confusion to the debates over the framing of fairy-tale policy in the early decades of Soviet Russia. At stake was a powerful tool to cultivate the mind of the young reader and future citizen, and Soviet cultural leaders were acutely aware of the importance of reaching this audience, and their parents, with apposite propaganda devices. Illustrated children's literature offered "one of the most powerful mediums for revealing and propagandizing the idea of socialism," but the fairy tale of the past, with its magical world-view, came under intense scrutiny as an appropriate weapon in the state's ideological arsenal.[2] The fate of the fairy tale was taken as critical by the differing stakeholders, including state leaders, parents who earnestly followed published lists such as "What to Read to Children," and, of course, Soviet children themselves, but fluctuations in cultural policy around the fairy tale were extreme in the 1920s and 1930s.[3]

The attack on the fairy tale began in earnest in the early 1920s. Perhaps its most well-known critic was Lenin's wife, Nadezhda Krupskaia, who was immensely influential as deputy commissar of enlightenment, and chair of the Central Committee on Political Education, and who put together an important manual that led to the exclusion of fairy tales from library shelves.[4] Other opponents of the fairy tale included prominent literary and cultural groups like LEF (Left Front of Arts), RAPP (Russian Association for Proletarian Writers), and Proletkult (Association for Proletarian Culture), who came out against folklore, calling it "a remnant of patriarchal ideology."[5] In 1924 a resolution was

Figure I.1 Nikolai Lapshin, illustration to *How Baba Yaga Was Destroyed* (1918), an early Soviet tale in which the most terrifying Russian fairy-tale villain, the witch Baba Yaga, is eradicated once and for all. Illustration in coloured linocut wood print; text by Nadezhda Lyubavina. (See also colour plate 3.) Reproduced with permission of the State Russian Hermitage Museum.

taken on the fairy tale at the third All-Russian Congress of Preschool Education, calling it "a hindrance in the development of materialist thinking."[6] The Russian *skazka* (fairy tale) included three discrete types, all of which were objectionable to Krupskaia on different ideological grounds. Most undesirable was the magical fairy tale (*volshebnaia skazka*), which promoted a non-realist perspective in children. The folk-tale (*narodnaia skazka*) was problematic because it reflected the reactionary world-view of the Russian peasantry. Equally controversial was the literary fairy tale (*literaturnaia skazka*), a product of writers from the nobility and therefore representative of an obsolete, conservative point of view.[7] Beloved Soviet children's writer, translator, and critic Kornei Chukovsky looked back at the 1920s, the period of fiercest debate over the fairy tale, in his book *Little Children* (1928; retitled, in its third edition, *From Two to Five*, 1933) and characterized the battle in terms of an epic struggle waged between ideologues like Krupskaia, on the one hand, and artists like himself and the writer Maxim Gorky, on the other. Chukovsky's account, however, needs to be taken with a grain of salt because it was written after Krupskaia had already lost the battle and over-emphasizes his own role as a framer of fairy-tale policy. Krupskaia is portrayed as holding an extreme materialist position, mirrored by that of parents in a 1929 Kremlin kindergarten group who believed that fairy tales were inappropriate as tools for upbringing because they promoted a culture of fantasy that was fundamentally alien to revolutionary values. Chukovsky positions himself as the leader of the opposition in this debate, as an artist who recognized that fantasy was an inalterable developmental stage and that, in a world purged of published fairy tales, children would unquestionably invent their own.[8] This point of view, that the fairy tale was not simply a cultural product but a state of mind, would be developed with far-reaching consequences during the Stalinist era. In point of fact, Chukovsky overstates Krupskaia's hard-line position on the fairy tale. Although Krupskaia was a proponent of progressive realist art and repeatedly spoke about her belief that mysticism and fantasy were harmful to the developing mind of the young Soviet citizen, she was by no means an opponent of the fairy tale, full stop.

In 1926, in a speech to an All-Russian conference on the children's book, Krupskaia spoke about the difficulty of dealing with the literature of the past and with fairy tales "steeped in mysticism, belief in God and miracles, propagating monarchism, national enmity [and] chauvinism."[9] Quite simply, much of the content of the traditional fairy tale was ideologically incompatible with the cultural goals of the new worker's state. In a letter to Gorky of 1932 she once again underlined the fact that she was not against the fairy tale per se: "The fairy tale that helps to understand life, – yes. I'm absolutely for it. The mystical fairy tale and story – not under any circumstances."[10] But did the fairy tale, when purged of mysticism and magic, spell in essence the end of the fairy tale? In reality, Krupskaia wielded her influence to promote a modest diet of folk- and fairy tales for children, including many of the oral tales collected by Alexander Afanasiev and published in eight volumes in 1855–67, some fables

(*basni*) by Ivan Krylov, and tales by Dmitry Mamin-Sibiriak, Lev Tolstoy, and Hans Christian Andersen.

The status of Pushkin, Russia's national bard and author of many of
the nation's best-known and most beloved poems, stories, plays, and
fairy tales, was undecided and rather tenuous under Lenin. Krupskaia's
"quiet purge" of Pushkin's works from public and school libraries during this period made it difficult for child readers to access his work.[11] At
the same time, Pushkin was commemorated by members of the artistic
and academic intelligentsia in 1921 and 1924 celebrations. Strangely, in
this topsy-turvy atmosphere, Pushkin scholarship matured for the first
time into a fully grown academic specialty, thanks largely to a Soviet lift
on imperial-era censorship, making the period 1900–30 a golden age for
Pushkin studies.[12]

It is in the context of this unsettled background for the father of the
literary Russian fairy tale that Krupskaia's public campaign against
the magical fairy tale took place. The battle encompassed much more
than the Pushkin problem, however; it had to do with the fundamental question of how Soviet children should be raised as readers and
shaped as cultural consumers. Both Chukovsky and Krupskaia were
avid theoreticians of child behaviour and development, but they
approached the subject from opposing points of view. Krupskaia was
an adherent of pedology, an educative theory that held sway from the
early 1920s to the early 1930s and was characterized by Chukovsky as
a group of "miserable theoreticians of child-guidance, contending that
fairy tales, toys and songs were useless to children of proletarians."[13]
Pedologists insisted that all children's literature be "class-conscious,"
and their point of view on the traditional fairy tale is best summed up
by a representative book title from 1928: *We Are against the Fairy Tale.*[14]
The program of the pedologists was bolstered by other groups promot-
ing materialist culture such as the avant-garde First Working Group of
Constructivists Productional Cell for Children's Books.[15] Artists from
this group, like Olga and Galina Chichagova, dedicated themselves to
a modern alternative to the fairy tale and, in addition to illustrating
several "production books" that demystified the workings of the modern world for children, designed a 1925 poster titled *Down with the Old
Types of Mystical and Fantastic Fairy Tales in Children's Books!! For the New
Children's Book!!*[16]

Krupskaia and Chukovsky both spent most of the 1920s working
tirelessly for the Soviet child. While Krupskaia did high-profile work,
directing the efforts of children's librarians and library collections
and overseeing children's presses and journals, Chukovsky wrote witty
and enchanting poems for children, many of which would become the

best-loved picture books of the Soviet and post-Soviet child's library. In essence, Krupskaia's approach to child development was to shape and direct, and Chukovsky's was to observe and record.[17] Krupskaia's top-down approach, with the state determining and then recommending appropriate material for child readers, overturned the work of the Institute of Children's Reading and its first director, Anna Pokrovskaia. Pokrovskaia emphasized a child-centred approach to the field, studying children's responses to stories and poems in storytelling hours and polling children on *their* favourite works, to create lists of suggested reading. But the concept of the child reader as an arbiter of taste came under attack in 1922, and by 1923 the Institute of Children's Reading had been renamed and placed under the aegis of the Commissariat of Enlightenment (Narkompros), of which Krupskaia was deputy commissar.[18] On one point, however, all these adversaries were in absolute agreement: children's literature in the early revolutionary period was of an unacceptably low quality, and it would be the task of the new Soviet era to focus attention, funding, and expertise on the child reader. This goal was, to a large extent, fulfilled in the 1920s and 1930s as publishing houses for children were established for the first time in Russia, and beautifully illustrated children's books were made available for mass consumption.[19]

In fact, it was neither Krupskaia nor Chukovsky but writer and activist Maxim Gorky who set the course for the fairy-tale policy that was consolidated under Stalin. A well-respected author, editor, and publisher, Gorky had a vast influence on cultural policy in the Leninist and early Stalinist years. Unlike Krupskaia, however, he was a proponent of the fairy tale of the past. He did not share her qualms about ideologically incorrect content, because, for him, written fairy tales showed the influence of centuries of oral tales that were authentically the work of the "labouring masses." Nor did he object to magical content, seeing flying carpets as a sign of man's yearning for technology and mastery of the natural world in order to lighten the load of labour.[20] In this sense Gorky saw the goals of the revolution and the goals of the fairy tale as connected, or rather he understood the revolution as having fulfilled the yearnings encapsulated in the fairy tale by turning flying carpets into airplanes and magical potions into helpful medicines. Gorky's take on the fairy tale anticipated a concept that would be relentlessly repeated under Stalin: "We were born to make the fairy tale come true." This line from a song called "The March of the Aviators," written in 1923 but elevated to immense popularity during the 1930s, in turn anticipates the famous Stalinist motto – and reflection of totalitarian culture – of the 1930s: "The Fairy Tale Has Become Reality."

Readers familiar with Gorky's role as the architect of socialist real-ism, the mandatory literary style for publishing authors in the Soviet Union, unveiled at the First All-Union Congress of the Writers' Union in 1934, might be surprised by the proportion of his speech devoted to the fairy tale during this momentous congress.[21] Moreover, the central position of children's literature in Stalinist society was underlined by the co-report given by well-known children's author Samuil Marshak, who had become the editor of the Children's Section of the State Publishing House in 1924. For Gorky, folk-and fairy tales, including ancient myths and legends, were the only authentic record of the dreams and aspirations of the labouring masses. These proletarian aspirations, he argued, were lost in the "high literature" that reflected the ideology of the ruling classes.

Gorky praised the fairy tale's "flights of whimsical fancy" that "spring from the achievements of labour," and anticipated the worship of hero-workers (Stakhanovites) of high Stalinism by calling the fairy tale the source of the "most profound, striking and artistically perfect types of heroes."[22] These observations were not fashioned in honour of the congress but were a reiteration of the position held by Gorky on the fairy tale throughout the 1920s.[23] His comments at this high-profile event did, however, signal that his stance had prevailed over Krupskaia's.

Writing Out the Magical Fairy Tale

One result of Krupskaia's public scourging of the traditional fairy tale was that it created an aesthetic environment in the first decade follow-ing the revolution that encouraged inventive and experimental fairy-tale material.[24] One of the earliest tales of the period, *How Baba Yaga Was Destroyed* (1918), was dedicated to discrediting a terrifying villain of Russian folklore once and for all. Baba Yaga, a hag who flies through the air in a mortar and lives in a hut standing on chicken legs deep in the forest, appears in countless traditional stories and tales. In many versions, heroes and children who find themselves in her hut have to defend themselves from being devoured, but in the 1918 story by Nadezhda Lyubavina, a plucky Soviet boy dispatches this enemy by declaring that he no longer believes in her. No match for this practi-cal Soviet world-view, Baba Yaga disappears, never to frighten children again. In the *lubok* (woodcut) illustration by Nikolai Lapshin, Baba Yaga is shown trying to snatch the child, who easily defends himself with a raised, victorious fist (fig. I.1). Lapshin's flattened, two-dimensional composition and use of the woodcut tie this work both to the traditional

folk form of the *lubok* and to the neo-primitivist aesthetic then prominent in the Russian avant-garde. Further, the dominant colour fields of
black and white enhance the thematic association of black-handed Baba
Yaga as an evil character with the Soviet boy – appearing white in negative space – as the good hero.

Constructivist book art with its admiration for technology dominated
the new Soviet children's book in the 1920s, and "synthesism" between
word and image became a hall-mark of the new book art for children
under Lenin.[25] Words and pictures came together to create a whole
new fairy-tale realm of colourful, concrete objects from the child's contemporary world. The "production books" created by poet Nikolai
Smirnov and artists Olga and Galina Chichagova for the First Working Group of Constructivists Productional Cell for Children's Books
revealed the mysteries of the machine world to their young audience,
with titles like *How People Travel* (1925), *For Children about Newspapers*
(1926), and *Where Do Dishes Come From?* (1926). Leading constructivist
artists like Alexander Rodchenko lent their talents to explicitly political
children's books like *The Childhood and Schooldays of Ilych* (1925), about
Lenin's childhood, by Lenin's sister Anna Ulyanova, and *The Homeless
Commune of the OGPU* (1928), about the good works of the secret police
in creating working communes for homeless children.

By 1929, urban mothers were being urged to hone their skills as folk-
and fairy-tale storytellers in special courses offered by the Department
of Children's Reading in the Institute of Methods of Pedagogy. After
the years of suspicion around the fairy tale under Lenin, the language
of the fairy tale was now considered crucial for transmitting a love of
nature and the simplicity of village life to city children who were living "in the close quarters of overfull apartments, in the noise of street
life." Meanwhile, during the new storytelling hours at libraries, clubs,
schools, and city squares, urban storytellers also offered themes closer
to the daily life of the city child: "machines, machine operators, fire-
men, chauffeurs, Red Army soldiers."[26]

The Repression and Resurgence of Magical Thinking

Perhaps the most crucial and entirely unforeseen consequence of the
battle for the fairy tale in the 1920s was the uncovering of magical thinking as an explosive cultural category that could be developed by Stalinist cultural leaders beyond the borders of children's literature. In their
battle over the fairy tale Krupskaia and Chukovsky foregrounded magic as the single most contentious element of the debate. Magical content was anathema to Krupskaia, her measuring stick determining the

traditional fairy tales that would be permitted or purged as she shaped the new canon of children's literature. In the 1926 article "On the Question of the Children's Book," Krupskaia insisted that children's literature must be "realistic in the extreme," following her guiding principle of "no blue cows or green dogs."[27] Such a utilitarian approach demanded that the fairy tale show real life "as it is," protecting the child from such harmful possibilities as dying and coming back to life.[28] It was this prohibition on magical content that Chukovsky found most objectionable in Krupskaia's campaign against the traditional fairy tale in the 1920s.[29] For him, magical thinking was an unavoidable developmental stage best characterized by the eight-year-old boy who kept going to see the movie *Chapaev* in the hopes that one more viewing might help avert the death of the hero.[30] While theorists like Anne Wilson have proposed that magical thinking emerges as a projection of the hero's or heroine's deepest wishes and desires onto the narrative, Hugh Crago argues that magical thinking is in fact a reflection of the prelogical mind of the child reader.[31] This is the developmental stage in which wishing you are invisible by closing your eyes is enough to make you disappear.[32]

Thanks to Krupskaia, Chukovsky, and a public battle for the fairy tale, magical thinking was tagged in the 1920s as a volatile, subversively persuasive element of the fairy tale. Krupskaia believed that she could eradicate this "harmful" psychological state in proletarian children by creating a literature that was deeply realistic and reflective of the "real world." While both Western and Soviet scholarship have since found with Chukovsky that magical thinking is a childhood stage that cannot be diverted, with or without fairy tales to read, it is Stalinist culture that seems to have appreciated most deeply that magical thinking, as a way of seeing and understanding the world, is not just for the child reader.

Anne Wilson argues that magical thought tends to "erupt" in societies that foreground rationalism and materialism and that magical rites involving initiation and sacrifice become appealing in societies that have gone through rapid urbanization and change, leaving individuals with a need for belonging and membership.[33] Marxist, atheist, Leninist Russia was precisely the kind of society that emphasized the rational and material. The official break with Russian Orthodoxy in 1917, Stalin's forced restructuring of agricultural practices through collectivization in the countryside, and the rapid mass industrialization of the five-year plans beginning in 1928 left Russian culture vulnerable to the upsurge of magical thinking. There is a deep connection between the public suppression of magical thought in fairy tales, and in culture generally, in the 1920s and the eruption of magical thought in stories and mass media by the mid-1930s. During the Great Terror (1936–8) print media was mobilized to tell a story of the "enemy of the people" that was presented to the public using fairy-tale structures. In her 1978 study of Soviet socialization and children's literature Felicity O'Dell recounts an article in an April 1938 edition of the children's journal *Murzilka*, titled "Three Cheers for the Soviet Secret Service," which deals with the heroic efforts of Soviet secret police chief Nikolai Yezhov in dealing with Right Opposition members Nikolai Bukharin, Alexei Rykov, and Mikhail Tomsky. As O'Dell points out, what is remarkable here is not just the appearance of this topic in a children's journal but the fact that its black-and-white fairy-tale telling of events, featuring kindly NKVD chief Uncle Yezhov and three wicked adversaries, is virtually indistinguishable from the telling of the story in adult publications like *Pravda*.

In other words, fairy-tale logic and magical thinking were becoming the dominant cultural categories for adults to decipher political events in the 1930s, and, at the same time, adult political themes were finding their way increasingly into children's literature via fairy-tale narratives. In Arkady Gaidar's popular 1935 children's novel *The Tale of the Military Secret, Malchish-Kibalchish and His Solemn Word*, the boy hero is tasked with fighting and unmasking enemies of the people. He must remain in an ever-vigilant state of war, remaining true to the cause, overcoming physical discomforts through heroic sacrifices, up to and including his own death. In Stalin-era narratives like these, the boundary between the magical and the real, the possible and the impossible, and the child and the adult was repeatedly violated by the fact that "fairy tales" analogous to *The Tale of the Military Secret* appeared regularly as serious news on the front pages of *Pravda* and *Izvestiia*.

Katerina Clark has shed light on how the use of folkloric and fairy-tale elements in the literature and print media of the 1930s created a "fantastic age" out of an "ethos ... charged with fantastic symbols."[34] Mark Lipovetsky calls this "the profound assimilation of the fairy-tale mentality by Soviet ideological discourse." He believes that Soviet culture seized upon the "utopian aspect of the fairy tale" and put it to use in the service of nourishing totalitarian ideology.[35] But the ground was prepared for this onslaught of Stalinist magical thinking in public discourse by its *erasure*, or at least attempted erasure, in the utilitarian 1920s. Thanks to Krupskaia's efforts, the public suppression of magical thinking took place at the highest levels and on a number of effective fronts. Libraries were mobilized to become what Denis Kozlov has called "disciplining agencies, vigilantly pruning their collections, guarding access to printed matter and monitoring public taste."[36] In the state-run publishing industry, editors similarly safeguarded Leninist cultural exigencies by removing the word "magic" from the title of such well-known works as Vladimir Propp's *Morphology of the Folktale* (originally titled *Morphology of the Magical Folktale*) in 1928.[37] With its public cultural campaign aimed at suppressing magical thought, Lenin-era Russia created a vulnerable emptiness into which the mass "fairy-tale mentality" of the Stalinist state could surge. By the mid-1930s the state had seized upon fairy-tale thinking as a compelling way to enthral, entice, and persuade its "children," the Soviet public. The appearance of the slogan "The Fairy Tale Has Become Reality" can be understood as an eerily self-reflective moment of the state's acknowledgment that the battle lines drawn in children's literature under Lenin had become the battle lines defining an entire culture under Stalin.

In the next two chapters I look at the astonishing progression of images in two magical fairy tales from the tsarist era that were able, for different reasons, to elude Krupskaia's ban: Alexander Pushkin's *Tale of the Priest and His Worker Balda* (1830) and Petr Ershov's *Little Humpbacked Horse* (1834). Both works rose to immense popularity in the period of the 1920s to the 1950s, when they were reimagined by Soviet-era illustrators. The successive reinvention of key figures such as the priest, the peasant, the tsar, and the magical horse shows how children's reading and literature constructed a new visual lexicon, connecting to important shifts in cultural policy and mediating the past to come in line with the priorities of the present.

Chapter One

The Poet, the Priest, and the Peasant

The Tale of the Priest and His Worker Balda (1830) stands out among Push-kin's fairy tales because of its simple peasant labourer hero, its biting anti-clerical satire, and the fact that the tale's negative portrayal of the priest made it unpublishable during Pushkin's lifetime. But it was precisely the depiction of a stand-off culminating in a "worker's" triumph over a church authority figure that made the work appealing to Lenin-era editors and publishers, even at a time of debate over the role of the fairy tale in a socialist state, and despite a substantial removal of Pushkin's works from public and school libraries in the 1920s. The opportunity to connect to two burning issues of the post-1917 era – the anti-religious campaign and the role of the peasant – transformed *Balda* into a timely classic. Its illustrated editions can be read as a site of negotiation between the values of the imperial past and those of the Soviet present, particularly in the depictions of its two central characters, the peasant and the priest.[1] A sur-vey of successive illustrated versions ranging over half a century shows that the priest's fortune fell in accordance with the ferocity of the post-1917 anti-religious campaign, necessitating his portrayal as an overt vil-lain that was, at times, skinny, intellectual, fat, cringing, cowardly, or old (fig. 1.1). Rather than depicting a figure whose authority was overturned, as pre-revolutionary illustrations tended to do, Soviet iterations showed the priest's power as already diminished from the outset. In contrast, the figure of the peasant, who had been shown as roughly equivalent to the priest in age and dim-wittedness in both pre-revolutionary and Lenin-era illustrations, suddenly became a strikingly young, vigorous, and advantaged adversary after 1928. Paradoxically, the Stalin-era renditions of a strong, healthy farm worker emerged at the same time that the Soviet countryside was being violently collectivized. If the Russian fairy tale represented a version of "the past," then Soviet illustrations were able to draw an idealized vision of socialist transformation upon the familiar

Figure 1.1 V. Spassky, alternative cover to Pushkin's *The Tale of the Priest and His Worker Balda* (1830), published as a double issue with Demian Bednyi's Sovietized sequel, *The Tale of the Farm Labourer Balda and the Final Judgment* (1919). (See also colour plate 4.) Author's collection thanks to a gift from Dr Alison Rowley.

landscape of that past. Illustrations of these two politically charged figures, the priest and the peasant, unambiguously followed the modulations of the campaigns to consolidate state atheism and restructure rural Russia, resulting in long-lasting shifts in the way that readers viewed this tale. The period 1917–53 entrenched a visual reversal of fortunes for the figures, a legacy still indelibly marked into today's versions of Pushkin's peasant and priest.

After the 1919 call at the Eighth Party Congress to prop up the propaganda role of Russian classics, illustrations quickly emerged as an effective way to tie a work of the past to the important affairs of the revolutionary present. Without the length of Marxist forewords and at a time of back-lash against scholarly commentary, illustrations were instant visual cues that could guide the Soviet reader, selecting and accentuating certain themes while suppressing others.[2] In the words of a Soviet textbook for schoolteachers, Russian fairy tales could no longer be simply an "echo from the past" but must also act as a living art of the Soviet era, a "voice of the present."[3] This new dual purpose to the fairy tale, reflecting *then* while representing *now*, informed intriguing decisions about how *Balda* would be illustrated from the 1920s to the 1950s, when state policy on the tale's villain and hero (the priest and the peasant), not to mention Pushkin himself, underwent dramatic upheavals.

Balda is a fairy tale about a peasant *batrak*, or hired farm labourer, taken on by a lazy, greedy priest who tries to cheat him out of his pay, thus engaging with the Soviet-approved theme of unjust master-servant relations. Balda "works for seven" (and "eats for four"), becoming indispensable in the priest's household. Seeking to employ Balda's labour for free, the priest assigns his worker a seemingly impossible task. He makes Balda responsible for collecting three years' worth of quit-rent from a group of devils on the land, a task that Balda accomplishes by outwitting his opponents, both diabolic and godly, winning for himself the right to give his master a humiliating "three raps on the head." We know exactly how Pushkin pictured his peasant Balda. and the priest Ostolop because he sketched them while writing the tale.[4] Pushkin's Balda is happy and well fed, while his priest is old, ill-tempered, and crafty (figs. 1.2 and 1.3). Both representations are in line with the humorous, irreverent tone of the tale, itself the product of a friendly "composition competition" between Pushkin and the writer Vassily Zhukovsky. Zhukovsky later became responsible for the first appearance of the work in print, although in order for him to receive permission for publication, the priest had to be changed to the more acceptable satirical object, the merchant.[5] As a result, *Balda* was printed exclusively until 1882 and as late as 1900 as *The Tale of the Merchant*

Figure 1.2 Alexander Pushkin's sketch of a smiling Balda, in competition against the young devil, 1830.

Figure 1.3 Alexander Pushkin's sketch of the priest Ostolop, about to receive his punishment of three flicks on the forehead from Balda, 1830.

Figure 1.4 Mikhail Nesterov's illustrations of the "merchant" Kuzma Ostolop (*left*) and Balda (*right*), published by A.D. Stupin in 1889.

Kuzma Ostolop and His Worker Balda. Before the revolution, *Balda* was republished thirty-six times, including sixteen times in illustrated editions. In all of these illustrations the priest does not appear as himself, but rather as the merchant Kuzma Ostolop, but many illustrators, notably Mikhail Nesterov in 1889, solved this problem by depicting the figure in the long beard and black dress typical of the parish priest and member of the "white" (or married) clergy (fig. 1.4).[6] The line between priest and merchant was so ambiguous in Nesterov's illustrations that the drawings remained unchanged even after the tale could revert to its original title, *The Tale of the Priest and His Worker Balda.*

Balda and the Anti-religious Campaign

After 1917 and throughout the 1920s when fairy tales from the imperial past were the subject of public debate, *Balda* was reprinted only seven times, five of the reprints being illustrated. Depictions of the priest underwent dramatic changes. He was unquestionably the villain of the work, but his inconsistent portrayal – at times as an exploiting overlord, at others as a weakling whose time had passed – coincided with a period of intense reworking of the relationship between church and state. One of the first reforms of the officially atheist Bolsheviks after the revolution was the disestablishment of the Russian Orthodox Church. A decree of January 1918 ended state support of the Church and nationalized all of its property, but allowed the Church to retain buildings and religious objects necessary for the celebration of religious rituals.[7] At the Eighth Party Congress in 1919 the Bolsheviks stated their intention to "liberate" the minds of the toiling masses from religious prejudice but not to offend the "religious susceptibilities of believers."[8] This contradictory blend of state atheism and official religious tolerance was characteristic of the 1920s. While the Constitution of 1918 guaranteed freedom of conscience and "freedom of religious and anti-religious propaganda," in practice the Lenin era saw anti-religious violence as Komsomol members, largely young men, and village Soviets took it upon themselves to forcibly close and plunder churches. In response, at the Twelfth Party Congress in 1923 the party issued a call for tolerance towards religious figures and ceremonies, and priests found themselves, paradoxically, under the wing of the state that had severed their financial support. At the local level, parish priests were still a visible part of village life in the 1920s and were often the single largest expenditure item, after vodka, in a *mir*'s budget.[9] But their image in the popular imagination, songs, and folklore tended to be as lazy, venal, and drunken members of society. In satirical journals of the day such as *Crocodile*, *Red Pepper*, and *Red Raven* the clergy were routinely depicted as "alcoholics, avaricious

parasites, warmongers and sadists," and these were not even the journals specializing in anti-religious propaganda.[10]

For politically committed writers and artists, one solution to the problem of the ideologically incorrect fairy tale of the past was to update
and modernize it in accordance with party policies. This approach
resulted in the creation of a Sovietized sequel called *The Tale of the Farm
Labourer Balda and the Final Judgment*, put out by the State Publishing
House in 1919. The author of this *Balda* sequel, which appeared in a
double issue alongside Pushkin's original, was Demian Bednyi.[11] The
edition was illustrated by V. Spassky, whose cover illustration parodies
the compositional conventions of the World of Art artist Ivan Bilibin,
an earlier illustrator of Pushkin's tales, by employing stylized lettering
and an ornately framed scene that depicts the "fairytale beasts" of the
tale. However, the stunned look of these beasts and the fact that they
are completely prosaic forest animals, as opposed to magical creatures,
foreground the satire of this edition (see fig. 1.1).

Bednyi's sequel connected directly to contemporary policy debates
over the peasant, and Balda was reconceived in the Bolshevik class par-
lance of the day as a *bedniak*, or poor peasant. The *bedniaks* and *batraks*
were favoured by the Bolsheviks by dint of their exploitation by the
kulaks, or prosperous peasants, and organizations called the Committees for the Poor were set up in the countryside to support them. Bednyi's sequel was a tale of redemption for this disadvantaged peasant,
who would have accounted for about 35 to 40 per cent of the peasant
population after the Russian Civil War (1918–20).[12] Although Pushkin's
original is a kind of revenge tale, with Balda winning the right to "rap"
the priest three times on the head, causing his employer to lose the
power of speech, his mental faculties, and even, it is suggested, his life,
Bednyi's sequel begins by re-establishing Balda's lowly position. Not
only does Spassky depict Balda as aged, stooped, and cowed at his ini-
tial meeting with the priest (fig. 1.5), but the peasant is shown in the
sequel being whipped at the behest of a new landowner, who casually
watches the maltreatment while smoking a pipe and wearing a dress-
ing gown (fig. 1.6). Balda then dies and lies in the ground for a hundred
years; he is called back to life by the trumpets of the Red Army and wit-
nesses the paradise on earth that has been established by the Soviets,
including the Committee for the Poor, which ministers to clean, well-
fed peasants, and the sight of happy peasant children going to school.

Bednyi's tale of "the final judgment" clearly affirms what religious
philosopher Nikolai Berdyaev saw as the official replacement of a religious with an ideological, but no less fanatical, faith after 1917. Published during the civil war in 1919, Bednyi's tale and Spassky's images

Figure 1.5 V. Spassky's illustration of Balda meeting his future
employer, the priest Ostolop, 1919.

Figure 1.6 V. Spassky's illustration of Balda's humiliating punishment
by a new, malevolent landowner, 1919.

belie the fact that the countryside was in chaos and that the only apocalypse taking place was the one in which communists were widely
rumoured by peasants to be agents of the Antichrist. Bednyi's Soviet
sequel to Pushkin's tale is largely an exercise in wishful thinking. The
Committees for the Poor, which had been set up to recruit *bedniaks* and
batraks as Soviet allies, were used to facilitate forced grain requisitions
from the peasants in the period 1918 to 1920 and, in contradiction to
Spassky's depiction, were deeply hated by rural populations (fig. 1.7).
Due to their profound unpopularity, the Soviets were forced to close the
committees by 1920.[13] As for Spassky's depictions of schools for peasant
children, universal primary school education (grades one to four) was
still eleven years away, and in 1919 the Russian countryside was largely
illiterate (fig. 1.8).

Pointing out the glaring disparities between Bednyi's sequel (as represented by Spassky) and the political and historical reality of 1919
ignores the fact that the work and its illustrations were intended to
have a primarily utopian function. Bednyi's vision was of a countryside
that, following Soviet reforms, would come into being, and the consumers of his images were certainly not intended to be peasants, who
could compare them to their everyday existence. Bednyi's fairy tale
set an important precedent for the Stalinist era, when a state cultural
policy of heroic nationalism made idealized depictions of the peasant
and the countryside part of a larger nationalist discourse. Like Bednyi's
tale, Stalin-era images often completely missed the satirical function of
Pushkin's tale, delivering straight-faced renditions of the peasant experience that relentlessly repeated how much things had improved in the
countryside thanks to the advent of Soviet power. Illustrations showing
the party as the helpmate of the peasant countered a sense that the "real
civil war was not between Reds and Whites, but between the state and
peasants."[14]

Bednyi served on the editorial board for a number of prestigious collected editions of Pushkin's works in the 1930s, but his Balda sequel
was never republished after 1922, and in the Lenin era Spassky's image
of a work-worn, downtrodden Balda competed with other visual interpretations of this Russian peasant. In contemporary emigré publications, for instance, we see a very different take on the work. In 1919
Balda appeared in a luxury edition of Russian fairy tales translated into
French, with illustrations by Jean Lébédeff. Lébédeff's version shows a
sly and vigorous Balda galloping on a white steed, the symbol of the
White opponents to Soviet rule and their desire to return to Russia as
victors in the civil war. A 1921 version published in Berlin shows a
large, strapping Balda confronting a rather pitiable priest. Intriguingly,

Figure 1.7 This 1919 illustration by V. Spassky showing peasants gathered
around the headquarters of the Committee for the Poor, with its images
of order and plenty, belies the reality of the Russian Civil War, which had
plunged the countryside into chaos. The "ghost" Balda can be
seen witnessing the scene, on the left.

Figure 1.8 In V. Spassky's 1919 illustration, happy primary schoolchildren play in front of a well-kept school. In reality, universal public education was not implemented until 1930.

Figure 1.9 Illustration of the face-off between peasant and priest by an
unknown artist. Published in Berlin, 1921.

Balda bears a remarkable resemblance to the proletarian-born writer
Maxim Gorky in this version and appears to be a commentary on the
bullying figure of the pro-Bolshevik intellectual and his pitiless attitude
towards faith and tradition (fig. 1.9).

In Soviet illustrated versions of *Balda* of the 1920s it was not yet compulsory to represent Balda as a positive character, although the priest
tended inevitably to be the object of parody. Granilshikov's 1925 illustrations make Balda into an imbecilic figure and the priest Ostolop into
a skinny intellectual wearing spectacles (fig. 1.10). This interpretation in
fact connects to the oral folk origins of the Balda tale where, some folklorists believe, Balda derives from a figure of bear-like strength that is
matched only by his immense stupidity.[15] In other illustrations from the
1920s, Balda ascends to a position that he would hold unflaggingly in
the Stalinist era, as a proud folk hero and inevitable victor of the stand-
off with his employer and master. In illustrations of 1926 and 1928 Balda
stands at least a foot taller than the priest and is unstooped, unwrinkled,
and determined. These illustrations emerged against a background of
high-profile debate over the role of religion in the countryside, as the
League of Godless, a volunteer atheist organization that had emerged in
1925, made ever-greater incursions into the village and claimed, at least

Figure 1.10 A. Granilshikov's pin-headed but large-gutted version of Balda
from 1925, facing off against an overbearing, bespectacled priest.

officially, to have grown from 86,000 members in 1926 to 465,000 members in 1929.[16] Faith battled anti-faith at the local level as the mass youth group Komsomol introduced secular alternatives to Easter while evangelical groups, in turn, organized religious alternatives to the Komsomol. *Balda* was a topical work in the 1920s as the Bolsheviks attempted to recruit peasants to their cause with a campaign of attention to rural issues called "Face the Village."[17] Although this attempt to seduce the countryside proved unsuccessful in 1925, illustrated versions of *Balda* from the 1920s bear witness to the fact that if the party could not bring actual peasants on side, it could certainly co-opt the image of the peasant for its own purposes. Under Lenin, the "worker Balda" was already beginning to rise from underdog to peasant hero.

After Stalin's consolidation of power in 1928 a number of high-profile cultural policies came together to make illustrations of a fairy tale depicting a peasant hero and a priest villain more important, and also more contradictory, than ever before. *Balda* flourished in the Stalin era (1928–53), enjoying seventy-five book republications, forty-eight of which were illustrated, as well as translation into multiple national languages of the Soviet Union, including Armenian, Karakalpak, Kazakh, Kirghiz, Mari, and Udmurt, and the languages of the Indigenous northern populations such as Chukchi, Evenki, and Nenets. In this way, the image of the peasant Balda was not only consumed by Russians but also exported to the non-Russian citizens of the Soviet Union. Beginning in the early 1930s, *Balda* was also adapted for stage and screen, becoming the subject of a film score by Dmitry Shostakovich (1934–5) to accompany an animated film by Mikhail Tsekhanovsky (begun in 1933, but unfinished, and almost completely destroyed during the war); a children's drama stylized as puppet theatre (1939); and an immensely popular ballet with music by Mikhail Chulaki, staged in 1940, 1941, and 1946.

Balda as Stalin-Era Peasant

The life of the peasant and the village priest was violently transformed in the 1930s thanks to the collectivization campaign that began in the winter of 1929–30 and an anti-religious campaign that spun out of control. The ferocity of these efforts reflects the fact that the anti-religious campaigns of the 1920s had been piecemeal and unco-ordinated and were judged to have been largely ineffective in transforming the peasant into a non-believer.[18] After a period of relative quiet in the countryside, coinciding with Lenin's New Economic Policy (1921–9), the suddenness and speed with which peasant villages were coerced into a system of state-run collective farms that were required to sell a fixed

percentage of grain at lower-than-market prices left the Russian countryside in turmoil. The catastrophic upheaval of the collectivization
campaign resulted in a famine in 1932–3 that was unreported.[19] This
extreme opposition of the image and the reality of the countryside was
a hallmark of the Stalinist era, a period in which the phenomenon of
the Potemkin village, a village faked for the sake of appearance, was
perfected and professionalized. Historian Sheila Fitzpatrick writes: "If
the typical Russian village of the 1930s was hungry, drab, depopulat-
ed, and demoralized, there was another village, happy and prosperous, bustling with people, and enlivened by the cheerful sounds of the
accordion and balalaika, that existed in imagination."[20]

The fake village with the happy, satiated peasant was pedalled,
mainly to educated urban readers, through media such as book illustrations, as part of a complex cultural construct. The peasant and the
countryside represented folk tradition, a bridge between past and present, and a crucial link between Soviet power and its supposed origins
in "the people" (narod). For these reasons the peasant and the countryside, whether in depictions of the past or on the kolkhoz (collective
farm) of the present, had to be represented as idyllic, harmonious, and
thriving. Illustrations to works like Balda could, and did, fulfill this cultural imperative under Stalin, as a heroic national past was shown to
culminate in the glories of the present.

Outstanding kolkhoz workers became the village counterpart to the
Stakhanovites, or model urban shock workers, of the 1930s. These
heroic peasant workers were displayed at prestigious national congresses of outstanding kolkhoz workers in 1933 (ironically, at the height
of the famine) and in 1935, as well as at smaller annual conferences. It
was during a conference of December 1935 that Stalin made his famous
pronouncement that "Life has become better and more cheerful," an
assertion that was shored up by the presence of outstanding peasant
workers like Nikor Shestopalov, who was an award-winning tractor
driver from Stalingrad, a bedniak, and a former illiterate. Fitzpatrick
argues that it was precisely during the peasant congresses, held at the
Kremlin in Moscow, that the role of the "professional peasant" and the
publicity image of Stalin as the kindly, paternalistic leader of a great
nation of rural and urban workers were consolidated.[21] As the two leading peasant celebrities appearing regularly beside Stalin in media pho-
tographs of the 1930s were women – Pasha Angelina, a norm-busting
tractor operator, and Maria Demchenko, an outstanding sugar-beet
sower – illustrated images of peasant men like Balda filled an important gap in the public imagination. In the countryside this gap was lit-
eral because young peasant men had responded to the collectivization

Figure 1.11 Illustration of Balda and the priest by A. Surikov. Published in Moscow in 1937 in Mari, a language spoken mainly in the Mari Republic and Bashkortostan, but also the Kirov oblast', Tatarstan, Udmurtia, and Perm regions. This illustrated edition is a tribute to how far Balda had made incursions into the reaches of the Soviet Union.

drive by emigrating to urban centres en masse. As a result, the number of young peasant men was much lower than that of young peasant women in the countryside in the 1930s.[22] *Balda* became part of a carefully crafted image of the peasant and the village in illustrations like A. Surikov's from 1937, which show a tall, broad-chested Balda in silhouette against a background of pastoral calm, plenty, and leisure, with peasant women buying and selling food, and a male figure resting and chatting. In this illustration the floating fields of light blue and white in the background convey a sense of tranquillity to the viewer, while the use of silhouettes in the foreground leaves out the individualized emotions on the faces of the priest and the peasant, suggesting a pleasant sense of quiet and calm (fig. 1.11).

Depictions of Balda's powerful physique, conveying the benefits of a robust diet, reflect the imagined prosperity typical of Stalin-era images of the countryside. In an illustration published in Irkutsk in 1937, Balda's peasant clothing has been drawn with shading that suggests a suit of armour, transforming him into a kind of village counterpart to the *bogatyrs* (epic folk heroes) who were being revived in *byliny* (epic songs) during the same period (fig. 1.12). Book illustrations from the 1930s had to play a dual role and could not afford to depict the past while neglecting the cultural imperatives of the present. Consequently illustrations like Sidelnikovsky's from 1937 show a countryside that is well off enough to provide a horse for Balda (fig. 1.13), but in reality, the lack

Figure 1.12 Illustration by an unknown artist, showing Balda with a padded, muscular physique. Published in Irkutsk in 1937.

Сказка о попе и о работнике его Балде

Figure 1.13 This title-page illustration by B. Sidelnikovsky for an edition of *Balda* published in Omsk in 1937 shows Balda mounted on the kind of swift-footed steed that had virtually disappeared from the Stalin-era countryside.

of horses to use as draft animals – a result of horses having been con-
scripted during the First World War, commandeered during the civil
war, and confiscated during collectivization – was a serious deficiency
in the countryside of the 1930s. Peasant men and women under Stalin
literally had to do the work of animals, and this had a deleterious effect
on agricultural output. Images of robust physiques and swift-footed
horses, however, sent to urban readers an important message of well-
being in the Russian countryside.[23]

The surfeit of illustrations from 1937 reflects the cultural importance
of the first Stalin-era Pushkin anniversary, which reached a zenith in
terms of the sheer magnitude of speeches, articles, readings, dramatizations, newly formed proletarian reading groups, and other cultural
activities greeting the arrival of "Pushkin for the masses." The 1937
jubilee was to be celebrated all over the Soviet Union, accompanied
by the inclusion of Pushkin in the literature curriculum of every public
school and by the publication of over thirteen million copies of works
by and about Pushkin in Russian and other national languages of the
Union.[24] Pushkin was firmly established as the founder of the glorious
tradition of Russian literature and made part of a zealous campaign
to revive the classics. At the same time, the championing of a heroic
national past confirmed the importance of the folk-tale and the fairy
tale, and works like *Balda* became significant because they emphasized
the role of *narodnost'* (national folk character) in Pushkin's works. This
narodnost' was evidenced through Pushkin's close relationship to his
peasant-born nanny Arina Rodionova, and the fairy tales that he heard
from her, like *Balda*, came into particular favour in the 1930s. *Balda* was
touted as one of only three fairy tales, along with *The Tale of the Fisherman and the Fish* and the unfinished *Medvedikha*, written by Pushkin in
authentic folk style.

Stakhanovite workers were encouraged to "master Pushkin and
transmit their knowledge to other workers," thus proving that the
masses could attain "culture," a major goal of the 1930s.[25] Although the
state-sponsored image of Pushkin was supposed to saturate entirely
the population of the Soviet Union so that, in theory, Russian peasants would have viewed illustrated versions of *Balda* as themselves (or
themselves as *Balda*) for the first time, in reality the instructional plan
and accompanying materials did not always extend into regional and
rural centres.[26]

At the same time that Balda's star was on the rise, the priest's, at
least in official representations, was on the decline. Komsomol members, largely young village men, began an aggressive attack on religion
beginning in 1927, and a state-sponsored anti-religious campaign that

resulted in the mass closing of churches, the arrest of priests, and violation of religious artifacts began in earnest in January 1930.[27] This anti-
religious campaign took on a momentum of its own as the Red Army
was used to strip monasteries of valuables and sacred objects (fig. 1.14),
and was marked by a venom and fervour that outstripped the expectations of the party and even the League of Militant Godless leader Emelian Iaroslavsky. About half of the working churches of 1929 had been
closed by 1933, and Komsomol activists staged public acts of sacrilege
such as the mock execution, by shooting, of saints depicted in icons.[28]
Starting in 1931, the anti-religious journal *Bezbozhnik* (Godless) included
a page specifically for children, encouraging them to "wage a struggle
against religion within the family."[29] Special cut-outs showed children
how to make their own anti-religious toys, including cardboard dolls
of drunken clergy, or Easter cakes (*kulich*) from which an exploiting
rich peasant would jump like a jack-in-the-box. In schools children set
up "godless corners," atheist alternatives to the sacred corner in which
religious families traditionally displayed icons. These imitated those
godless corners being set up on factory floors all over the Soviet Union.
In 1938 atheism became an official part of the school curriculum.[30]

The response to these state campaigns, particularly among older
peasant men and women, was a revival of religious faith and support
for the Orthodox Church. The census of 1937 showed a majority of
peasants declaring themselves as believers, although this proved to be
a wedge issue with urban centres, where, conversely, two-thirds of the
population above the age of sixteen declared themselves to be atheists.[31]
The guarantee of freedom of religious belief and the restoration of civil
rights for priests in the 1936 constitution resulted in a brief revitaliza-
tion of visibility for the church and the village priest in 1937. But when
priests, on the strength of their new-found support and constitutional
rights, began to emerge as potential candidates in the 1937 elections
to the Supreme Soviet, the party responded with a new wave of mass
arrests and church closures. Correspondingly, illustrations published to
meet the Pushkin jubilee year of 1937 tended to become more damag-
ing in their depiction of the priest and more violent and carnivalesque
in their depiction of his punishment by Balda. In A. Konetssky's 1936
illustrations the priest is marked and made ridiculous by an enormous cross on his chest (fig. 1.15), and in the final illustration of the
series he is shown to be a cringing coward hiding beneath the skirts
of his enormously overfed wife (fig. 1.16). N. Filatov's 1938 illustration explicitly makes the priest into a satanic figure with two horns,
whom Balda "raps" with one hand, while reproaching him with the
other. Many illustrations from the Stalinist era show the priest not only

Figure 1.14 The demolition of the St Simonov Monastery and the removal of religious artifacts by Red Army soldiers, 1927. Reproduced from the David King Collection with the permission of the Tate Gallery (London).

Bir kyni вarojan вazaroja...

Figure 1.15 The priest wears an outlandishly large cross in this illustration by A. Konetssky to accompany an edition of *Balda* published in Kazakhstan in 1936.

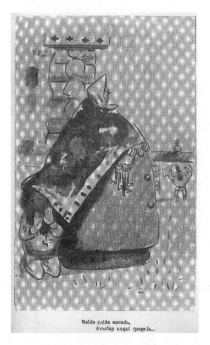

Balda çolda вaradь,
Aвьrlap ьnqьl qaoja.ıь...

Figure 1.16 In this illustration by A. Konetssky, the priest is barely visible underneath the skirts of his wife, whose large set of keys suggest that she is the head of the household.

threatened with retribution but physically overcome after this physical punishment has been delivered. An illustration by V. Vlasov from
1935 shows the priest knocked off his feet by the force of the blows, and
in 1936, Svidersky showed a sinister Balda looming over a completely
vanquished priest.

The revival of folk- and fairy tales and the heroes of the past went
along with a new campaign, in the 1930s, to celebrate and sacralize the
present in folk-inspired songs and epic poems, which Frank Miller has
memorably termed "Stalinist fakelore." Folklore and fakelore came
together in one of the most captivating illustrated versions of *Balda*, by
the Palekh artist Dmitry Butorin in 1936. Palekh art itself, a distinctive
style of brightly coloured tempera painting with silver and gold detail
on a black lacquered background, encompassed many of the paradoxes
inherent in the Stalinist revival of the national past and is perhaps best
described as faux authenticism. On the one hand, Palekh work originated as a folk art style among icon painters beginning in the seven-
teenth century and could claim a legitimate peasant heritage, stemming
from artisans in the village of Palekh in the Ivanovo region northeast of
Moscow. On the other hand, the advent of officially atheist Soviet power
also destroyed the livelihood of traditional Palekh icon painters, who
then turned to the creation of miniature lacquered bead boxes, cigarette
cases, brooches, and other consumer goods for the mass market. Under
Stalin, the style was still derived from the traditions of icon painting,
but content reflected the strange blend of past and present inherent in
heroic nationalism. Scenes from traditional folk- and fairy tales and
byliny mixed with subjects such as "The Komsomols Depart for the
Civil War" (by K.S. Bokarev) or "Flourish, Kolkhoz Land" (by T.I. Zub-
kov). This transformation from religious painting to Stalinist objet d'art
has led Svetlana Boym to term Palekh miniatures an example of a "lacquered reality" emblematic of Stalinist cultural practices overall.[32] Like
the multilayered papier mâché of the signature lacquered boxes, Palekh
art became a palimpsest of folk tradition with a Soviet overlay, and
there is no more fitting artistic style for the Balda of the 1930s, that epic
peasant hero of the collectivized Potemkin village, than the Sovietized
faux-traditional version of Palekh art. Indeed Palekh art transformed
from the miniature to the monumental at precisely the same moment
that Balda was transfigured into an epic folk hero. Beginning in 1934,
Palekh art expanded into theatre back-drops, large-scale murals at the
Leningrad Palace of Pioneers, and book illustrations.[33]

It was at this cultural moment in the mid-1930s that Dmitry Butorin's Palekh illustrations to *Balda* emerged. These illustrations fulfil one
of the important functions of Soviet Palekh art by "preserving the old

within the new" and using the conventions of traditional icon painting to expand the narrative function of the work of art. Balda is tall,
dark haired, and bearded, like many of the *bogatyr* heroes that Butorin
depicted in other Palekh works.[34] There is no trace of irony or satire
in his illustrations; rather the two-dimensionality of the figures and
the way in which both Balda and the priest hold their fingers signal
the conventions of iconography. Although the three fingers signify the
bargain over the raps on the head, they suggest the traditional way in
which saints crossed themselves, creating a Balda that is much closer to
hagiography than comedy (fig. 1.17). Like all of Butorin's heroes from
Danko to Pushkin, Balda is dressed in red and is often shown either
flexing his muscles or rolling up his sleeves. Although in the first illustration of the series the figures in the background suggested rancour
in the tsarist countryside, with angry peasants haggling over goods,
pointing and making fists, in subsequent illustrations Balda subdues
the countryside by vanquishing devils with a large stick and whip-like
rope. These illustrations were published in the same period as articles
announcing the dekulakization (expropriation and mass deportation of
so-called prosperous peasants) in the countryside, and Balda with his
"whip" becomes a stand-in for Stalin's violent clean-up in the village.
In less than two decades, in the period between V. Spassky's illustrations in the civil-war era and Butorin's illustrations of high Stalinism,
Balda was transformed from an overworked underdog to a robust
warrior. In the late Stalinist period Balda progressed to a figure that
was younger, taller, stronger, and, increasingly, blonder than his cleri-
cal adversary. Mogilevsky's illustrations of 1944 show a handsome
young peasant holding three fingers up to a shorter and older scowling
priest (fig. 1.18). Svidersky's 1948 illustrations have the priest reaching only as high as Balda's shoulder. In Dekhterev's 1949 illustrations
a snub-nosed, clean-shaven Balda peers down at a foolish, overweight
opponent. Another set of illustrations, by Janus in 1949, fashions the
stand-off as puppet theatre – but the priest is the only puppet-sized
figure, and Balda is physically strapping, with long, curled blonde hair.

It was a tribute to Balda's immense cultural importance in the 1930s
that well-known film director Mikhail Tsekhanovsky was engaged by
Lenfilm Studios in 1933 to create an animated version of the tale with a
score by Dmitry Shostakovich. Shostakovich's six-act concert suite was
composed between 1934 and 1935, but the project was left unfinished
following Stalin's infamous denunciation of Shostakovich's 1936 opera
Lady Macbeth of Mtsensk District. Tsekhanovsky's animated film adaptation of *Balda* was mostly destroyed in the 1941 bombing of Lenfilm's
studios in Leningrad, but the short scene "In the Marketplace" has

Figure 1.17 Dmitry Butorin's Palekh illustration from 1936, showing Balda in
the red clothing traditional for heroes of iconography (see also colour plate 5).

Figure 1.18 A. Mogilevsky's 1944 version shows Balda as younger
and stronger than the priest.

survived and attests to the strong satirical edge of the work. Shostakovich's musical characterization of Balda is at first somewhat gruff and
unrefined, becoming bustling and joyous when Balda begins physical
work, and suggesting a victorious fate through the fanfare and celebration of the final movement, "Balda's Gallop."

Balda the strong, vigorous folk hero was revisited in the popular
ballet adaptation of Pushkin's tale, which premiered in 1940 and was
reproduced in 1941 and 1946. Mikhail Chulaki, a teacher of Mstislav
Rostropovich, composed the music for the ballet, which emphasizes the
folk elements of the fairy tale. The musical motifs associated with Balda
are "optimistic, life-embracing, clear, Russian," according to a 1940
article by Iu.A. Vainkop, and the theatre decorations for the ballet, by
A.A. Kolomoitsev, depict an idealized version of the Russian countryside populated by serene birch trees, a rainbow, and happy, colourfully
dressed peasants dancing to the accordion (fig. 1.19).[35] These harmo-
nized with contemporary images of the collectivized village in Stalinist block-buster musicals from the 1940s like Ivan Pyryev's *Cossacks of
the Kuban* (1949). One sketch even showed Balda transformed into a
Pushkinesque double, dressed as a peasant, glorifying in the pastoral
contentment of the village (fig. 1.20).

Figure 1.19 A.A. Kolomoitsev's sketch for theatre decorations to
M. Chulaki's ballet adaptation of *Balda*, 1940.

Figure 1.20 A Pushkinesque figure appears centre stage, ready to burst into
song and dance, in a sketch by an unknown artist for a ballet adaptation of
Balda. Published in M.I. Chulaki's book *The Tale of the Priest and His Worker
Balda*, Leningrad, 1946.

The original sense of Pushkin's fairy tale was that despite being disempowered and disadvantaged, the peasant – caught between the clergy and the devil – prevails against both adversaries through craft and cunning. This was a tale of wish fulfilment for the original folk audience of an oral version of the tale, namely, for the peasant himself. The Soviet illustrations to this work, so plainly altered from the way in which Pushkin himself had imagined and sketched his Balda and Ostolop, radically reoriented the tale's satirical and subversive message. The successive transformations of Balda into an opponent advantaged by height, youth, and strength means that no unexpected reversal takes place at the end of the visual text. Moreover, these depictions represent a clear appropriation by the state of the image of the peasant in order to speak about and on behalf of this supposed beneficiary of revolutionary advances for a mostly urban consumer of the tale. The dissonance between the imaginary and the actual would have been striking in the 1930s, when in reality this ostensibly advantaged peasant bore the brunt of the brutal collectivization campaign. Without changing a single word, Soviet illustrations shifted readings of the tale's happy ending. Instead of a cowed peasant underdog emerging on top contrary to all expectation, the success of the Soviet Balda was scripted from the beginning. Thus the satire of the tale fell flat, and a work that had once been banned for its subversive subtext became a vehicle for state messaging.

Chapter Two

Up, Up, and Away on the Little Humpbacked Horse

Few Russian fairy tales can rival Petr Ershov's *Little Humpbacked Horse* (1834), a remarkable survivor of rapid changes in political culture from the tsarist through the Stalinist periods, for its uninterrupted success or longevity. This whimsical and magical tale remained well-published throughout the years of Leninist rancour against the magical fairy tale, reaching a zenith from the mid-1930s to early 1950s when it was put out annually in enormous print runs by Soviet publishing houses and illustrated by leading lights in children's illustration like Yury Vasnetsov and Vladimir Konashevich. Among the factors supporting the tale's successful survival was the adaptability of its visual lexicon, which illustrators developed in accordance with the values of the present. Three images in particular lent themselves to expedient transformations. The tale's protagonist, Ivan the Fool (*Ivan-durak*), transitioned from a lazy simpleton to a pure-hearted but under-estimated hero, while the tsar became a character whose violent disposal in the finale went from unexpected to historically inevitable. The little humpbacked horse of this aerial adventure was recoded to emblematize the prestigious achievements of Soviet long-distance flying and polar exploration in the 1930s, as well as a favourite armchair-travellers' hobby for children known as *stranovedenie*, or country studies. The tale offered something for every political climate. Under Lenin, when it was paramount to break with the imperial past, many illustrators emphasized Ershov's satire of the fictional tsar Saltan by drawing grotesque caricatures that underscored this royal figure's caprice and stupidity. Under Stalin, when *narodnost'*, or national folk character, became an imperative quality for works of art, illustrators celebrated the tale's traditional folk hero, Ivan the Fool, underlining his strength and resourcefulness. Through its illustrated versions, this work from the past was refashioned to reflect the emphases of contemporary culture.

Figure 2.1 Front cover of *The Little Humpbacked Horse* with illustrations by V. Korablinov, published in Voronezh, 1950 (see also colour plate 6).

Perhaps what most resonated with producers and consumers of illustrated editions from the 1920s to the 1950s was the way in which this fairy tale about a magical flying horse who helps Ivan reach hero status, and eventually become tsar himself, corresponded to a concurrent national obsession with aviation and flight. In the 1920s Russian citizens were called upon by a mass propaganda campaign to help build the first Soviet civil air fleet; by the late 1930s the Soviet Union had launched itself to international renown by claiming over sixty world records including the longest, highest, and fastest flights, the first landing at the North Pole, and the first polar flight from the Soviet Union to the United States.[1] Aeronautics, airplanes, and flight were popular topics for illustrated children's books throughout the 1920s, 1930s, and 1940s.[2] Many of these books were non-fiction and featured all kinds of flying machines, including hot-air balloons, dirigibles, and Zeppelin airships, as well as airplanes.[3] Some were fantastical, like Roman Karmen's 1931 book about the aerosled.[4] This attention to flight highlighted the technological and military prowess of the Soviets, and republications of *The Little Humpbacked Horse* dovetailed nicely with the theme. This imperial-era tale was proof of Gorky's words at the First All-Union Congress of the Writers' Union that fairy tales encapsulated the yearnings of the past for abilities like flight, yearnings that had at last been fulfilled by the technological advances of the modern, Soviet era.

Front covers of *The Little Humpbacked Horse*, reaching readers in the hundreds of thousands in the 1930s, 1940s, and early 1950s, repeatedly featured a simple Russian boy soaring high into a starlit sky on the back of his magical companion (fig. 2.1). These iconic images forged connections between the tale and the daring aviation feats that were capturing the public imagination under Stalin. Ivan and his little humpbacked horse flew over mountains, coast-lines, and boreal forest in illustrations at the same moment that the nation was seized with a mania for *stranovedenie* (in this case, the study of the different geographical, climatic, and agricultural zones comprising the Soviet Union). This "cult of the motherland" became an "inseparable part of Soviet children's culture" under Stalin and functioned as a building block of patriotism in the 1930s.[5] As long-distance fliers like Valery Chkalov shattered world records, and millions of readers consumed the tale of an underdog rising to glory, this work became a symbol of Stalinist Russia's discovery of itself as a heroic nation.

The Little Humpbacked Horse (*Konek-gorbunok*) weaves together multiple folk motifs and characters in a whimsical adventure story. The hero of the tale is the traditional Russian folk hero Ivan the Fool, the simpleton third son who rises from obscurity to fame thanks to an epic quest that takes him sky-bound around the realm. Derived from the fiery mare Sivka-burka (or Sivko-burko), Ershov's loyal and wish-fulfilling little humpbacked horse has the added twist that he is tiny (only three arshins, or five-and-a-half-inches tall) and deformed, with two humps on his back and long ears like a donkey.[6] Other folklore figures in the tale include the volatile and easily fooled tsar, whom Ivan outwits and dethrones – in this case in a dramatic ending in which Ivan saves himself from being boiled alive by convincing the tsar to jump into the boiling vat. The legendary firebird and the lovely tsar maiden represent the glory and love that an unlikely hero can win for himself on a successful quest. Other elements of the tale, representing the enormous heights and depths that Ivan must attain on his journey, include the moon (Mesiats Mesiatsovich), a monarch who reigns in the sky; a magical but cursed whale, so enormous that he has an entire peninsula growing on his back; and a foul-tempered and wily ruff, a fish from the perch family, who reveals the secret underwater treasure that helps Ivan win the maiden.[7] The blend of traditional folk motifs with an "authentic" folk narrative featuring Siberian peasant idioms, added to the almost complete obscurity of Ershov as an author, led some Soviet critics to claim that he had not so much written *The Little Humpbacked Horse* as "remembered" and reassembled it from the tellings of countless peasant folk narrators in his Siberian childhood.[8] This interpretation fit well with the Stalin-era spotlight on oral folk narrators of traditional tales who also created "new" songs (*noviny*) that celebrated the long-distance and polar fliers who were the Soviet realization of an ancient dream to soar into the skies.

Virtually every article and foreword written about Ershov under Lenin and Stalin begin by saying that although everyone knows *The Little Humpbacked Horse*, almost no one knows the writer Petr Ershov.[9] Unlike Pushkin and Dostoevsky, who came with complex cultural baggage in the eyes of the Soviets, Ershov was virtually a blank slate to critics, and what *was* known about the biography of this Siberian native was easily shaped into a narrative consistent with Lenin and Stalin–era cultural directives. With the manuscript copy of the tale lost, only one contemporary memoir about Ershov in existence, and an archive that was not completely discovered until the late 1940s, Soviet critics were essentially free to fashion their own legend of him.[10] This legend followed a template that included his childhood in remote Siberia, his move to St Petersburg to attend university, his masterful creation of *The Little Humpbacked Horse* when he was a young man of only nineteen, the recognition of his talent by Pushkin himself, his return to Siberia, his never-fulfilled dream to write an epic poem called *Ivan-tsarevich* that would unite all the Russian fairy tales, and his death in obscurity in 1869. As Stalinism matured, the legend was salted with a socially conscious analysis that what united the 1830s (when the tale was first published) with the 1930s was a recognition of the importance of folklore and the life of "the people" and a turning away from scholarly and "high" artistic literature.[11] In both epochs an interest in folklore was taken as a sign of political progressiveness.[12] For Stalin-era children's literature critic and journal editor A. Babushkina, *The Little Humpbacked Horse* proved the long-standing "blood enmity" between tsar and people, and the latter's revolutionary desire to replace a bad tsar with a good leader.[13] In Babushkina's view, Ivan the Fool is a double character: on the outside, as a peasant would appear to the aristocracy – lazy and clumsy; on the inside, as one preserving the true qualities of the people: "intelligence, keenness of wit, enterprise, humanity."[14]

Critical evaluation of Ershov's hero changed radically from the late nineteenth to the mid-twentieth century. Although a review of *The Little Humpbacked Horse* in an 1884 edition of the journal *Fatherland Notes* called the tale "dangerous for children" because its hero championed "stupidity, idleness and uselessness," a Stalin-era textbook for teachers of 1946 praised the educative value of the work for children, calling its hero "brave, loyal and simple."[15] In the same period, illustrators profoundly transformed the image of Ivan and of the humpbacked horse. Ivan became younger and younger in ensuing decades. Whereas it was typical for illustrators of pre-revolutionary versions to depict him as an adolescent or young man, by the late 1930s and 1940s he was shown almost exclusively as a child about the same age as the "young schoolboy" for whom children's publishers designated these editions. This corresponded with a change in intended audience: in the tsarist period and throughout the 1920s the tale was published as a Russian fairy tale in three parts, but by the 1930s, when children's publishing houses had become well established, the work was more often subtitled "a fairytale for children." In the 1920s it was common to depict Ivan in a satirical way, as a kind of village idiot with drooping mouth or in-turned feet (fig. 2.2). But under Stalin, although the tsar often remained a satirical figure, depictions of Ivan steadily became more earnest and serious. The simple peasant shirt and bast shoes in which he was shown in the 1920s were replaced under Stalin by more festive national dress (fig. 2.3). Likewise, his steed transformed from the 1920s to the 1950s: under Lenin the little humpbacked horse was deformed, donkey-like, and ridiculous, often measuring only to Ivan's knees; starting with Yury Vasnetsov's illustrations of 1934, the little humpbacked horse becomes both heroic and folkloric, with a tall bristly mane and a prancing step. By the late

Figure 2.2 Ivan appearing very much the fool, and the little humpbacked horse with donkey ears, in this illustration by A.F. Afanas'ev, published in Moscow in 1924.

1940s and early 1950s, illustrators were fashioning him as an adorable child's toy with wide luminous eyes, a pony instead of a donkey.

Even before the revolution the immense popularity and seeming innocuousness of *The Little Humpbacked Horse* had been harnessed for political purposes. In 1906 censors mistakenly approved a parody of the tale by S. Basov-Verkhoiantsev, called *The Little Galloping Horse* (*Konek-skakunok*). In fact, the reworked fairy tale invoked the recent civil disorder of 1905 and described a coming revolution in which all the riches and power would pass to the workers. This politicized parody was immediately republished after 1917.[16] In the 1920s, when the magical fairy tale became a matter of controversy, a children's theatre production of *The Little Humpbacked Horse* by the Young Spectator's Theatre minimized the fantastical in the tale by using only concrete objects and toys. The flying horse, talking moon, and whale were shown as handmade, child-like folk art objects, referencing the neo-primitivist art popular in the early revolutionary period. The script adhered almost completely to Ershov's original text but was narrated by old peasant "grandfathers" who interacted with the main characters, pulling them into the realm of the real. Director A. Briantsev insisted that there was "nothing magical" about the play, which debuted in 1922 and remained popular with young audiences well into the Stalinist era.[17]

Figure 2.3 A more heroic version of Ivan published in Riga, Latvia, in 1952. Illustration by M. Karpenko.

During the imperial era forty-four editions of *The Little Humpbacked Horse* were published, twenty-six of them illustrated. In the 1920s the proportion of illustrated editions went up dramatically: of eighteen separate publications, fourteen were illustrated. Deriding the tale's fictional tsar was common to illustrators of the Lenin era. In an edition of 1924 illustrated by various artists of the Studio of the Academy of Arts, the Romanov's double-eagle coat of arms is displayed even inside the tsar's canopy bed, but the insignia is shrouded in a dark storm cloud (fig. 2.5). In particular, artists made the most of the final scene of the fairy tale, when the tsar is boiled alive. In the same edition of 1924 the tsar is shown in a ridiculous posture, bent double about to dive into the vat, displaying his naked buttocks to viewers in a biting caricature. Another take on the scene of the tsar's demise, by an unknown artist in 1917, takes an allegorical rather than satirical perspective. In this illustration the tsar,

Figure 2.4 The toy pony version of the little humpbacked horse, popular
from the late 1940s. This illustration by N. Kochergin was published by the
State Children's Publishing House in 1953 in 50,000 copies, and again by the
Karelian State Publishing Agency in 100,000 copies (see also colour plate 7).

powerful and tragic, dies slowly in the vat while around him "workers"
chop and haul wood to intensify the fire, and "cooks" approach with
wooden spoons to finish off the strange stew. In the foreground a man
in Lenin-style cap sits and watches the tsar's execution by the people.
Above this naturalistic scene, and contrasting it completely with its folkloric stylization, Ivan (now the tsar) and the tsar maiden preside over a
fairy-tale ending (fig. 2.6). The clash of these two compositional worlds –
the folkloric one with its ornamentation and detail, and the "factual"
foregrounded one with its representational lines – conveys the sense that
where the tale left off, revolutionary history stepped in.

Air-Minded: The Little Humpbacked Horse in the 1920s

Readers began to identify *The Little Humpbacked Horse* with the creation,
development, and triumphs of Soviet aviation from the mid-1920s. In
1925 a Soviet parody of the tale appeared called *The Little Flying Horse, An
Aerial Fairy Tale* (*Konek-letunok, aero-skazka*), featuring a front cover with
a jubilant young boy astride a hybrid horse-airplane (fig. 2.7). Published

in Siberia by the O.D.V.F., the Society for Friends of the Air Fleet, this imitation of *The Little Humpbacked Horse* was intended as a vehicle for the campaign to develop and finance Russia's first civil air fleet. Civil aviation was founded in February 1923 with the creation of the O.D.V.F. as well as the Volunteer Air Fleet (Dobrolet), the precursor to Russia's commercial carrier Aeroflot.[18] Dobrolet's mandate was to expand an air fleet that could meet the nation's growing infrastructure objectives: delivering the mail more quickly, supporting agriculture, developing aerial photography, and discovering new air routes to Siberia. With these urgent goals in mind, in March 1923 the O.D.V.F. initiated a campaign to make Soviet citizens more "air-minded."[19] This included hosting air shows, establishing a newspaper dedicated to aviation news called *Airplane*, and instructing workers that it was patriotic to support aviation.[20]

In order to raise the revenue necessary to pay for this fleet, the O.D.V.F. launched a mass campaign to sell shares to the public, beginning at one ruble, fifty-two kopeks. The poster for the campaign featured the slogan "Build the Air Fleet of the U.S.S.R!" and showcased a pilot in a billowing red scarf, pointing up to a sky filled with dozens of soaring biplanes. *The Little Flying Horse, An Aerial Fairy Tale* was part of this lofty venture in the 1920s to build up the civil air fleet by appealing to readers and potential investors. In this work written by Andrei Kruchina, the hero, Ivan, is the third son of a Siberian peasant. He is a shining example of Soviet values as a "fool" who loves reading and eschews church services. He leaves home to fulfil his dream of flying an airplane and trains as a Soviet pilot in Tobolsk, the city in which Ershov grew up. Ivan becomes an aerial postman, bringing important packages from Siberia to the prestigious Council of People's Commissars in Moscow. He eventually returns to his peasant village and uses his airplane to heroically save the harvest by spraying it with insecticide; he also rescues his aunt Maria by flying her to the nearest hospital, more than a hundred kilometres away. The appealing image of the little humpbacked horse, or rather his modern counterpart the little flying horse, was used to entreat readers to "write to the O.D.V.F" so that "the people can strengthen the air fleet," and the fairy tale was firmly identified in the public imagination with the real-life feat of connecting the nation via a network of aerial pathways.[21] Of course, this cultural message was not always consistent. *The Little Octobrist Scamp* (*Oktiabrenok-postrelenok*), an illustrated children's book of 1925 by Nikolai Agnivtsev with illustrations by Ivan Maliutin, identified the little humpbacked horse as a superstitious relic of the past that needed to be debunked along with Baba Yaga and flying carpets. Nevertheless, whether the horse was transformed into an airplane or updated and

Figure 2.5 Ivan appears before the angry Tsar Saltan, who sleeps under the emblem of the imperial family. The illustrators are listed as "various artists of the Academy of Arts," in an edition put out by *Siniaia ptitsa* in 1924.

Figure 2.6 The tsar is boiled alive while the workers stoke the fire in this illustration by an unknown artist, published by the Levine Publishing House in 1917.

Figure 2.7 Cover image of *The Little Flying Horse, An Aerial Fairy Tale*,
illustrated by an unknown artist in 1925.

replaced by one, as in Avgintsev's story, *The Little Humpbacked Horse*
was routinely identified with the growth of Soviet aviation.

The campaign to increase support and appreciation of Soviet civil
aviation called for a series of visits by pilots and airplanes to far-flung
communities. The star of these tours was a biplane known by its nick-
name, the Konek-Gorbunok (Little Humpbacked Horse). Built by V.N.
Khioni in 1923, the Konek-Gorbunok (officially the Kh-5) was rejected
for military service but proved ideal for dazzling members of the public
by taking them up into the air for the first time, thus galvanizing their
air-mindedness. By 1927, Konek-Gorbunok airplanes formed approximately one-third of the Dobrolet fleet, and the air-mindedness inspired
by them and *The Little Flying Horse* became the precursor to the air
mania of the 1930s.[22] The O.D.V.F. and Dobrolet were subsumed by the
V.O.G.V.F., the All-Union Civil Air Fleet, in 1930 on the eve of Soviet
Russia's most glorious decade in aviation. This early chapter in Soviet
aviation history cemented several new cultural tendencies that originated under Lenin but took off under Stalin. Opening and mapping

new aerial routes between Russia's east and west transformed exploration into something that took place not just on the ground but in the air. Dobrolet's activities connected Moscow to Siberian cities in an unprecedented way. By 1929, regular airmail service to Irkutsk had reduced mailing times from six days to thirty-six hours.[23] Between 1930 and 1935, established routes pushed even further into Siberia: to Yakutsk in the north and Khabarovsk in the south.[24] Previously remote spaces became seen, mapped, and accessible. During the same years in which the "unknown" Siberian author Petr Ershov was being introduced to the public by Soviet critics, the twin connection of *The Little Humpbacked Horse* to aviation and Siberia – the land-mass hosting the Russian Arctic – meant that Stalin-era illustrations to this nineteenth-century fairy tale were poised to address two of the most heroic ventures of the epoch: long-distance flying and polar exploration.

Air-Obsessed: The Little Humpbacked Horse under Stalin

Soviet Russia's passion for flight and flying reached full throttle in the 1930s, and the little humpbacked horse became entrenched as one of its emblems. Stalin signalled the importance of aviation by declaring 18 August to be Aviation Day, an all-Union holiday, in 1933. Aviators and flying machines were honoured with postage stamps in 1938 and 1939 and in plays, movies, and books throughout the 1930s.[25] These were tributes to the remarkable feats of Soviet aviation. In 1937 a team led by pilot Valery Chkalov set a new long-distance record, flying over the North Pole from Moscow to Vancouver in Washington state. A month later, a team led by Mikhail Gromov flew even farther. In the same year, the Soviet Union became the first to land an aircraft at the North Pole and the first to establish a scientific outpost there. The following year, in 1938, Valentina Grizodubova led a team that set a long-distance record in women's aviation. Thus, in a short period at the end of the 1930s, Soviet pilots made history in the air and in the Arctic many times over.[26] These outstanding achievements in aviation showcased the technological prowess of the Soviet Union, and Stalin linked himself closely to the victories. He was fashioned as the "Father of Pilots" in the press; the pilot heroes themselves became known as "Stalin's falcons." Chkalov's famous transpolar route of 1937 was called "Stalin's Route" (*stalinskii marshrut*), a name emblazoned on the side of the aircraft and displayed to the world when it became the centrepiece of the Soviet Pavilion of the Arctic at the 1939 World's Fair in New York.[27]

Historian Kendall E. Bailes argues that these successes in aviation were a crucial legitimizing tool for Stalin. If, after 1917, the Bolsheviks had declared power in a way that was "fundamentally new to political practice" by "claim[ing] legitimacy not only as the avant-garde of the industrial proletariat but on the basis of their ability to transform nature and society," by the 1930s they still had to make good on that promise.[28] The sixty-two world records in aviation garnered by Soviet pilots between 1933 and 1938 were put to use in the service of "winning support for [Stalin's] regime at home and abroad, and of counterbalancing the effect of the purges."[29] *The Little Humpbacked Horse* played an important role in this myth of national heroism, not only because it thematized the drama playing out on the world stage (against all odds, Russian heroes rise to glory), but because as a product of a previous age it represented a wish that had been fulfilled by the advent of Soviet power. With a beginning that had finally received a happy ending, it became part of a created tradition that validated the coming of Stalinism. It is not surprising then that *The Little Humpbacked Horse* reached new heights in the 1930s and 1940s and the early 1950s, with fifty-six publications, forty-nine of them illustrated.

During this period the work was targeted specifically at very young children, a new generation eager for heroes and encouraged to become increasingly air-minded. In 1937, *Siskin* (*Chizh*), a children's journal for the very youngest readers, published a two-page feature called "Who Are They?," showing pictures of fairy-tale characters "that all children know." At the very top is Ivan, imagined as a very young boy, flying on a magical horse.[30] In issues of 1938, images of children (particularly boys) in flight became a standard feature. The polar aviator Shirshov published an open letter urging children to "get A's" so they could "become pilots, sailors, academics, and then go to the Arctic." Children read the story of a boy named Seriozha who was taken up in an airplane over seas, fields, and forests by a female pilot named Auntie Masha. The back cover of another issue from 1938 shows an aerial formation spelling the word "Stalin" in the skies over the Kremlin. This illustration referenced the November 1937 celebrations marking the twentieth anniversary of the revolution, when airplanes over the Kremlin spelled not only "Stalin" but also "Lenin" and "USSR."[31] In the late 1930s, publishing houses for children and adolescents put an emphasis on books by and about polar aviation, and the media underlined the link between hero pilots and the children they inspired.[32] The story of a Russian boy who flies all over the "kingdom," winning riches and glory along the way, was very much to the point in the 1930s and reflected the real-life celebrity of long-distance aviators like Valery Chkalov. For children's journals like *Siskin*, *The Little Humpbacked Horse* functioned as an ideal link between the child's imaginary world and the goals the state hoped to inspire in its young citizens.

Figure 2.8 Tatiana Glebova, cover of *The Little Humpbacked Horse* put
out by the State Publishing House in 1929.

Stalin-era artists like Tatiana Glebova, a student of Pavel Filonov,
made clear in their illustrated editions of *The Little Humpbacked Horse*
that the fairy tale was about "today." Glebova became a children's illustrator in 1926; her first set of illustrations to *The Little Humpbacked Horse*
appeared in 1928 and was republished in 1929 and 1933. The work is
notable for its contemporary look: her interpretation of Ivan is much
closer to Filonov's analytic realism than folk stylization thanks to her
simple lines, pencil shading, and the two-dimensionality of the boy and
the horse (fig. 2.8). The flattening of the two major figures in the composition, and simplification of the image to imitate a child's drawing,
clearly mark this cover art as part of the avant-garde aesthetic that was
to be eclipsed by the demand for greater representational and three-
dimensional composition once socialist realism had been mandated.
Glebova's tsar is completely devoid of opulence or splendour: he sleeps
in an unadorned double bed with no curtains on his window, and the
kingdom is rendered in a series of modernist angles. She reworked

Figure 2.9 Yury Vasnetsov's whimsical cover image for the 1934 Schoolchild's
Library edition of *The Little Humpbacked Horse*.

these illustrations for an edition put out by the Young Guard publishing agency in 1933, enhancing the folkloric style of her work through
added colour and design, making her back-drops appear more whimsical and dreamlike. Taken as a sign of Soviet culture's authentic link
to the people, this folk stylization became an increasingly entrenched
feature of children's illustrations in the 1930s. For *The Little Humpbacked
Horse*, its highest expression came in the illustrations by Yury Vasnetsov, whose work presaged the iconic look of Soviet children's books
well into the 1970s.

Vasnetsov's illustrations to the tale were published in 1934, 1936, 1938,
and 1945 in significant print runs. A student of the avant-garde artist
Kazimir Malevich in the 1920s, Vasnetsov became a children's illustrator at the State Children's Publishing House in 1928 under the direction
of the important children's book artist Vladimir Lebedev, and he illustrated a number of prestigious works by Tolstoy, Chukovsky, and other
prominent writers of children's books. He initiated the post-war trend

of having Ivan appear to be the same age as his very young reader and of emblazoning the cover with the evocative image of Ivan and his horse soaring across the sky (fig. 2.9). Vasnetsov's illustrations to *The Little Humpbacked Horse* reflected a broader tendency to have folklore fully saturate contemporary culture, with airplanes fashioned as "steel firebirds," and the Moscow subway system as an "underground king-dom" praised in a 1935 *novina* (new song) called "Of the Miracle Stair-case," by A.V. Morozova.[33] These images enhanced the heroic value of everyday Stalinist culture, raising it to an epic level by plugging it into a fabricated fairy-tale past. This tendency also meant that silly and satiri-cal elements in the fairy tale were reduced or purged in illustrations. After Vasnetsov, the little humpbacked horse was generally shown as plucky rather than ridiculous, simply a smaller version of his attractive older siblings (fig. 2.10). During the war years, images of heroism, avia-tion, and love of the motherland became even more relevant, and *The Little Humpbacked Horse* continued to appear in illustrated editions of 1941, 1942, 1944, and 1945. Despite an overall drop in publication runs during the war years, this fairy tale was put out in quantities as high as 225,000. All these publications were aimed at young children and acted to cement patriotism through fairy-tale images of heroism and the motherland.

Stranovedenie: A Child's Cult of the Motherland

The Little Humpbacked Horse found an important place at the heart of Stalin-era literary culture because the tale connected to contemporary priorities on three counts. First, it referenced a national folkloric past that was easily linked to the achievements of the present. Second, its images of flight stimulated heroic aspirations in young readers while the tale became a symbol of shared national triumphs in aviation. And third, the story of a Russian boy flying to and discovering distant parts of the realm reflected the national frenzy for *stranovedenie* (coun-try studies), a field targeted at children in the 1930s, with the aim of making all corners of the motherland known and loved by its citizens. Although Leninist Russia had maintained an international focus, by the mid-1930s "the subject of labour and class struggle [was] ousted by that of the Soviet Motherland, [and] the image of the revolutionary state was substituted with descriptions of the country's beauty, spaciousness and the happy childhood it provided."[34] *Stranovedenie* originated in the early twentieth century as a field of study dedicated to the geography, climate, agriculture, and ethnicities of the Russian Empire. In the 1920s *stranovedenie* was still defining and consolidating itself as a discipline,

Figure 2.10 Yury Vasnetsov, illustration in the 1938 publication of
The Little Humpbacked Horse.

but in the 1930s it surged as geography and history were revived in the elementary school curriculum.[35] The idea was to provide children with a shared sense of a Soviet homeland that, despite vast territorial variations and the presence of multiple ethnic groups, was presented as largely a Russian construct.[36] To put it another way, Russianness was used as the equalizing factor that united a large, disparate territory known as the Soviet Union. Outside the classroom a popular series of expeditions for children called "Learn More about Our Motherland!" became a mass trend of the 1930s. The children's newspaper *Pionerskaia Pravda* ran geographic competitions and games for children from all parts of the country in issues of 1938, 1939, and 1940, and Komsomol characters featured regularly in adventure and exploration films of the decade.[37] Children who read or were read *The Little Humpbacked Horse*, following the adventures as the boy hero flew from one part of the land to another, uncovering its riches and solving its mysteries along the way, emulated the armchair travelling of *stranovedenie*. In this way the fairy tale connected seamlessly with a favourite leisure-time activity for Stalin-era children, becoming a cipher for the ritual of discovering and celebrating the motherland.

This ritual could be enacted in a variety of ways, including reading the letters of children living above the Arctic Circle in the popular book *We Are from Igarka* (1938) or honouring the country's forests, fields, and rivers in the 1936 hit "Song of the Motherland."[38] An important goal of *stranovedenie* was its attempt to efface the border between centre and periphery, Moscow and the edges of the empire, by making all citizens equally and knowledgeably Soviet. The Papanovites, the team of Arctic researchers led by Ivan Papanin, who established a camp at the North Pole in 1938, reported that they carried on Soviet cultural practices even in the polar wilderness, reciting Pushkin at night and standing to sing the "Internationale."[39] *The Little Humpbacked Horse* also contributed to the act of erasing boundaries and connecting the nation. With its Siberian-born author and local Siberian vocabulary, the tale familiarized young urban readers with a part of the country that had only been fully connected by rail to European Russia since 1916.[40] Illustrators of the work in the 1930s and 1940s revealed a landscape of wooden huts, coniferous forests, and sea-coast that was fittingly Siberian. Just as the Konek-Gorbunok airplane and *The Little Flying Horse* of the 1920s had become associated with the creation of new, regular air routes from Moscow into Siberia, linking the country together in a way it had never been before, so too did illustrations of the Stalin era make Siberia appear to be closer and more familiar than ever.

The Little Humpbacked Horse even helped to make visible the Siberia that was off the map, the Siberia of Stalin's Gulag archipelago, when Magadan, the administrative centre of the Gulag empire, produced its own edition of the fairy tale in 1947. Millions of prisoners disappeared into Gulag camps in the Stalinist era, many of them located in the part of Siberia above the Arctic Circle. The most infamous of these was Kolyma, a gold-mining camp located in the Magadan region of northeastern Siberia. In 1938 the great Russian poet Osip Mandelstam was sentenced to eight years in Kolyma and died on the way there. Camp survivor Varlam Shalamov, who served sentences from 1929 to 1951, described in his *Kolyma Tales* (first published in English translation in 1966 and in Russian in 1978) how prison labour was used to mine gold out of the permafrost with pickaxes. Accessing the rich mineral deposits of the Kolyma river basin was one of the main objectives of Dal'stroi (Main Administration for Construction in the Far North), created in 1931. In 1938 Dal'stroi inherited the prestigious empire of Arctic exploration operated by Glavsevmorput (Chief Directorate of the Northern Sea Route) and in the same year came under Stalin's large Gulag administration, governed by the NKVD, the secret police.[41] Dal'stroi was centred in Magadan, a Siberian town that had only been established in 1929 but which rapidly expanded as it became the major transit point for the transfer of millions of prisoners to Gulag camps.

As its population boomed with an influx of Soviet bureaucrats and their families, Magadan became eager to establish itself as a legitimate urban centre like any other in the Soviet Union. In 1939 it amended its special extraterritorial status by applying for and winning the right to call itself a "city." The Soviet Kolyma Publishing House, which existed from 1936 to 1954, was one of a series of cultural institutions, including a newspaper, a magazine, and a theatre, intended to normalize the city's position. In 1947 Soviet Kolyma, produced its own handsome edition of *The Little Humpbacked Horse* in a print run of five thousand, with well over fifty illustrations (fig. 2.11). The edition is typical for this period with its folk stylization, naive Ivan, plucky little horse, and angry bearded tsar. The work also captures the call for post-war optimism in an illustration that shows Ivan and the little humpbacked horse at the foot of a mountain that towers over the forest. Instead of representing it as an impassable obstacle, the illustration shows a road to what appears to be the very top of the world that opens up for the two companions, just as the sun shines from behind the dark clouds (fig. 2.12). For Magadan, a city desiring to establish its authenticity and ordinariness in the post-1945 period, there was perhaps no more fitting calling card than the fairy tale whose hero, in the eyes of Stalin-era

Figure 2.11 Front cover of *The Little Humpbacked Horse* published by the Soviet Kolyma Publishing House in 1947 in the Siberian city of Magadan, the administrative centre of Stalin's Gulag archipelago. Unknown artist.

Figure 2.12 The Russian peasant and his plucky companion climb to the
summit as the sun emerges, in this illustration from the 1947 edition of
The Little Humpbacked Horse published in Kolyma.

critics, epitomized simplicity and honesty and whose story embodied
the optimism and heroism of the epoch.

Overall, illustrations to this tale from 1917 to 1953 make overt what
had traditionally been concealed in the character of Ivan the Fool.
Intrinsic to this peasant protagonist was a duality between appearance
and true nature. To the outside world and particularly to those above
him in rank and superiority, he appeared to be a talentless dim-wit,
but the tale suggested hidden heroic qualities. Soviet illustrations made
those explicit for the first time, but this had the effect of reducing the
multidimensionality of the tale. Instead of Ivan's being uncovered as a
hero at the end of the adventure, after his courage and loyalty had gone
unrecognized by dismissive brothers, ignorant tsars, and sycophantic
servants, no real reversal took place. By and large in the period under
study, the visual text showed him as a hero all along and proposed that

his rise and the tsar's downfall were inevitable. What had been a tale of revelation became instead a fairly obvious parable of the revolution. *The Little Humpbacked Horse* operated as what neo-Marxist, fairy-tale theorist Jack Zipes would classify as a tale of class conflict and subversion, in which alternative social hierarchies are proposed as a kind of utopian reordering of society.[42] Although the tale had once been considered, by late nineteenth-century critics, a dangerous lesson about imagined social upheaval, its Soviet illustrated versions bolstered the Stalin-era critics' argument that *The Little Humpbacked Horse* intuited unavoidable revolutionary change. Through its illustrated versions this work was able to achieve the ideal form for fairy tales: an expression of the present rather than an evocation of the past.

PART II

The Afterlife of Russian Classics

The Lenin-era state recognized very early the significance of Russian literary classics.[1] The 11 January 1918 Decree on the State Publishing House declared a publishing monopoly on the great works of Russian literature for a period of five years, as well as the intention to produce a full academic collection of classics and shorter, popular editions of classics that would be accessible to the working classes.[2] Although Lunacharsky and the Commissariat of Enlightenment were unable to bring these volumes to fruition, and the state monopoly on classics was never enforced, this early decree shows some important intentions of the state regarding literary classics.[3] Firstly, the literary greats of the past were appropriated on behalf of the people as their rightful heritage. But before the people could access that heritage, the state required the texts to be reframed, either by abridging them to increase their comprehensibility and popular appeal or by buttressing them with appropriate forewords and critical commentaries.[4] It was paramount that these critical commentaries be written from an approved point of view: the decree cautioned that the full academic collection of Russian classics could not be produced until the membership of the Academy of Sciences was "democratized."[5] The January 1918 resolution established that the literary artifacts of the past would not simply be reproduced on their own terms; they had to be explicated, contextualized, and legitimized. Yesterday would have to be annotated by today. As to Russian classics for the adolescent and child reader, some were produced by the private publishing houses that still existed in the 1920s; there was no state edition of classics for children until the early Stalin era.[6] From 1917 until the end of the 1920s the most republished classics overall were those of Tolstoy. His works were republished 140 times, as compared to those of Chekhov (sixty-five times), Gogol (thirty-one times), Pushkin (eighteen times), and Lermontov and Turgenev (each seventeen times).[7] In the 1920s a precedent was set for Dostoevsky's books being the least republished Russian classics, with only twelve new editions of his work.[8]

In the 1930s, when the State Children's Publishing House came into operation, a more detailed picture emerges of the classics that were produced specifically for adolescent and child audiences. At this point Pushkin ascended to the top of the list of the most republished classics for children (thirty-eight book editions), followed by Chekhov (nineteen) and Tolstoy (eighteen); then a steep drop to Lermontov (eight), Gogol and Turgenev (four each), and, tailing the others again, Dostoevsky with two. It is worth commenting in this introduction on this dearth of Dostoevsky editions because his notable scarcity among the pantheon of classics (reversed in the post-Stalin years) speaks volumes about the state and its difficult relationship with the literary past.

The Spurned Classic

Dostoevsky was a troublesome figure to reconcile with Soviet values thanks to the religious conviction that permeates his later writing, his personal and professional affiliation with conservatives and reactionaries, and the lampooning of revolutionaries in his novel *Demons* (1871). Although in the 1920s, before state publishing had been fully consolidated, it was still possible to be an admirer of Dostoevsky's writing, and even to produce critical works dedicated to Dostoevsky's thought as a religious philosopher, such as Alexander Dolinin's 1922 *Dostoevsky: Articles and Materials*, by the 1930s Dostoevsky could only be read and studied by caveat – in "Marxist interpretation" or with a "critical attitude."

In the 1920s and 1930s, five works by Dostoevsky became part of Soviet children's reading. Excerpts from *Brothers Karamazov* (1880) were issued by children's presses in 1928 and 1947, the latter illustrated by V. Ladyagin. *Crime and Punishment* (1866) was republished twice for the adolescent audience, in the series Classics for the Middle School in 1923 and by the Children's Literature Publishing House in 1934.[9] *Notes from the House of the Dead* (1861) was republished as part of the School Series of Classics, with a lengthy and critical foreword, in 1935.[10] One of the real contradictions at the heart of Dostoevsky's Soviet afterlife is that the few works that were made part of children's reading from the 1920s to the 1950s were precisely the novels from the objectionable later period of Dostoevsky's literary output. Thus the state reproduced and distributed those very texts that it deemed unacceptable, albeit with long forewords explaining in detail why the works were unsuitable.

Further, this same period of greatest stricture against Dostoevsky's writings also witnessed the flourishing of Dostoevsky scholarship, as previously unpublished manuscripts, drafts, and letters were made available for the first time.

Dostoevsky's fate in the state-produced textbook *Russian Literature* was no less dire. Although he appeared in his own chapter of the 1938–9 edition, he was severely criticized as a writer who had fatally misdiagnosed the cure for tsarist society's ills, choosing religious and moral solutions over political and revolutionary ones. Teachers who were training at pedagogical institutes in 1938 were reminded in the section that concluded the Dostoevsky chapter, called "The Reactionariness of Dostoevsky's Views," that they had "to study Dostoevsky, but in no way to learn from Dostoevsky."[11] By 1940, students were neither studying nor learning from Dostoevsky. Although sections on Gogol, Tolstoy, Chekhov, and other Russian classics remained, Dostoevsky's section was removed from the textbook for secondary schools and, by extension, from the pantheon of great Russian authors of the past, for over a decade. Dostoevsky was not officially rehabilitated until the seventy-fifth anniversary of his death in 1956, when he finally joined Pushkin, Tolstoy, and other classics as a "great Russian writer." In the schools, however, the fallout was longer lasting. As late as 1969, D.L. Sorkina, the author of *Dostoevsky in the Schools*, lamented "a complete absence of books about the writer."[12]

The Celebrated Classic

Dostoevsky was the exception among classics, however. In the 1930s Pushkin emerged at the head of a wider campaign to rehabilitate the national past and revive a literary canon that was touted as the forerunner to the great achievements of the present. The co-opting of Russian literary classics constituted one of Stalin's greatest cultural projects in the 1930s. Together with a restoration of historical figures like Alexander Nevsky and Peter the Great, the Stalinist repositioning of the past aimed at selecting a Red canon and a heroic national past fitting to the grand aspirations of the regime.[13] As David Brandenberger and Kevin Platt have argued, in the 1930s a "usable past" was constructed by carefully selecting certain figures to ascend to a Stalinist pantheon of heroic precursors. This usable past was bolstered by the folk-inspired songs and epic poems that Frank Miller has memorably termed "Stalinist fakelore." Alongside the larger-than-life heroes from the mythic past like Ilya Muromets and Mikula Selianovich, the new Stalinist heroes of long-distance flights and Arctic exploration were celebrated in the so-called *noviny* (new songs) that imitated the folk traditions of the *stariny* (old songs). These heroes penetrated every layer of society right down to the nursery. In 1937 the day care of a Kharkov tractor factory featured a mobile of a polar long-distance airplane suspended from the ceiling, above a portrait of Stalin overseeing the toddlers at play.[14]

By the mid-1930s, Pushkin's star had already risen and fallen quite spectacularly in republications and reassessments of his works. Whereas in 1887, the year marking fifty years since his death, the end of copyright restrictions on his writings had translated into a huge surge in republications and sales, this bestselling status, as we have seen, was dramatically curtailed in the 1920s.[15] The end of the nineteenth century had also seen the start of the tradition of publicly celebrated Pushkin anniversaries, a cultural phenomenon that would be hyperextended into the enormous all-Union Stalinist Pushkin jubilees of 1937 and 1949, when Pushkin was touted as "the founder of new Russian literature" and the "most contemporary of our contemporaries."[16] These occasions, which are examined in the next chapter, in turn justified republications of classics in huge circulations, many of them illustrated and for child audiences. But while leading intellectuals had argued in 1887 against commemorating the anniversary of Pushkin's untimely death, feeling it would be in bad taste to mark that event, under Lenin and Stalin this sense of nicety was repudiated, and the anniversary years of the twentieth century established a firm emphasis on the poet's death.[17] If, from the late nineteenth century to the late 1920s, the image of Pushkin was appropriated at times by the state, and at others by the intelligentsia, by the late 1930s the party had established a firm monopoly on Pushkin, who was fashioned into the "friend of the people" and the founding father of an illustrious national literary tradition that had continued into Stalinist times. During the Second World War, Pushkin played an important role for the state as an emblem of Russia's cultural greatness that was opposed to the images of bestial, cultureless fascists. In 1943, Vera Inber published a poem called "Pushkin Lives!" (Pushkin zhiv!), which describes a survivor of the siege of Leningrad who does not want to abandon his Pushkin collection during a Nazi bombing raid. As he is pulled from the wreckage, he is clutching a half-burned copy of a Pushkin work to his chest, and when he regains consciousness, his first words are, "And Pushkin?" A friend reassures him that "Pushkin lives!" Not only Russia's national bard but many Russian classics enjoyed a robust return to life in the 1930s after the ambiguities of the 1920s. Although the creation of Soviet illustrated children's literature had been the major achievement of the 1920s, a large body of state-produced children's *reading*, originating in the past but mediated for the present by illustrations, was the accomplishment of the Stalin-era 1930s.

Classics in the Stalin-Era Public School

In grades eight and nine the Russian classics were presented to adolescent students through the public school textbook *Russian Literature*. This textbook, which began publication in 1936, presented literature as a "fight" (*literaturnaia bor'ba*) that was taking place in the nineteenth century shoulder to shoulder with battles for greater social and political justice.[18] An updated edition of this textbook was published every year until 1941, when publication was suspended until 1946 because of the war, then subsequently continued. The final pre-war edition of 1940 begins with the death of Pushkin in 1837 and conceptualizes Russian literature in terms of heirs to his legacy, especially as endorsed by progressive literary critics like Vissarion Belinsky. Stand-alone chapters were dedicated to Turgenev, Chernyshevsky, Tolstoy, Nekrasov, Saltykov-Schedrin, Uspensky, and Chekhov. All editions of the textbook established a format that began with Pushkin in the nineteenth century and ended with Chekhov in the twentieth century. The conclusion to the textbook established that the classics were precursors leading to the father of Soviet literature, Maxim Gorky. The author of this conclusion, A. Zerchaninov, wrote: "The nineteenth century left our epoch an enormous artistic heritage. To study it, value it, love it – this is our duty, one of the most essential conditions of growth for our great socialist culture."[19] Thus a firm connection between the past and the present was established, or, rather, the purpose of the past was elucidated as the artistic foundation of what would later be built by the Soviets. This position represented a significant departure from the early years of the revolution, when the past was regarded as a legacy to be accepted only grudgingly. But by the post-war era, future teachers of Russian literature were informed in the textbook for teacher training colleges that the function of artistic literature was to "acquaint us with the life of the past."[20] The textbook edition of 1947 insisted: "Artistic literature acquaints us as much with the past as with the current life of society."[21]

Classics in War Time

During the Great Patriotic War (1941–5) the importance of Russian classics was further entrenched. The state called up Russia's literary lions – Pushkin, Tolstoy, Lermontov, Turgenev, and, yes, Dostoevsky – in order to claim that their great achievements were worth safeguarding from cultural incursion. In these years Pushkin remained the most republished classic with eleven book editions of his work produced. Chekhov was republished seven times, followed by Lermontov (six), Tolstoy (four), Gogol (three) and Turgenev (two). Dostoevsky's works were not republished at all during the war, yet Soviet adult literary culture finally found some common ground with Dostoevsky. For a brief window lasting until 1947, Dostoevsky was reconceived as a great patriotic writer whose anti-German comments could now be taken as a timely warning against the rise of a fascist, Teutonic enemy. His *Diary of a Writer* was republished just before the war, in 1940, and bolstered by articles like Emelian Iaroslavsky's "Fyodor Mikhailovich Dostoevsky against the Germans," published in the journal *Bolshevik* in 1942. The importance of using Dostoevsky as a spokesman for anti-German sentiment even justified a temporary cessation of the campaign of criticism against *Demons*. Instead of castigating the work for its parodic portrayal of revolutionaries, staunch party critics like V.V. Ermilov now discovered in the novel "a brilliant portrayal of the precursors of Fascism" and even titled his 1942 article in the journal *Literature and Art* "The Great Russian Writer F.M. Dostoevsky."[22] Unfortunately Dostoevsky's rise in fortune coincided with the years in which no new edition of the public school textbook was produced, and so he remained the spurned classic for students in high school.

Overall, classics were a small but growing segment of the overall output of the Children's Literature Publishing House. Whereas classics accounted for 9 per cent of all children's literature published by the state in 1933, this had grown to 15 per cent by 1940.[23] Still, this relatively small percentage was strategically important as part of a larger state-sponsored revival of the heroic past and therefore represents a mighty minority of works included in the child's library. In the following two chapters I look at two important works of children's reading, Pushkin's *The Bronze Horseman* and Tolstoy's *Anna Karenina*. In longitudinal studies of the positioning of these works in adolescent literature, the public school system, and popular culture more widely, I show that illustrations were fundamental to new conceptualizations of the works as domains of the child's library, as well as fundamental to shifts in the presentation of images of Pushkin himself, of the city of St Petersburg or Leningrad, and of separated mothers like Anna Karenina.

Chapter Three

The Bronze Horseman Rides Again

Six illustrated editions of Alexander Pushkin's *Mednyi vsadnik* (*The Bronze Horseman*) by five different artists were published during the Stalinist period, 1928–53.[1] In the 1930s and 1940s the poem rose to a new significance as the state aggressively promoted its author in Pushkin jubilees of 1937 and 1949 and rehabilitated one of its leading characters, Peter the Great, as a ruthless but admirable hero from the national past. Illustrations were used as a strategic method of forging connections between Pushkin's early nineteenth-century poem and the cultural priorities of Stalinist Russia, cueing Soviet readers on the correct interpretation of key ideas like "tsarist literature" and "St Petersburg." Illustrated editions could speak to contemporary events in compelling ways, as when illustrations of *The Bronze Horseman* in 1949 turned Pushkin's story of a terrifying 1824 St Petersburg flood into a reader, after the siege of Leningrad, on how to weather catastrophe and begin the project of rebuilding a damaged city. While socialist-realist representations of Pushkin's text became compulsory from the mid-1930s, in practice the modernist illustrations of Alexander Benois, first published in the luxury art journal *Mir iskusstva* (World of art) in 1904, were being republished as late as 1948. In this chapter I explore how Stalin-era publishers cannily repositioned Benois's illustrations to bring them in line with the state's cultural agenda, and the ways in which publishers in the 1930s and 1940s employed newly commissioned illustrations of *The Bronze Horseman* to make the poem resonate with new cultural meaning. I will also look at the fundamental shift that took place between the 1920s and 1930s, turning *The Bronze Horseman*, for the first time, into children's reading and a cornerstone of the public school curriculum.

In the 1930s Pushkin ascended to unprecedented heights at the head of the canon of new Russian literature and the object of zealous 1937 and 1949 anniversary celebrations. At the same time, graphic illustrations began to play a crucial role in articulating a correct approach to the great works of the tsarist era. Illustrations accompanying works of classical Russian literature were given top priority in the late 1930s.[2] As the 1937 Pushkin jubilee year approached, and Soviet publishing houses were preparing to flood the reading public with millions of anniversary-edition copies of Pushkin's works, illustrated editions of Pushkin's writings, including *The Bronze Horseman*, found themselves at the very centre of a political and cultural firestorm about how to formulate the new principles of socialist-realist art and articulate the cultural goals of the state.

A Modernist Classic Refashioned

Despite the prominence assigned to illustrations of Pushkin's works, this area stood at a critical juncture as late as 1936. At the *Exhibition of Soviet Illustrations to Artistic Literature, 1931–1936*, which opened at the Museum of Decorative Arts in Moscow in 1936 and was intended to showcase the success of the socialist-realist school in graphic art, first-rank socialist-realist illustrations of Pushkin's works remained a notable and regrettable blank.[3] The incomplete transition from modernism to socialist realism in artistic practice prompted the decision to republish the only existing full-length illustrated version of *The Bronze Horseman*, by the artist Alexander Benois, despite the fact that he had permanently left the Soviet Union for France in 1924, and his work derived from an artistic school now labelled as reactionary, bourgeois, and narrowly focused on aesthetics.[4] The illustration *After Him Gallops the Bronze Horseman*, for instance, highlights the nightmarish sense of foreboding in the work through its ominous colour blocks and its use of perspective and size. The natural and man-made landscape dwarfs the figure of the hero, placed on the right-hand edge of the composition, conveying a sense of being threatened from all sides and literally pushed off the page. The tiny size of the fleeing hero compared to his surroundings suggests his complete vulnerability to devouring, irrational forces (see fig. 3.1). To mitigate these undesirable features, two shrewd publishing choices were made. Whereas the original Benois illustrations had been commissioned by an elite group of bibliophiles and had appeared in what Soviet leaders regarded as the decadent art journal *World of Art*, the 1936 republication of Benois's work, which was readily attributed to him, was put out by the State Children's Publishing House.[5] In fact, one half of the illustrated editions of *The Bronze Horseman* produced during the Stalinist era were put out by children's publishing houses, two illustrated by Benois (1936 and 1945) and one by Mikhail Rodionov

Figure 3.1 Alexander Benois, *After Him Gallops the Bronze Horseman*. Stalin-era editors selected Benois's second version of the illustration (created in 1916; first published in 1923), which augmented the apocalyptic undertones of the work through its galloping storm clouds.

(1949). As a result, the Benois illustrations entered a Soviet afterlife that was carefully managed to create an entirely new reader, the Soviet twelve- to seventeen-year-old, who had not yet been born when Benois's series first appeared in 1904.[6]

The second strategic publishing decision was to significantly reduce the size of Benois's series, making the 1936 and 1945 republications of his illustrations controlled *selections*. In fact, 1936 did not mark the first time that Benois's series had been altered, because the artist himself had created three different versions of *The Bronze Horseman* illustrations over a period spanning nearly two decades, from 1903 to 1922, with each one destined for a distinct reading audience. The original version of the series, composed in 1903, contained a large enough number of illustrations – thirty-three – to make the graphic work a sustained visual accompaniment to Pushkin's text. Benois was lauded at the time for his careful reproduction of period details from St Petersburg in the 1820s.[7] Like Pushkin's poem, the illustrations often digress from the main plot to record asides about the tsarist capital and minor literary figures of the day such as Count Khvostov. When these illustrations were published in the journal *World of Art* in 1904, they produced the impression of an elegant edition from the nineteenth century, complete with illuminations, tail-pieces, and stately coats of arms. This contrasted sharply

Figure 3.2 What the reader did not see in 1936. Alexander Benois's illustration of Evgeny pursuing Fortune, and in turn being pursued by the Grim Reaper. Published in 1904 and 1923.

with Benois's second series, a taut six-illustration pamphlet put out in an inexpensive "people's edition" by the St Petersburg Literacy Society in 1912. These illustrations, composed in 1905–6, tend to foreground the terror and calamity of the flood. Benois's third series, created 1916–22, contained thirty-five illustrations that largely amalgamated the work of the first two series. It was published by the Committee for Popularizing Artistic Editions in 1923.[8]

Left out when editorial decisions were turned over to Stalin-era publishers in 1936 were the historical embellishments such as crowd scenes on Mars Field or tsarist officials standing on a flooded embankment, as well as mythological images of Triton, Fortune, or the Grim Reaper (fig. 3.2). The 1936 illustrations eschew leisurely digression, focusing on the physical action of the poem. With only thirteen illustrations selected from the original thirty-three, they present a leaner, less emotive interpretation of *The Bronze Horseman*, a poem that treats the young hero, Evgeny, who during the life-imperilling flood of 1824 crosses to the other side of the raging Neva river to find his fiancée, Parasha. Discovering that she has perished, Evgeny moves from grief to madness and finds himself at the foot of the bronze equine monument to Peter the Great, where he raises his fist at the autocrat whom he blames for the disaster.[9] The Bronze Horseman then descends from his pedestal and pursues Evgeny to his death. The 1936 edition of Benois's series subdues the terror evoked by the artist in earlier versions of the work, foreshortening the scenes depicting Evgeny's madness and cutting back the spine-tingling images of his pursuit by the supernatural Bronze Horseman. The original sequence of ten illustrations ·taking the reader from Evgeny's discovery of Parasha's destroyed home, through his distraught wandering, to the base of the Bronze Horseman monument, and then in flight through the dark streets of St Petersburg is whittled down to four sharp images. In 1936 Evgeny does not sleep on the streets, the Bronze Horseman's outstretched arm does not appear to move, over three illustrations, until it is pointing ominously at Evgeny, and his dead body is not discovered or shown. In general, the 1936 edition of Benois's work emerges as more plot driven and rational than its three predecessors and, with its enormous circulation of 300,000 copies, aimed at reaching a significant number of young readers.

The 1945 post-war edition of Benois's illustrations, put out as part of the Schoolchild's Library series and containing only five illustrations, furthered the course set out in 1936 and eliminated any illustrations depicting flood victims, Evgeny's insanity, the confrontation between tsar and citizen, the animation of the Bronze Horseman, and the pitiless pursuit of his human prey (fig. 3.3). In 1945 the entire story in pictures consists of Peter the Great contemplating the future site of St Petersburg, Evgeny walking home in the rain, two "period" silhouettes – one of the Bronze Horseman monument seen from the rear, and one of sails on the Neva – and finally the collapsed hut where Evgeny's body is found, a reproduction so tiny that the body cannot be seen. The result, even taking into account war-time retrenchment, is an astonishingly sanitized and bland illustrated version of *The Bronze Horseman*.

In addition to the "cleansing" process whereby mystical and irrational elements were diminished in the series, and Benois's work was fundamentally reconceived as illustrated literature for the adolescent reader, a factor that may have contributed to the inclusion of these modernist drawings in Stalinist mass editions of the 1930s and 1940s was a Leninist initiative for repackaging the images for mass consumption. In the 1920s, selected images from Benois's series were popularized for the mass market as picture postcards produced by the St Eugenia Society (fig. 3.4). The commercial success of the St Eugenia Society's

Figure 3.3 One of the images of madness and pursuit excised from the 1936 and 1945 republications of Benois's illustrations to *The Bronze Horseman* (see also colour plate 8). Published in 1923.

wares, with the most popular postcards selling out in quantities of fifty or sixty thousand, prompted the Leninist government to take over the venture and rename the society the Committee for Popularizing Artistic Editions, which was subsumed under the State Academy of Material Culture.[10] The St Eugenia Society acted as a kind of bridge reconciling the elite aesthetics of the World of Art group – the society kept close ties with members and featured their art prominently in its products – and the early Soviet mass market.[11] The Stalinist repackaging of Benois's *Bronze Horseman* series built upon this early success at redirecting Benois's work from the elite to the everyday consumer, yet it remained problematic, ambiguous, and insufficiently focused on social utility. The Stalinist editorial project of effacing unacceptably dramatic, supernatural, and sublime elements was achieved at the price of cutting an increasingly large proportion of the series between 1936 and 1945, and Benois himself remained a problematic figure as a leader in the World of Art movement and a permanent emigrant from the Soviet Union as of 1924. The need for a socialist-realist visual interpretation of *The Bronze Horseman* remained.

Figure 3.4 This image of imperial-era splendour was reproduced as a postcard by the Committee for Popularizing Artistic Editions in 1923 but was left out of the 1936 and 1945 editions of Benois's *Bronze Horseman* illustrations.

The Bronze Horseman Rides Again as Soviet Classic

The first Stalin-era commission for illustrations to *The Bronze Horseman* was assigned to the artist Alexei Kravchenko and appeared in 1936. Put out by the Artistic Literature Publishing House, these new illustrations formed an adult companion piece to Benois's so-called children's illustrations. Although the state was eager for work that would exhibit the "victory of realistic principles in book art," Kravchenko's series of five wood engravings did not yet fulfil that aspiration.[12] Kravchenko's images were unsuitably emotional and lyrical, with characters arrested in dramatic and highly stylized postures. Yet in two senses this work showed an intriguing attention to Stalinist cultural practices. Kravchenko's representation of Evgeny, for instance, shows a conflation between Pushkin's tragic hero and the poet himself. In the first illustration of the series Evgeny's wind-blown hair falls down over his cheek in a simulation of Pushkin's famous sideburn (fig. 3.5). Evgeny cuts a poetic figure with his black frock coat, stylized gestures of arms raised as if in oration, and long, romantic eyelashes (fig. 3.6). In this way the conflict in the poem, where Peter the Great pursues and harasses his citizen from atop his bronze steed, can be read as taking place between *Pushkin* and the tsarist state.[13] If in Benois's depiction

Figure 3.5 Alexei Kravchenko's "Pushkinian" illustration of Evgeny, 1936.

Figure 3.6 Kravchenko's 1936 poetic representation of Evgeny, who stands in a storm-tossed boat but appears in a posture more appropriate to reciting verse.

of Evgeny the hero's face is generally obscured, signalling his role as an "everyman," Kravchenko's series draws a parallel between the downtrodden hero and Pushkin's fate at the hand of his tsarist master. Kravchenko's illustrations articulate an important goal of the 1937 Pushkin jubilee, casting Pushkin as the victim of tsarist autocracy, whose "spirit of civic protest" had been unjustly crushed, and who, suffering and unrecognized under Nicholas I, was only now, in Stalinist Russia, being acknowledged as a "friend of the people" and "the most contemporary of our contemporaries."[14]

The second intriguing way in which the Kravchenko illustrations support the Stalinist incarnation of the Pushkin myth is in the representation, or rather the *non*-representation, of St Petersburg. The city is a looming, magical, and malevolent presence in the Benois illustrations. It is the imperial capital that Peter the Great founded on low-lying marshland, creating the ideal conditions for the catastrophic deluge that overcame the city and its populace. Commissioned in 1903, Benois's original series was intended to mark St Petersburg's two-hundredth anniversary, and Benois was selected for the job because of his reputation as a specialist in St Petersburg architecture and decoration. Benois himself used the illustrations to rescue the city from its nineteenth-century image as a dull bureaucratic centre and explore his own aesthetic construction of St Petersburg as a place of wonder and terror.[15] By 1936, however, as the colossal Pushkin jubilee approached, official policy was to play down Pushkin's connection to St Petersburg, now renamed Leningrad, and make Moscow the centre of festivities. St Petersburg was rejected because it was the place "where Pushkin was murdered," although this concern for impropriety did not appear to affect the rest of the jubilee celebration, which marked the very occasion of his death.[16] In fact, of the eight Pushkin anniversaries celebrated in 1880–1999, the six jubilees of the twentieth century established a firm emphasis on Pushkin's death.[17] St Petersburg virtually disappears as the setting of the poem in Kravchenko's series. While in Benois's illustrations the signature buildings and embankments of the city had appeared prominently, only once in Kravchenko's series can we recognize a Petersburg landmark, the spire of the Peter and Paul Fortress, barely visible through the darkness and rain.

Benois's and Kravchenko's 1936 illustrated editions of *The Bronze Horseman* were published while the Stalinist cultural line on graphic illustrations, as well as the Pushkin myth, was still in the process of consolidation. In fact, neither artist's work really fulfilled the mandate to discover "progressive ideological content," "positive images," and a "base in the *narod*."[18] Like the drawings by the retrospective-minded

Figure 3.7 Alexei Kravchenko
was often selected to illustrate
scenes of the supernatural, such
as this illustration to Pushkin's
The Queen of Spades (1939–40).

Benois, the *Bronze Horseman* illustrations by Kravchenko signalled a
backwards glance to the 1830s, when engravings on wood, such as his
own, had emerged as a leading technique in book illustration.[19] But
it was no longer acceptable, by the mid-1930s, for artists to approach
an illustrated work of classical Russian literature as a period piece.
This kind of "archaeological" approach to the text was expected to be
replaced by ideologically driven images that could "speak our contemporary language."[20] Kravchenko's dramatic neo-romanticism lent itself
to images of the mystical or the grotesque, and in the late 1920s to 1930s
he was often commissioned to illustrate works portraying the supernatural that were being republished thanks to the important place of
their authors in the classical canon. These works included Gogol's "The
Portrait" in 1929 and Pushkin's *Stone Guest* in 1936 and *The Queen of
Spades* in 1939–40 (fig. 3.7). Kravchenko's signature style, when applied
to illustrations of historical socialist importance like the shooting down
of members of the Paris Commune (1924), lent a heightened emotional

Figure 3.8 Kravchenko, *Paris Commune: The Shooting of the Communards* (1924).
As in the illustration for *The Queen of Spades*, dramatically raised arms depict
helplessness before a larger, malevolent power.

and elevated epic status to the works (fig. 3.8). Ultimately, however, his
work remained outside the aesthetic boundaries of socialist-realist art,
and the search for a more contemporary rendering of *The Bronze Horseman* continued. The appearance of Benois's and Kravchenko's illustrations in the run-up to the Pushkin anniversary year of 1937 may be
attributed to the Stalinist goal of using the jubilee to attract figures from
the pre-revolutionary intelligentsia back to Stalinist social practices.[21] It
was in this period, the same one in which Anna Akhmatova was permitted to publish an article on Pushkin (her first appearance in print
since 1922), that the illustrations of two artists connected to the modernist World of Art group found their way into a prominent role in the
first Stalinist Pushkin celebration.[22] Not until 1949, the second Stalinist
Pushkin jubilee, were the precepts of socialist-realist book art finally
fulfilled in illustrated editions of *The Bronze Horseman*.

Weathering the Storm of the Siege

The 1949 jubilee has generally been understood as a moment of tire-
some repetition rather than an opportunity for laying down new stra-
ta of cultural meaning. Cultural historians Karen Petrone and David

Brandenberger, in their recent work on Stalinist public celebrations, position the 1949 Pushkin jubilee as an extended replay of 1937, with essentially the same forced festivities aimed at a population already exhausted and benumbed by the Pushkinian frenzy of the 1930s. Yet for survivors of the siege of Leningrad (1941–4), illustrated editions of *The Bronze Horseman* marking the 1949 anniversary year transformed the jubilee into more than 1936 redux; they made the work that Pushkin subtitled *Peterburgskaia povest'* (A Petersburg story), and its accompanying visual text, urgently relevant. Readers who had lived through the aerial bombardment of Leningrad could discover in the story of a terrifying storm raining down upon their city, battering buildings, destroying homes, and claiming innocent victims, the chance to affirm their recent sacrifice and pay tribute to their ordeal. Moreover, in the atmosphere of enforced forgetting that attended the party's post-war crack-down on Leningrad exceptionalism and siege commemoration – culminating in the devastating purge of top Leningrad party officials, known as the Leningrad affair (1949–53) – the three 1949 illustrated editions of *The Bronze Horseman* offered a unique opportunity to counter the erasure of siege representation by showing "storm survivors" in unmistakable Leningrad settings.

The state had begun to control the way the siege was memorialized as early as April 1945, with the Leningrad Writers' Union leading a campaign of criticism against authors who depicted the war as "local, personal, painful or absurd – in short, as anything other than a 'great struggle.'" In the post-war decade the party ruthlessly positioned itself as the master narrator of the story of the siege, focusing on a policy of "universaliz[ing] the Leningrad epic" at the expense of local and individual tributes by siege survivors.[23] By 1949, localistic publications and posters depicting not only the siege but any sense of Leningrad singularity were being purged.[24] Following the visit of Central Committee Secretary Georgy Malenkov to the newly created Museum of the Defence of Leningrad in February 1949, the museum directors were arrested and an order issued to overhaul the exhibits so that the role of Stalin in the war could be emphasized. By 1953, the museum had been liquidated, and its unique collections, containing more than thirty-two thousand items of siege memorabilia, destroyed. The cultural repression that had started in 1945 with Leningrad's writers of the siege then spread into a broader xenophobic and anti-Semitic campaign against "cosmopolitanism" that culminated in a political purge of the city's leaders. The Leningrad affair ultimately resulted in six defendants being sentenced to death by shooting, and over two thousand Soviet workers losing their employment.[25]

Despite this savage and prolonged campaign to prevent a self-narrated Leningrad memorialization of the siege, the cultural significance of the 1949 Pushkin jubilee made it possible to publish illustrated

Figure 3.9 Benois's image portrays the chaos and terror wrought
by a storm. Published in 1923.

editions of *The Bronze Horseman* that included images of a heroic population recovering from disaster in identifiable Leningrad locations. In
effect, the celebration of Pushkin trumped the ban on Leningrad exceptionalism because Stalin had made the poet both pivotal to claims
of Russian national greatness in war-time speeches and a symbol of
the motherland's salvation during the post-war recovery.[26] The 1949
Bronze Horseman illustrations could be read, overall, as images of all-
Union strength in the face of adversity, but the unmistakable setting of
the "storm survivors" also permitted select illustrations to double as
clever circumventions of the Leningrad-exceptionalism ban, and this
likely did not escape readers who had until recently earnestly dedicated themselves to the task of commemorating the epic struggle of
Leningraders during the blockade.[27] The fact that in 1949 the Museum
of the Defence of Leningrad had been visited by one million people,
about the same number as the city's war-time population, and the fact
that it was second only to the Hermitage in visitation, suggest that
Leningraders were anxious to pay tribute to their experience.[28] Illustrated editions of *The Bronze Horseman* offered readers a way of honouring that need.

Figure 3.10 Mikhail Rodionov shows efficient rowers and an organized
rescue of a flood victim in his series published by the State
Children's Publishing House, 1949.

All three 1949 illustrated editions of *The Bronze Horseman* signal a turn
towards the post-war mandate for optimism and patriotism. Despite the
prominence of the Pushkin anniversary, the immense human losses of
the war meant that two out of three of the illustrators were relatively
unknown. The edition of *The Bronze Horseman* put out by the State Children's Publishing House featured eleven illustrations by the well-known
Soviet graphic artist Mikhail Rodionov. But the edition published by the
Pushkin Society used the work of Mikhail Grigor'ev, whose artistic reputation had been established in Leningrad theatre decoration; and the
edition put out by Lenizo selected the work of recent art-school gradu-
ate Igor Ershov, who had illustrated *The Bronze Horseman* for his 1947
diploma project at the Leningrad Art Institute.[29] All three illustrators to
The Bronze Horseman developed the theme of "weathering the storm."
Benois had emphasized the floodwater's ability to isolate and terrify the
civilian population (fig. 3.9), but post–siege of Leningrad illustrations
highlight the idea of working together to rise above the catastrophe. They
show scenes in which flood victims act calmly to assist others. If outstretched arms in Benois's series signalled fear and helplessness, Rodionov shows arms reaching out to save fellow citizens (fig. 3.10). In one
illustration Ershov depicts a boat full of people with determined faces,

Figure 3.11 Igor Ershov's 1949 illustration depicts a courageous group of survivors, sitting with indomitable expressions in a storm-tossed boat. The woman calmly holds a bundled baby, while the men lean towards survivors on a roof seen in the background, presumably planning to bring them safely into the boat.

banding together against the crisis. One of the figures stands against the wind and leans towards a group of survivors on a rooftop, suggesting a planned rescue (fig. 3.11). Benois's illustrations highlighted overturned boats, flood victims clinging helplessly to whatever they can or drowning, but Ershov does not show a single body in the water.

The 1949 illustrations by Mikhail Grigor'ev pick up on the motif of co-operation in the face of tragedy, showing flood victims working together in an organized assembly line to save household items, even as flood-water streams through an open window (fig. 3.12). For the first time ever in an illustrated edition of *The Bronze Horseman*, Grigor'ev depicts the process of cleaning up after the storm and returning to the comforting customs of everyday life, with sweepers tidying the streets, a woman airing out bedding, and survivors greeting each other and

Figure 3.12 Mikhail Grigor'ev's illustration depicts household members working together to save valuable items from water damage, 1949.

Figure 3.13 Grigor'ev's depiction of the return to normal civic life, 1949.

shaking hands (fig. 3.13).[30] The three 1949 illustrated editions of *The Bronze Horseman* mark an attention to post-war emphases on the importance of *trud* (labour) and rebuilding, motifs that were part of the crucial push to complete the first post-war Five-Year Plan (1946–50) and repair the Soviet economy.[31]

Several core cultural shifts came together in the Stalinist period to launch *The Bronze Horseman* into unprecedented cultural prominence. Thanks to the state initiatives for Pushkin jubilees and the program to co-opt Russian literary classics, the poem enjoyed enormous print runs in the 1930s and 1940s.[32] Mikhail Grigor'ev's 1949 illustrated *Bronze Horseman*, put out as part of the Academy of Sciences' project to publish Pushkin's complete works, was published in 100,000 copies, over five times the average for a book published even ten years later.[33] Illustrated versions of *The Bronze Horseman*, which had been associated with luxury editions in the pre-revolutionary period, were thus transformed into "Pushkin for the masses," reaching far greater numbers of readers than ever before.[34] At the same time, a new target audience was created. Although the Stalinist era was not the first to recognize the strategic importance of reaching the juvenile reader, it *was* the first to achieve state-run publications of Russian classics for children and adolescents; thus young readers in the Stalinist era were the first generation to have access to richly illustrated children's literature for mass consumption.[35]

Pushkin in Public School

While *The Bronze Horseman* was reaching a larger and younger reading audience, it was also finding a new niche at the core of the public school curriculum. This was made possible by Stalinist educational reform, which replaced the chaos of the 1920s with the establishment of universal compulsory education and a standardized curriculum.[36] The Stalinist demand for an educative (*vospitatel'nyi*) function to illustrated children's literature made works like *The Bronze Horseman* apposite as pedagogical tools, and beginning in the 1930s the poem appeared in the state-issued textbook *Russian Literature*, targeted at the fifteen-year-old Russian eighth grader.[37] An examination of successive versions of this textbook appearing in the period 1936 to 1959 shows the advance of *The Bronze Horseman* to a prominent role in the creation of a post-war Russian nationalist agenda. In the 1930s *The Bronze Horseman* did not appear as a text for individual study; rather, the poem was included as one of Pushkin's "Works of the 1830s," with a focus on how Pushkin's works thematized the poet's position on capitalism, feudalism, and other socio-economic questions.[38] In the 1938–9 edition the poem merits a short individual entry that addresses a theme that would be developed relentlessly in the 1940s: the clash of individual and state interests. In the late 1930s the emphasis was on Pushkin's dream of finding a balance between individual happiness and the greater social good, but in subsequent editions of the textbook throughout the 1940s this position was continually adjusted until Pushkin emerged as a proponent of state power at the expense of the individual.[39] According to the 1948 authors of the textbook, the poem is mainly a defence of Peter the Great, whose acts to "strengthen Russia" were completely supported by Pushkin.

Evgeny dies because he does not understand the "historical laws of the development of Russia," and Pushkin, supposedly, depicts the full legitimacy of this historical process, which suppresses everything "personal" and "private."[40]

By the end of the Stalinist era this line had changed considerably. The 1953 edition of the textbook for teachers training at pedagogical institutes, also titled *Russian Literature*, takes the position that regardless of Peter the Great's advances, autocracy is against the interests of the people and inevitably leads to revolt.[41] The 1959 student textbook goes even further, stating that Peter is guilty of standing in the way of "the happiness of the common people" and that Evgeny is "correct in his revolt against the government that has ruined his happiness."[42] Thus in the period between the Great Terror and Stalin's death, 1936–53, the poem stood as an integral part of the middle-school curriculum, but its "meaning" was continually updated. What had been a vindication of the expendability of the individual in the grand scheme of historical necessity in the post-war years became a treatise on curtailing limitless power in 1953 and beyond.

Another major shift in the presentation of *The Bronze Horseman* to Soviet schoolchildren coincided with Russia's entry into the Second World War. Beginning in the 1940s, *The Bronze Horseman* was presented in tandem with Pushkin's epic of the "great northern war," *Poltava* (1828), in a two-part national saga of visionary state building. The companion textbook used for pedagogical institutes was unequivocal about how *The Bronze Horseman* should be presented by teachers to their classes in the immediate post-war period. Evgeny should be positioned as the inevitable victim of a greater "historical process," namely Russia's victorious march forward, now linked to the expansion and consolidation of Russian national territory after Peter the Great's 1709 victory over Sweden's Charles XII at Poltava.[43] Pushkin himself, according to the textbook, was certain of the legitimacy of the great Russian state-building project and in *The Bronze Horseman* justifies Peter the Great's ruthlessness as the diligent and selfless execution of state demands.[44] Indeed, a contemporary article corroborated that "Pushkin never doubted the great destiny that awaited Russia."[45] In this light, the inclusion of Benois's signature modernist illustration *After Him Gallops the Bronze Horseman* in the school textbooks of 1939 and 1948 becomes readily understandable (fig. 3.1). Any anxiety about the apocalyptic undertones suggested by an animated statue pursuing a terrified human prey is allayed by the clear directive to students that the monumental leader is justifiably chasing down an unwelcome individualistic obstacle to the regime's larger goals. The proportions of the illustration, with an enormous symbol of state power in the foreground and a tiny individual figure fleeing towards the edge of the page, creates a clear picture for the viewer and encourages a perspective on the poem from up high on the state steed. The value of Benois's illustration in establishing a grandiose dimension of state values clearly outweighed, for Soviet editors, the more subversive eschatological imagery of the illustration, with its four storm clouds galloping across the sky like the Horsemen of the Apocalypse, and the second cloud appearing to protrude from Peter's mouth like the trumpet of the archangel.[46]

The Stalinist use of *The Bronze Horseman* in the creation of a nationalist narrative, what Benedict Anderson would call the mobilization of print media in the service of a calculated shaping of an "imagined community" of readers, becomes readily apparent when we consider that the *Poltava–Bronze Horseman* unit is noticeably absent from textbooks designated for grade-eight students of non-Russian Soviet schools of the same period.[47] Instead, those students were offered *Evgeny Onegin* (a text aimed at Russian students in grade nine) with an explanation that Engels had learned Russian by translating the poem. Thus the great narrative of Russian expansion was dampened down for students of the non-Russian republics, and Pushkin's importance was instead underlined by his international reputation with great thinkers.

At the Centre of the 1949 Jubilee

The Bronze Horseman's central role in the Russian public school curriculum in the 1940s was augmented for purposes of the 1949 jubilee celebration, when students from grades six to ten recited the work in oratory contests, and entire schools viewed illustrated editions via slide shows.[48] A 1949 guide for teachers who were preparing for the anniversary makes clear the extent to which Pushkin and *The Bronze Horseman* had penetrated the public school system. In addition to suggested activities for grades eight to ten, including oral reports, circle reading groups, dramatizations, analyses of Pushkin's works, and excursions to Pushkin museums and Pushkin areas, on 6 June all schools were to hold a special assembly and hear speeches from the school director, teachers of literature, and the students themselves.[49]

During the Pushkin jubilee even elementary school children were targeted as suggested readers of *The Bronze Horseman*. A special 1949 exhibition guide produced by the State Children's Publishing House for schools and libraries included posters dedicated to individual works, as well as instructions on how to present them to children. The *Bronze Horseman* poster was aimed at children in grades five to seven but "could be shown" to students as young as grades three to five (ages ten to twelve in Russia). The top of the poster featured an "endorsement" of the poem by the radical nineteenth-century literary critic Vissarion Belinsky, emphasizing the clash of the "grandiose" and the "simplistic" within the work.[50] At the centre was a period black-and-white lithograph of the Bronze Horseman monument, and, below, these lines from the poem: "Stand in beauty, Peter's city / Remain as unbending as Russia." The overall effect of this state-sponsored exhibition for schoolchildren was of a sober yet majestic work of art that had become part of a larger, national epic, one aimed at increasingly younger audiences.

The 1949 Pushkin celebrations mobilized public education on an unprecedented scale. Although the Russian school system had participated in the state-sponsored Pushkin anniversary of 1889, with copies of Pushkin's works being distributed to schoolchildren for free, neither universal education nor a standardized curriculum existed at that time.[51] The piecemeal delivery of a state-sponsored image of Pushkin in 1889 was upgraded, by 1949, to an all-encompassing campaign. In accordance with post-war cultural shifts, the emphasis was placed on Pushkin as an "ardent patriot" whose works were "permeated with patriotism."[52] In general, the post-war period was pivotal in placing *The Bronze Horseman* at the centre of Stalin-era literary culture, and this was developed simultaneously in multiple ways. While public school textbooks made the work central to a Russian nationalist narrative, and jubilee exhibits continued to lower the age of target audiences, illustrated editions made possible a deep sense of connection to the siege and the suppression of its story. The poem remains an important part of the school curriculum in Russia today, where it is targeted at the grade-seven, fourteen-year-old reader – the same adolescent group first selected by Stalin-era editors and educators.

The mass, organized readings and slide shows of *The Bronze Horseman* during the jubilee years, the huge print runs of illustrated editions, and the significance attributed to the poem in public school textbooks meant that text and reader came together in a way that was unique to the Stalinist era. In the 1930s and 1940s *The Bronze Horseman* suggested something particular to reading audiences, and illustrations helped to develop these new connotations, as readers during the Great Terror of 1936–8 contemplated the theme of the unhappy relationship between citizen and state; siege survivors, prohibited from commemorating their epic struggle, were heartened by images of their city recovering from disaster. Stalin-era book illustrations repositioned the way in which Soviet readers imagined themselves, their role as citizens, and their relationship to the spaces they inhabited. As for the *Bronze Horseman* illustrations by Alexander Benois, they remained in their Stalinist incarnation for another eleven years after Stalin's death in 1953, a testament to the art of reinventing the past.[53] Benois himself remembered *The Bronze Horseman* illustrations in one of his last letters, a response to Soviet art historian Alexei Savinov in 1960. Benois was unaware of the Soviet repurposing of his work and considered *The Bronze Horseman* illustrations to be a project from the distant past.[54] Ironically, they were kept alive in the book's Soviet afterlife, inspiring new illustrated interpretations of *The Bronze Horseman* that continued to connect the poem to issues of contemporary political and cultural importance.

Chapter Four

Anna Karenina and the Mother-and-Child Reunion

The scene depicting Anna Karenina's embrace of her son, Seriozha, appeared in virtually every Soviet republication, every newly illustrated edition, and even many public school textbook sections on Tolstoy (fig. 4.1.). When only one illustration from the novel could be selected for reprinting or illustration, this was often the one chosen. Anna's embrace of her son was emotionally powerful: it signalled the sorrow of parting what should never be parted – a mother and child. But why did they have to part? When Soviet editors and publishers included this illustration in the Schoolchild's Library Series of 1939, or the grade-nine textbooks of 1940 and 1948, it was supposed to highlight the fact that imperial-era conservatism and religious strictures around divorce had been lifted, making Soviet-era repetitions of this farewell embrace unthinkable. The scene dovetailed nicely with claims that Anna's tragedy could have been circumvented had she only been allowed to find a place in the workforce and make a useful contribution to society as a working mother. Therefore, Anna, her mistakes, and her sufferings – ultimately her failures – as a mother were fashioned into something of a foil for Soviet women, particularly wives and mothers. Tolstoy's suitability as a classic, which was maintained unabated, and Anna's story as a touching favourite to read and view in the 1930s, meant that Anna maintained a high profile throughout multiple decades in which the importance, role, boundaries, and duties of motherhood were a topic of public debate, decree, and legislation. For young readers, images of Anna epitomized a complex and changing set of criteria around personal and social responsibilities for women.

Lenin wrote no less than five articles about Tolstoy between 1908 and 1911, underlining his importance as a writer and cultural figure.[1] For Lenin, Tolstoy represented a passionate critic of Russia's political and social ills at a pivotal moment between the emancipation of the serfs in

Figure 4.1 Mikhail Vrubel, *Anna Karenina's Meeting with Her Son* (1878),
reproduced in the Academia edition of *Anna Karenina* (1936) and the textbook
for grade-nine students *Russian Literature* (1940 and 1948).

1861 and the first Russian revolution in 1905. He was, in Lenin's estimation, a "mirror of the Russian revolution" and the mouthpiece for the worsening political and moral crisis that could be felt in the factories, on the estates, and also in the households and bedrooms of the nation. The domestic crisis, in particular, is reflected in the novel *Anna Karenina* (1873), which thematizes the rights and responsibilities of mothers and wives and the conflict between personal and public duty. These remained vital social questions as Lenin offered unprecedented legal and political rights to Soviet women and, increasingly, co-opted motherhood as a state interest. Through its portraits of the adulteress Anna, the young bride Kitty, and the exhausted mother Dolly, *Anna Karenina* explores the situation of women and such controversies as access to divorce, the use of birth control, and maternal obligations once a marriage has dissolved. As a constant presence in the grade-nine textbook beginning in the late 1930s, accompanied by pedagogical texts that emphasized new expectations for young Soviet women, *Anna Karenina* brought these issues to the fore for adolescent readers.

A lovely, vital society woman in a loveless marriage to an older, prominent bureaucrat, Anna Karenina must leave behind her eight-year-old son, Seriozha, in order to pursue her passionate love affair with Alexei Vronsky. Anna's beloved son is caught in the conflict of personal freedom, maternal instinct, and social duty, a dilemma that became increasingly relevant to Lenin-era "Annas" as the state sought to release women from childcare duties and place them in the workforce en masse. In the Stalinist era this renegotiation between private and public obligation deepened as the state endeavoured to "forge an alliance with mothers through [its] definition of motherhood as a noble and rewarded service to the state, rather than as a private matter proceeding from the relationship between husbands and wives."[2] Tatiana Pletneva, in a 1927 article titled "Conversations with Readers about Motherhood" in *Women's Journal*, addressed the complexity inherent in Soviet motherhood; under this umbrella issue were included the questions of "female individuality, motherhood as a social function," and "the social requirements of motherhood." Although the conflict of the personal versus the social was very much acknowledged, Pletneva summed up that "the proletarian revolution doesn't at all lead to the unbridling of individuality but, on the contrary, to the strictest subordination of personal interests and personal behaviour to the interests of the entire society."[3]

Anna Karenina spoke to issues of contemporary relevance to Soviet women and also to adolescent girls, the future wives and mothers of the nation. It became one of the most popular republished classics, and

it fully saturated popular culture in 1937 when the Moscow Art Thė-
atre staged a stunningly successful dramatization of the novel, which
travelled from Moscow to Paris, and "everyone," including Stalin, was
reading, viewing, and discussing *Anna Karenina*.[4] Soviet book editions
of *Anna Karenina* were aimed at both adult and young readers and
illustrated by some of the most prominent contemporary book artists,
including Nikolai Tyrsa and Alexander Samokhvalov. The novel was
published by the State Children's Publishing House in 1934 and 1954
in print runs of at least fifty thousand, and as part of the Schoolchild's
Library series with illustrations by Tyrsa in 1939. Perhaps the most rec-
ognizable illustration in the novel, under Lenin and Stalin, was Mikhail
Vrubel's imperial-era illustration *The Meeting of Anna Karenina with Her
Son*, created in 1878. This depiction of Anna embracing her son was
reproduced in the public school textbook *Russian Literature* in 1940 and
1948 (see fig. 4.1), and also appeared in the prominent, if unfinished,
Stalinist Literary Encyclopaedia project as well as in adult editions of
the novel.[5] Every textbook for the grade-nine student between 1938
and 1953 included a prominent section on Tolstoy and *Anna Karenina*.
Although illustrated editions for young readers began to be produced
only in the late 1930s, the novel's themes of the rights and responsibilities of Soviet women were heavily discussed beginning in the 1920s.

Anna Karenina from the 1920s to the 1950s

Anna Karenina was republished seven times under Lenin and sixty-sev-
en times under Stalin, making it entrenched as firmly in adult reading
as in children's reading and the public school curriculum. Avant-garde
groups working in the first decade after the revolution, like Mayakovsky's futurists, at first rejected Tolstoy and the literary greats of
the past, but in attempting to forge a new Soviet literary form, they
returned, by the end of the 1920s, to the idea of precursors and models. The ideal of the New LEF collective (as the group called itself after
1927) was a kind of literary realism that they conceived of as "a red Lev
Tolstoy."[6] Lenin and Bolshevik cultural leaders championed Tolstoy
because he had been born to wealth but had rejected it, had advocated
for peasant rights and education, and, unlike Dostoevsky, had been a
reactionary and a revolutionary in the right order.

At the same time that Tolstoy came to occupy a central place in
the Lenin-era canon of classics, *Anna Karenina* began to speak to an
important new set of state gender initiatives. In the 1920s, new laws,
propaganda campaigns, and cultural shifts began to transform motherhood into a "social rather than private matter."[7] As early as 1926, in

the journal *Questions of Motherhood and Infancy*, author V. Lebedeva was writing that "motherhood is the social function of women – this is our watchword."[8] Olga Issoupova has looked at how Lebedeva's article "highlights three key Bolshevik positions with regard to maternity: first, that motherhood was not a private matter, but a social one; second, that motherhood was the 'natural' destiny of women; and third, that it was a function which was to be facilitated and rewarded by the state."[9] This was achieved by encouraging the mass entrance of women into the labour force, thus transferring them from private dependence on fathers and husbands to the "protection of the state."[10] Progressive laws of 1918 and 1926 allowed for divorce and for property to be held by women, but as Sarah Ashwin argues, these laws were aimed not only at liberation but also at substituting the authority of the party for that traditionally held by the church.[11] The public school textbooks of the 1930s made it clear to young readers that had Anna Karenina been the beneficiary of these advances, she need not have suffered from the social stigma of adultery or have been separated from her beloved son. The emotional force of that tragic separation emerged in illustrations depicting Anna's embrace of Seriozha, a mother-and-child reunion that was, at the same time, a moment of painful leave-taking.

Illustrated editions of *Anna Karenina* for both young and adult readers in the 1920s, 1930s, and 1940s invariably included this heart-wrenching moment when Anna, having left her husband, must sneak into her own house and wake her peacefully sleeping little boy to wish him a happy birthday. Anna's embrace of Seriozha stands as a pivotal scene because it exemplifies the thorny moral dilemma at the heart of the book. As Loralee MacPike has shown, Tolstoy conformed to the conventions of the adulterine novel by having the gender of Anna's offspring of her legitimate union with Karenin be male. Later in the novel, when Anna gives birth to the child of her illegitimate union with Vronsky, the child is female. In nearly all examples of the novel of adultery, including *Anna Karenina* and Flaubert's *Madame Bovary* (1856), "female adultery is intolerable, leading not only to marital breakdown but to the humiliation of both partners and usually also to the death of the wife."[12] Conventionally in these novels, "good women bear sons, bad women daughters who cannot carry on the male line, thus ensuring that negative qualities in the parents (particularly the mother) will not be part of the moral 'genealogical continuity.'"[13]

Anna's birthday embrace of her son, and her hurried exit from the house in which she is no longer welcome, articulates this paradigm and becomes a symbolic moment of parting between mother and son, and therefore of farewell to the traditional family and legitimate morality.

This scene appears in nearly every Soviet illustrated edition of the work because of its emotional power and the centrality of its message.

In the 1938 textbook for pedagogical institutes, Anna's suicide at the end of the novel is discussed in connection with the epigraph to the novel, "Vengeance is mine; I will repay" (Romans 12:19). Teachers were instructed that Anna's death was the result not only of "her own inner worries" but also of the painful and untenable position in which imperial society placed her.[14] According to the authors, Anna's tragedy was the consequence of both her "refusal of the duty of a wife and mother for the sake of the narrowly egotistical happiness of love" and society's inability to provide her with a larger goal upon which to focus her energy.[15] In the textbook for grade-nine students of 1938–9, Anna's lack of useful, fulfilling work is also noted, and her pursuit of selfish passion is blamed for extinguishing in her the world of "higher, complex, poetic" interests.[16] The clash between Anna's maternal feelings and her consuming love affair is seen as the central conflict of the novel: she must choose between being a mother and being a lover. With Anna's suicide, the authors argue, Tolstoy condemned aristocratic society for "destroy[ing] the moral bases of life, specifically the principles of spirituality and the inviolability of marriage."[17] The contemporary reader, even the fifteen-year-old reader of this textbook, was expected to note the improvements since Anna Karenina's time when "almost all roads of social activity were closed to women and she could only prove herself in love, the family and in personal life."[18] This take on the new opportunities and responsibilities of wives and mothers, as it was positioned for adolescent students, dovetailed with the messages directed at adult readers in women's magazines of the period.

The textbook of 1940 reiterates that society "dooms" Anna because she cannot escape from her situation by taking "the path of social struggle and work" that is now available to Soviet mothers.[19] The authors lament the fact that for Tolstoy a woman's place is "not in the department," "not at the telegraph counter," but in the family.[20] In actuality, Stalinist society did not differ much from Tolstoy's in its judgment that a woman's great "service" to the country was children. The line on Anna Karenina for Stalin-era students was that imperial society should be condemned for limiting a woman's freedom – but that freedom was now defined as the duty to bear and rear children *and* to contribute labour outside the home. In fact, the textbook message for adolescents merely reiterated what journals had been telling Soviet women since the 1920s: "Society demands of the woman ... that [she] recognize herself not as a lonely, torn-off individual ... but as a member of society, connected through society to the general interests and required to take those interests into account."[21]

The idea was that the new generation of Soviet mothers, secure and connected to society as the "brick-layer[s] of the future society," would be spared Anna Karenina's isolated, cut-off fate.[22] Both Tolstoy and the writers of the Stalin-era textbook could agree that Anna's principal crime was that she "destroy[ed] the family for the sake of personal happiness."[23] On the question of freedom versus duty for wives and mothers, both came down heavily on the side of duty.[24]

Mikhail Vrubel's depiction of the embrace of mother and child, *Anna Karenina's Meeting with Her Son*, republished in the textbooks of 1940 and 1948, highlights Anna's failure as a mother. Executed in 1878, just five years after the first appearance of *Anna Karenina*, the illustration captures the public discord aroused by the novel at the time. Vrubel's illustration shows an obsessive embrace of an innocent son and a psychologically ill mother. Anna is dressed with an excessiveness that appears out of place in the nursery. Dark circles under her eyes attest to her mental disquiet, as do her consuming gaze and the distressed way she is squeezing her son's cheeks. The yellow hue of the illustration underlines the sense of tension and illness in this scene. Vrubel, a young artist of only twenty-two years of age when this illustration was created, was no doubt responding to the lively debate that *Anna Karenina* had sparked in the journals of the day. On the one hand, liberal critics complained of Tolstoy's pitilessness for his heroine, but, on the other, in liberal journals such as *Vestnik Evropy* (The messenger of Europe), authors like A. Stankevich responded to Anna's plight by condemning her for the childish pursuit of empty pleasure: "If only this grown-up child loved, wished for, and understood anything other than treats and caresses, we can't help but think, finishing *Anna Karenina*! If only the majority of women had serious goals in life, if only they didn't see in life only fun and amusement, if only they understood that in the self-denial and self-sacrifice of the mother and wife there is more virtue and greater moral gratification than chasing after phantoms according to the call of their appetites and fantasies!"[25]

Readers could connect these changes to the ways in which a favourite classic was being reinterpreted: the take on *Anna Karenina*, in Soviet textbooks, was that Anna's tragedy results from the stifling set of choices offered to mothers in imperial Russia. She cannot divorce her husband without great difficulty, and she cannot work outside the home – this is what forces her to sneak into her husband's house in order to embrace *her own child*. Adolescent Soviet readers were expected to experience the poignancy of this scene while feeling grateful that an enlightened government had eliminated the stigma and causes of that heartbreak. In effect, the state *had* solved Anna's dilemma, but it had done so by symbolically taking over and modernizing the "Karenin" role. Divorce and wages were granted by the state, and in exchange, motherhood was co-opted for state purposes. During the collectivization and industrial-ization drives of the 1930s the state soothed a ravaged nation, cemented identity, and forged unity by employing images of motherhood.[26]

Maternity was raised to an issue of "national resonance," culminat-ing, during the war, in the "twinning of motherhood and nation," as images of the family and state were taken to be one and the same.[27] The embrace of mother and son was used for its emotional force in Iraklii Toidze's 1943 war-time propaganda poster For the Motherland! (Za rodinu-mat'!), which likened motherhood to the earth and Mother Russia, and a young son to the nation. Toidze's image of a determined mother dressed in flowing red, holding a male child in a pose that suggested protection but also the heart-breaking possibility of sepa-ration, became a convention of war-time posters under Stalin.[28] This trope, familiar to every adolescent reader of Anna Karenina in the public schools, borrowed from traditional Russian Orthodox imagery show-ing Mary and the infant Jesus, but also from more recent images of a mother and son closer to home – Anna and Seriozha.

Anna Karenina at the Moscow Art Theatre

The novel's 1937 dramatization by famous director Vladimir Nemirov-ich-Danchenko at the Moscow Art Theatre sparked a broad Anna Kar-enina fever that lasted throughout the 1930s and 1940s. This revival inspired new illustrations for young readers, such as the 1939 edition illustrated by Nikolai Tyrsa for the Schoolchild's Library series, which depicted Anna as a frivolous, preoccupied mother, as well as republi-cations of Vrubel's portrayal of a disturbed mother in the textbooks of 1940 and 1948. The Kremlin top brass, including Stalin, Molotov, Kaga-novich, Voroshilov, and Zhdanov, all attended the opening night of Anna Karenina in April 1937. The show was an immense success, and its lead actors, Alla Tarasova (as Anna, fig. 4.2) and Nikolai Khmelov (as Karenin, fig. 4.3), were "passionately applauded" by the entire hall and named "People's Artists of the USSR" by the end of the month.[29] The play was selected to travel to the Paris Expo (Exposition Internationale des Arts et Techniques dans la Vie Moderne) in August 1937; it contin-ued to run for decades in Russia and was filmed in 1953. Its stunning success can be attributed to the mass campaign under Stalin to revive Russian classics and underlines the interconnections between adult and adolescent culture. Full-figured Alla Tarasova as Anna epitomized the new womanly image of Soviet women appearing in women's jour-nals and coincided with a conservative shift in expectations for wives and mothers. Humourless Nikolai Khmelov embodied Karenin to the

1-е действие   5-я картина
А н н а: — Я несчастлива?
Анна — А. К. Тарасова   Вронский — М. И. Прудкин

Figure 4.2 Alla Tarasova as the stylish and full-figured Anna, shown here in a still from the 1938 Moscow Art Theatre production of *Anna Karenina*. On the left is Vronsky, played by M.I. Prudkin.

Figure 4.3 Nikolai Khmelov's grim, humourless Karenin became iconic when his portrait appeared in the textbook for grade-nine students in 1940, 1948, and 1949.

extent that his image appeared in the textbook for grade-nine students in 1940, 1948, and 1949.

In the second half of the 1930s the question of family and marriage began to take on a central role in magazines like *Working Woman* (*Rabotnitsa*). Pregnant and breast-feeding women appeared more often, as did women occupied with traditional tasks like sewing or embroidering, often against the background of a "luxury" interior or a vacation resort.[30] Meanwhile, motherhood and childbearing became increasingly regulated by the state. As of 1930 abortion was allowed only by permission of a special commission, in 1935 it became a user-paid service, and in 1936 it was banned altogether (until 1953).[31] In 1934 abandonment of children was criminalized. Women (and not men) became "criminally responsible in cases of abandonment, which was considered to be a crime comparable to murder."[32] By 1936, an article by Kaminsky had declared that "motherhood is the highest form of service to one's people and the state."[33] Anna's dilemma, with her role as mother being patrolled and delimited by the state, was not at all outmoded in the minds of Stalin-era women, or of their daughters and sons. In this era of retreat from the gender advances of the 1920s, the role of wives was being increasingly defined and rewarded by the state.[34] Anna Karenina was certainly not a model wife, but she fit seamlessly into the culture of the 1930s because she problematized expectations for wives, just as those expectations were receiving greater attention than they had ever before.

Anna in Illustrations for Young Readers

Prominent artist Nikolai Tyrsa's illustrated edition of *Anna Karenina* appeared as part of the Schoolchild's Library series in 1939. These illustrations show an elegantly dressed Anna whose wifely indiscretions have cost her her son (fig. 4.4). Anna wears a hat, signalling that she is a part of the *haut monde* but not natural in the nursery. In the novel Anna takes off her hat before embracing her son, but in these illustrations the hat remains as a further obstacle standing between mother and child. Anna's Soviet illustrators – Tyrsa in this children's edition and Samokhvalov in adult editions from the same period – often depict her looking away from her son, although in the novel Tolstoy has her looking and speaking directly to him.[35]

In Tyrsa's version Seriozha embraces his mother from the heart while she turns her head both pensively and coquettishly to one side. Tyrsa has also made an interesting use of colour and shading: Anna's clothes, hat, eyes, and hair are drawn in black, and Seriozha's curls, nightgown, bed-clothes, and bare feet are white, suggesting his purity

Figure 4.4 Nikolai Tyrsa's illustration of the famous embrace of mother and son, which appeared in the Schoolchild's Library edition of *Anna Karenina* in 1939. Seriozha buries his face in his mother's neck while Anna, in full makeup, elaborate sleeves, and a stylish hat, looks sadly to the side.

and innocence (see fig. 4.4). According to the textbook for grade-nine students of 1938–9, "Anna perishes because she isn't able to acclimatize herself to the lying and duplicity [of society]. That's how the contemporary reader would understand her tragedy."[36] The 1940 textbook compares Anna with another heroine of Russian literature, Pushkin's Tatiana Larina from *Eugene Onegin*, who is also a "prisoner" of her marriage vows but who stoically honours them.[37]

The Tolstoy Anniversary of 1953

Soviet-era dedication to Tolstoy as a great writer was unflagging, but republications of his works, including *Anna Karenina*, received a boost in 1953 in honour of the 125th anniversary of his birth. A collected-works edition was published in 1952 by the state publishing agency Artistic Literature in an immense print run of three hundred thousand, and *Anna Karenina* was published in a separate edition in 1953 by the State Literary Publishing House in an equally impressive quantity of two hundred thousand. Artist Aram Vanetsian was commissioned to create a special series of Anna Karenina illustrations for an anniversary edition of the journal *Ogonek*. Following the precedent set by the Moscow Art Theatre production, which was still popular some sixteen years after its première, Vanetsian's illustrations offer a melodramatic interpretation of the novel almost exclusively focused on Anna's tragic romance. Anna is captured in five particularly poignant scenes, three of which focus upon her embrace of her son or her suicide (fig. 4.5). In the same year, a special postage stamp was dedicated to the anniversary of Tolstoy's birth. With stamps celebrating the anniversary of his death issued in 1935 and 1960, Tolstoy became the Russian classic most honoured by the Soviet postal system from the 1920s to the 1960s in an impressive field of competitors that included Chekhov, Lermontov, and Turgenev. Only the revered father of Soviet literature, Maxim Gorky, had an equal number of postal tributes in the same period.

In a cycle of Tolstoy anniversary lectures in 1953, E.N. Kupreianova pointed to the farewell scene between Anna and Seriozha that was featured in textbooks of the 1940s as particularly touching and tragic, the "suffering of a mother and son, forced to separate, and the cruelty and unnaturalness of that separation."[38] Kupreianova followed the line on *Anna Karenina* consolidated under Stalin in the 1930s, underlining the importance of the novel in unearthing all of the injustice and inequality of women in family relationships, all of "women's legal, material and spiritual lack of rights" in the imperial era.[39] Karenin takes Seriozha from Anna because he understands that it is his duty to "punish his

Figure 4.5 The embrace between Anna and Seriozha by Aram Vanetsian, published in *Ogonek* as part of the Tolstoy anniversary celebrations in 1953.

wife who has broken the family law, a duty laid down on him by god and society."[40] According to Kupreianova, Tolstoy portrays the separation between mother and son as a "cruel violence on [Anna's] maternal feelings and human rights," but he also gives Anna responsibility for choosing the "egotistical thirst for personal happiness," over her child.[41] It is her knowledge of the "evil" that she has done in choosing Vronsky over the son, "who is not guilty of anything and is deeply loved," that drives Anna to suicide.[42] Tolstoy famously began *Anna Karenina* with the aphorism "All happy families are alike. Each unhappy family is unhappy in its own way." Kupreianova points out that in fact the unhappy families, Anna's and Dolly's, are those modelled on the "old principles of the aristocracy," while the happy families are those, like Levin and Kitty's, or the peasant couple Ivan Parmenov and his wife, formed under the principle of "shared work" and "true interrelationship."[43] Kupreianova credits the Stalin era with fully reforming society to create the proper conditions for a happy family. But, in reality, the role of wife had become increasingly regulated, and the role of husband had been supplanted by the state itself.

What would an adolescent girl, or boy, learn about motherhood and duty by reading illustrated versions of *Anna Karenina*? Tolstoy's imperial-era text had emphasized that as an adulteress Anna broke family, religious, and social law. She had transgressed before her husband, God, and society – and society was by far the least of the three. In the first three decades of Soviet power, a mother was no less bound by duty before personal interest, but she was expected to reprioritize so that state or social interests came first, the family's interests were subordinated to that, and religious duty was jettisoned altogether. She was urged to leave her child in state-sponsored care and join the workforce in the 1920s, and then to bear children to help the state during the war years. The embrace between Anna and Seriozha was a centrepiece of the visual narrative of this text between the 1920s and 1950s, and its purpose was to remind young readers of the agonizing choices that women were no longer forced to make. In the end, however, the choices of mothers continued to be judged and scrutinized, just by a Soviet yardstick.

PART III

War-Time Picture Books

In the 1927 picture book *What the Red Army Is For*, two young boys spy on military manoeuvres and wonder what, beyond singing songs and hiding in ditches, the purpose of the Red Army is.[1] They are taken to the commander, who tells them that the Red Army is there so that the workers and peasants can stand up against the enemy. When the boys ask why the enemy does not come if they are ready, the commander answers that the enemy does not come *because* they are ready. In the 1920s and 1930s the responsibility for being ready was shared by the Red Army and its young followers alike. By 1940, as Olga Kucherenko has argued, Russia had become a "nation in uniform," and no explicit dividing line between child and adult was drawn when it came to a sense of responsibility for defending the motherland.[2]

When Soviet Russia entered the war against Hitler in June 1941, children's literature took on the theme of patriotic struggle with renewed vigour. The Great Patriotic War (1941–5) disrupted but did not extinguish the production of children's books. Some 629 books were published by the State Children's Publishing House during the war years, reaching a circulation of 37.5 million, and 703 more titles for children were issued by other publishing houses.[3] Indeed, the children's press suffered less from war-time paper shortages than did other publishing areas. Throughout the war, for example, the Leningrad children's journal *Campfire* (*Koster*) only missed one issue.[4] Thus, even when resources were scarce, child readers were prioritized as an important audience to mobilize with feelings of patriotic duty. As could be expected from at least two decades of preparing children for the possibility of war, when war did arrive in 1941, children were not sheltered from its realities or separated from the rest of the people in the heroic struggle against the hated fascist enemy. War-time children's literature focused on heroic themes, and illustrations took their cue from overtly agitational war posters.[5] Although the State Children's Publishing House planned a full list of classics for publication during the war, very few of these were actually published, and with no new edition of the state literature text-book in the years 1941–6, children's literature led the way in instruct-ing, rallying, and reassuring the children and youth of the nation about the war.

War Time in the Schools

War-time Commissar of Education V.P. Potemkin saw instilling a sense of patriotic duty as the top priority of schools, but there were signifi-cant impediments to the smooth functioning of the public school sys-tem during these years and hence their ability to achieve even the most basic educational goals. War arrived just as officials were attempting to extend the years of compulsory education to seven in rural areas and ten in urban areas by 1942. Thanks to war-time realities, rural areas in fact remained with nothing further than primary schooling, and urban areas remained with seven years of compulsory education.[6] Some 5.3 million children in the six republics occupied by the Nazi army were lost to the Soviet school system altogether.[7] Attempts were made to evacuate school-aged children out of areas threatened by invasion, but in Leningrad the rapid German advance and lack of preparation meant that in July 1941 some four hundred thousand children needed to be re-evacuated after being sent by train into enemy territory. By Septem-ber 1941 the evacuation was cut off at about three hundred thousand children because the blockade had already been instituted.[8]

Celebrated children's writer Arkady Gaidar dedicated one of his famous "Notes from the Front," which was given high profile in the newspaper *Komsomol'skaia Pravda*, to wishing Soviet children good luck on their first day of school on 1 September 1941. Gaidar reminded chil-dren of their important duty to study hard and help others while their older brothers and fathers were away at the front, saying, "This severe, terrible year will show who among you is truly laborious, steadfast and courageous."[9] For the tens of thousands of children who remained in Leningrad during the siege, the school year began officially in Octo-ber for grades one to six but was interrupted by air attacks, the lack of Soviet teaching staff (almost half of whom were serving at the front), and, as the siege continued, starvation. Still, schooling continued in air raid shelters, despite the extreme cold of unheated rooms in winter, and sometimes in five shifts ending at 11:30 p.m. The student population was depleted as older students volunteered and were called to the front, and those fourteen years and older began to replace the disappearing labour force.[10] By the spring of 1942 the party had issued orders making it easier for children to stay in school, including exempting them from the general labour mobilization of February 1942 and offering grades five to seven at night schools for those working during the day.[11]

The war was also reflected in changes made to the public school curriculum. Although some subjects, like natural science and history, received less instruction time per week, Russian literature continued to receive top priority and focused on love of the nation rather than on devotion to the cause of communism.[12] Beginning in 1942, boys in grades five to seven received compulsory basic training, including assault training and marches of up to ten kilometres in length.[13] Subjects like geometry, trigonometry, physics, chemistry, and geography were militarized, and learning German was encouraged for the eventuality of taking prisoners. In his "Notes from the Front" Arkady Gaidar wrote with shame about a young Soviet boy who overheard Nazi soldiers discussing a map, but he had not learned enough German to report what was said, even though he had completed grade nine.[14] Russian-language classes received updated content such as "She captured a fascist," and history lessons aimed first and foremost at instilling a love of the motherland or, in the words of Commissar of Education Potemkin, "why I love it, what is dear to me in it, what I am defending, and why if necessary I am giving my own life for it."[15]

The First Picture Books of the War

The first children's picture book published about the war was *Your Defenders* (*Tvoi zashchitniki*) by Lev Kassil' in 1942, with illustrations by Adrian Ermolaev. The book was aimed at pre-schoolers but was frank, even explicit, in its depiction of war, showing explosions and bodily attacks. This stark realism, however, was tempered by the fact that only Nazi soldiers are shown dead; in the same location, the single wounded Red Army soldier depicted is receiving immediate medical attention from a brave field nurse. The explicit aim of the book was to instill pride and gratitude in young Soviets for the brave soldiers defending them, but its implicit goal, in this early period of the war, with the Red Army in retreat and the Soviet borderlands occupied by the Nazis, was to reassure children of the might and determination of their defenders. The soldiers in Ermolaev's illustrations are well clothed and equipped, caught in rapid forward motion with uniformly calm, purposeful expressions (fig. III.1). Child readers were shown, over twenty illustrations, that they were being defended by sea, by air, and on the ground; on skis, on horseback, on motorcycles, and by parachute; in forests and

in cities; by day and at night. The book showcased and perhaps inflated
the technological might of the Red Army, who attacked in fighter jets,
tanks, submarines, and trucks with anti-aircraft guns, rifles, grenades,
and even swords. While the content of the picture book is alarming, its
visual presentation is soothing: most of the Soviet soldiers are shown in
their winter camouflage smocks, making an elegant canvas of advancing, indomitable white warriors who are mowing down and calmly
stepping over the faceless, grey-uniformed enemy (fig. III.2).

Sergei Mikhalkov's *My Street*, published in 1943 with illustrations by
Iu. Pimenov and V. Vasil'ev, was another early war-time picture book,
this time focused on the home front. The light-hearted poem for pre-
schoolers tells the story of a father who returns from the front on a two-
day leave and takes his young son to visit the everyday places on their
street – the pharmacy, the barber, and the flower vendor. The aim of the
book was to normalize scenes of war for the young child, because in the
background of the quotidian Moscow neighbourhood appear scenes of
a nation embroiled in battle (fig. III.3). Trams and buses bringing people to work are joined by tanks and transport trucks bringing supplies
to the front; on the sidewalk, pedestrians walk alongside uniformed
army and naval officers. The work explicitly comforted children about
a feared enemy and the certainty of a safe future. The boy and his father
stop to view the famous patriotic propaganda posters displayed in the
windows of TASS (Telegraph Agency of the Soviet Union), prompting
the boy to observe gaily: "I see a portrait of Hitler / I know that he's a
cannibal / But I don't tremble in terror / I laugh happily / I hold Dad's
hand / I'm not afraid of Germans!" Carefree outings to visit exotic
animals at the Moscow zoo were replaced with viewings of different
beasts as father and son walked past an enemy plane that has been
shot down and displayed behind bars in the capital (fig. III.4). In the
park they see a strange "green elephant," which is actually a barrage
balloon, intended to act as an impediment to low-flying enemy aircraft.
The steadfast balloon, which come nightfall would "rise up, guarding
us / Like a faithful watchman," stands in for the real elephants, who
had been victims of the bombing raid of June 1941; the raid had caused
fires in the Elephant, Lion, and Monkey Houses and destroyed the
zoo's archives.

New Order in the Schools

By the end of the war, military themes and images explicitly governed
the child's world. A 1945 book for children going to school for the first
time, *For the School Child to Keep in Mind*, by Samuil Marshak with

Figure III.1 The cover of Lev Kassil's *Your Defenders*, illustrated by Adrian
Ermolaev, the first illustrated book for children about the war, 1942
(see also colour plate 9).

Figure III.2 Crack parachutists landing in white camouflage against a snow-
filled sky create an appealing landscape in Adrian Ermolaev's 1942
illustration to *Your Defenders* (see also colour plate 10).

Figure III.3 *This Is Dad, This Is Me, This Is My Street*. Title-page drawing to
Sergei Mikhalkov's *My Street*, illustrated by V. Vasil'ev and Iu. Pimenov, 1943.
The illustration infuses an everyday street scene, featuring pedestrians
and trams, with images of a nation at war (the barrage balloon
and the father in military uniform).

Figure III.4 Instead of visiting
animals at the zoo, young
children in Moscow view a
different kind of beast: a downed
Nazi fighter. Illustration by
V. Vasil'ev and Iu. Pimenov in *My
Street* by Sergei Mikhalkov, 1943.

Plate 1 Viktor Govorkov, "Thank You, Dear Stalin, for a Happy Childhood!" poster, 1936

Plate 2 "What I Should Read" poster with list of recommended children's literature, 1928

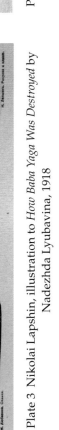

Plate 4 V. Spassky, alternative cover to *The Tale of the Priest and His Worker Balda* (1830) by Alexander Pushkin

Plate 3 Nikolai Lapshin, illustration to *How Baba Yaga Was Destroyed by Nadezhda Lyubavina*, 1918

Plate 5 Dmitry Butorin, Palekh illustration of Balda and
the priest, 1936

Plate 6 V. Korablinov, illustration on front cover of *The Little Humpbacked Horse*, 1950

Plate 7 N. Kochergin, illustration of Ivan the Fool and the little humpbacked horse, 1953

Plate 8 Alexander Benois, illustration showing a terrifying game of hide-and-seek, 1923

Plate 9 Adrian Ermolaev, cover of *Your Defenders* by Lev Kassil', 1942

Plate 10 Ermolaev, illustration of parachutists in *Your Defenders*
by Lev Kassil', 1942

Plate 11 Alexandra Jakobson, illustration in *Let Us Take the New Rifles*, 1941

Plate 12 Jakobson, illustration of girl nurses and wounded boy soldier, 1941

Plate 13 Aleksei Pakhomov, illustration to "Let Us Take the New Rifles," in *To Children* by Mayakovsky, 1959

Plate 14 Mikhail
Tsekhanovsky, cover
illustration of *Mail*, 1927

Plate 15 Tsekhanovsky, illustration from *Mail*, 1927

Plate 16 Tsekhanovsky,
back-cover illustration to
Mail, 1927

illustrations by Adrian Ermolaev, explained what to expect at school and how to behave. This was done by comparing teachers to naval commanders, classes to military companies that must be properly lined up, and the school bell to a naval whistle (figs. III.5, III.6, III.7, and III.8). Children's books like these reflected new, strict rules of conduct that had been planned for schools since the 1930s but only implemented in 1943. The stringent regulations, as in the military, emphasized "order, obedience, politeness and deference to authority" in order to temper the continuing social problem of abandoned and delinquent children.[16] As Julie deGraffenried has argued, post-war children's culture represented a jarring return to the social contract of the Stalinist 1930s, when the state had ostensibly provided a happy, protected childhood in exchange for good grades. Children were expected to return to this narrative after having been urged during the war to contribute military help and labour and to make sacrifices up to and including their own lives.[17]

The Child Martyrs

If the young readers of the war-time picture book were reassured about the war and its outcome, adolescent readers were instead encouraged to read, internalize, and emulate the stories of the so-called child martyrs, who were teenagers just like they were. The stories of child partisans, martyrs, and heroes entered the consciousness of the nation, becoming a lasting part of children's literature and continuing to resonate at the core of national identity long after 1945. A list of recommended reading for children published in 1950 featured books about child heroes like Shura Chekalin, who fought as a partisan in Tula and was captured, tortured, and hung by the Nazis in November 1941; Aleksander Matrosov, the teenage boy who used his body as a human shield so that other Soviet soldiers could continue to battle the enemy; and Zoia Kosmodem'ianskaia, the teenage girl who was tortured and killed by the Nazis.[18]

The first two parts of this book have looked at the role of illustrations in reimagining texts from the past for a Soviet child reader. It was not enough for these illustrations simply to depict the costumes, customs, and landscapes of a fairy tale or a nineteenth-century classic; they had to find a visual language that could bridge yesterday and today, to slip between the pages of a fixed text and dislodge its temporal moorings in order to highlight continuities with values important to the Soviet state. This was a complex task, as illustrations to fairy tales and classics at times distanced and defamiliarized the past in order to show

Figures III.5 and III.6 An orderly classroom of attentive first-graders is likened to a company in formation, receiving orders, in Adrian Ermolaev's 1945 illustrations to *For the School Child to Keep in Mind*.

the great social leaps forward that had been achieved, or they selected and highlighted commonalities that drew the cultures of the past and the present together. Book art therefore had a composite purpose of illustrating and of annotating, critiquing, and editorializing the texts from the past that they accompanied, becoming a gateway from the words of yesterday to the young minds of today. The illustrator's work was not just to represent but to repurpose. In this third and final part I look at the picture books produced for young readers during the Second World War and argue that the particular demands of this war-time period resulted in a new way of conceptualizing the past and a new

Figures III.7 and III.8 First-time schoolchildren were reminded that, just as soldiers saluted their officers, so were boys expected to raise their caps to their teacher, and girls to bow, in *For the School Child to Keep in Mind* (1945).

way of addressing the child reader. By the time of Hitler's invasion of the Soviet Union in June 1941, twenty-four years had passed since 1917, in other words a period long enough to produce a generation – in fact, the first Soviet generation. In the following two chapters I explore how war-time picture books configured the 1920s as a native, shared past with a native, shared library. I examine the transformation of Mayakovsky's "Let Us Take the New Rifles," originally published as a marching song for young Pioneers in 1927, into a mass-distributed picture book of the war-time period. These illustrated editions had a dual audience: the child readers of the 1940s and their parents, who had been Mayakovsky's first child readers in the 1920s. In the final chapter of this section I explore how, in response to requests from the now-grown first readers of his children's classic *Mail* (1927), Samuil Marshak created the sequel, *War-Time Mail*, in 1944, addressing this same dual audience and using the themes and images of the 1920s to inspire a sense of patriotic duty and pride during the war years.

Chapter Five

Mayakovsky Is Marching with Us

The great poet and artist of the revolution, Vladimir Mayakovsky, wrote thirteen poems for children in the period between 1925 and 1929. Most of these were negatively reviewed by critics at the time and were even recommended for exclusion from state library collections on the grounds that they were derivative and ill mannered. Nevertheless, some of Mayakovsky's children's poems were extremely well known during this period because of their appearance in the mass newspaper *Pionerskaia Pravda*. By the mid-1930s, concurrently with Stalin's reassessment of Mayakovsky as having been the leading Soviet poet in adult literary culture, he was reconfigured as an important children's author. Republications reflected this shift by moving from single works illustrated by an avant-garde illustrator, the norm in the 1920s, to prestigious collected editions for children with a single illustrator for multiple works. During the war this "best" and "most talented" poet was cited as having foreseen the national crisis of invasion – and its outcome in victory – in his 1927 poem "Let Us Take the New Rifles" ["Voz'mem vintovki novye"], in which he had called upon Soviet children to be ready when war came. War-time editions of this children's poem also targeted Mayakovsky's first readers of the 1920s, who were now parents, cueing them on their place as the first generation raised with Soviet values and as the generation now called upon to defend those values in war. This chapter looks at the significance of the war-time years in effecting a new association of a Soviet past with a Soviet present. Texts originating in the 1920s like "Let Us Take the New Rifles" were reimbued with meaning in the 1940s and used to bring together two generations of readers through works that were newly conceived as classics in a Soviet canon of children's literature. This new role was accomplished by war-time commissions for illustrated editions of Mayakovsky's poem that either augmented its prestige (through illustrations by leading

Figure 5.1 Alexandra Jakobson, illustration to Mayakovsky's *Let Us Take the New Rifles* (1941). (See also colour plate 11.) Cotsen Children's Library. Reproduced courtesy of the Department of Rare Books and Special Collections, Princeton University.

war-time artists like Aleksei Pakhomov) or transformed the work into a massively distributed picture book (illustrated by Alexandra Jakobson in 1941, 1945, and 1946) (fig. 5.1). When the children who as Pioneers of the 1920s had marched to Mayakovsky's "Let Us Take the New Rifles" read picture-book versions of the poem to *their* children in the 1940s, this work became the kind of shared intergenerational text that linked the post-1917 past to the war-time present.

In the 1920s eight of Mayakovsky's thirteen children's poems were published as picture books for pre-school-aged children (up to the age of five) or the young reader (five to ten years of age), all with different illustrators.[1] Two of them were published in the children's newspaper *Pionerskaia Pravda* with accompanying musical scores to be used in marches.[2] Like his famous civil war–era ROSTA posters, displayed in the windows of the telegraph agencies all over Russia, Mayakovsky's children's books were witty and politically engaged. They deal with the habits that distinguish a useful child member of society from an undesirable one (*What Is Good and What Is Bad,*) or the occupations to which children should aspire in a worker's state (*What Should I Be?*). Many of the illustrators of these books were, like Mayakovsky, left wing and avant-garde, showing an affinity with cubism (Irena Sunderland's use of perspective in *Let's Stroll* from 1926) or constructivism (Nisson Shifrin's schematic, overlaid uniforms in *What Should I Be?* from 1929). Mayakovsky's children's books received praise from increasingly sidelined experts in the field like Anna Pokrovskaia, but on the whole they were not well received by critics in the 1920s.[3] A 1925 review of Mayakovsky's first book, *The Tale of Petia, a Fat Child, and of Sima, Who Is Skinny*, called the book "stupid and rude."[4] Some of his children's books were kept out of public library collections because of unfavourable reviews from the Bibliographic Commission of the Central Children's Library.[5] As Fanni Ebin, the first and only Soviet author to produce a full-length study of Mayakovsky's works for children, put it in 1961, "almost all of [Mayakovsky's] poems for children were declared unsuccessful from an artistic point of view and dangerous from a pedagogical one."[6] At the same time, Mayakovsky was a regular contributor to mass children's newspapers like *Pionerskaia Pravda*, and children's poems like his 1927 "Let Us Take the New Rifles," set to music as a march, were popular with millions of Pioneers and schoolchildren.

Reconfiguring Mayakovsky for Stalin-Era Children

The way in which Mayakovsky was presented to children changed dramatically from the late 1930s. After his suicide in April 1930 the author was declared "the best, most talented poet of our Soviet epoch" by Stalin in 1935. In 1937 Mayakovsky's works began to be published in a new way. Collections for a very young reader, titled *To Children* [*Detiam*], were produced regularly up to and throughout the war years, with a single illustrator for multiple poems (fig. 5.2). In addition to republications of individual works, Mayakovsky "for children" appeared in collections of 1937 with illustrations by Natan Al'tman; 1941 with illustrations by Yury Pimenov; 1946 with illustrations by A.E. Gubin; and 1949 and 1953 with illustrations by Aleksei Pakhomov.[7] During the war Mayakovsky became the author most published in collections titled and dedicated "to children."[8] These volumes had a set order that began with "What Is Good and What Is Bad" and ended with "Let Us Take the New Rifles," and as a result, this short work accrued the sense of a final flourish and "last word." Bolstered with forewords by leading

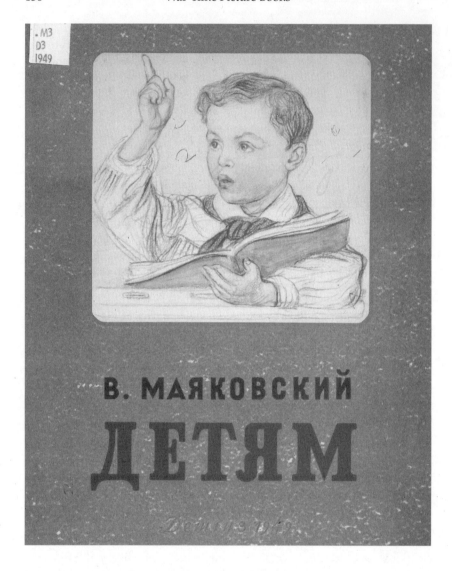

Figure 5.2 The cover of a work of Mayakovsky's collected children's poems, *To Children* (1949), illustrated by Aleksei Pakhomov.

Soviet children's writers like Lev Kassil', and illustrated by respected artists like the siege of Leningrad survivor Aleksei Pakhomov, the Mayakovsky for children of the 1940s was a far cry from the children's author of the 1920s, whose books had been visually avant-garde, controversial, and guarded from public library collections.

Nevertheless, war-time forewords to Mayakovsky's works for children unfailingly positioned the poet as a figure who *linked* the 1920s to the 1940s. This claim was supported by references to "Let Us Take the New Rifles," the work in which Mayakovsky had foreseen a coming war and urged children to be ready for it. Placing Mayakovsky as a "living connection" to the first decade after 1917 also fulfilled the important state goal of situating the war, as Stephen Lovell has argued, as the "delayed culmination of the revolution."[9] Works like "Let Us Take the New Rifles" were a call to arms but also a vindication of the years of warning and preparation for a "threat to [the nation's] existence."[10] This children's work took on a renewed importance and meaning in its second, war-time life because it epitomized the patriotic war-time call to guard the values of the revolution. The issue of war-time sequels to picture books of the 1920s, another facet of cultural bridging between the 1920s and the 1940s, is dealt with in the next chapter. "Let Us Take the New Rifles" was not a sequel to a work of the 1920s like *War-Time Mail* was; nevertheless, this repurposed text accomplished some of the same goals: it beckoned the poem's first-time readers, recalling a shared work of their 1920s childhoods in war time, and making the memory text part of their own children's childhood. Both were nostalgia products, but, more than that, they were able to reference a shared past that was set in an era of uniquely *Soviet* values, upbringing, and literary and visual culture. In war time "the past" at last advanced beyond the borderline of 1917, transforming it from an objectionable, ideologically foreign territory to a native, shared one.

From Pioneer March to Picture Book

"Let Us Take the New Rifles" was a work expressed in multiple, sometimes overlapping literary and visual forms from its first appearance in 1927 to its last Stalin-era publication in 1949. It was at times a poem, a marching song, a photomontage, a film scene, and an illustrated children's book. It first appeared in the 18 June 1927 edition of the weekly (biweekly after 1928) newspaper *Pionerskaia Pravda* for children aged nine to fourteen years and youth aged fourteen to twenty years. The words to the poem appeared beneath a musical score by K. Pokrasa in an edition dedicated to the celebration of the Week of the Defence of the

USSR. The poem foretells of the time "when" (not if) war will return, and marching and shooting games will transform into the real work of military defence and medical support for the wounded ("When / the blizzard of war / comes again – / we must be able to aim, / and shoot.") The page of *Pionerskaia Pravda* before "Let Us Take the New Rifles" bears the headline "Visiting the Red Army" and asks child readers to "write in and tell us how you keep a 'living connection' to the Red Army, and how you're helping it." The next issue, of 25 June, outlines nine things that every Pioneer should be doing to prepare for the defence of the USSR. These include staying healthy, being ready to administer first aid, doing formation drills, reading topography, signalling by radio, knowing how to put on gas masks, participating in marksmanship circles, and showing love, care, and devotion for the Red Army and the Red Fleet.

Preparation for war permeated children's sport following a 1925 party resolution titled "On the Tasks of the Party in Physical Education," which called for military preparedness in sport training for youth. A 1927 list published by sport pedologist M.A. Kornil'eva-Radina recommended replacing children's bourgeois games of the past with new games, named "Bomb" and "On the Brave Attack," that trained children in the principles of national defence.[11] Starting in 1934, a junior version of the mass sport program Ready for Labour and Defence (Gotov k trudu i oborone, GTO), called Be Ready for Labour and Defence (BGTO), was brought in explicitly for Pioneers and schoolchildren aged thirteen to fourteen years and fifteen to sixteen years.[12] Mayakovsky's poem, which appeared in this context of increasing emphasis on child military preparedness, was very well circulated. "Let Us Take the New Rifles" was published in three different children's newspapers in 1927, was given a new musical score by K. Korchmarev in 1928, appeared in a book of Mayakovsky's "adult" poems in 1928, and was published for children again in 1929.[13] Just a few days after Mayakovsky's death, an April 1930 article in Pravda noted that "Let Us Take the New Rifles" was sung in every Pioneer organization across the USSR.

In 1930 "Let Us Take the New Rifles" was represented visually for the first time, in a photomontage that appeared in the short-lived children's journal *Piatidnevka* (fig. 5.3). Published under the title "Pioneer song," the photomontage evinced a musical performance of the march at a Pioneer rally. Children in white Pioneer blouses with red kerchiefs blow trumpets, play a drum, and salute to the Pioneer motto: "Always ready!" Beginning in 1940, this marching song entered mass war-time children's culture when it was featured at the end of *Timur and His Team* (*Timur i ego komanda*, 1940), the blockbuster film based on the children's

Figure 5.3 Photomontage to accompany Mayakovsky's "Let Us Take the New Rifles" in the journal *Piatidnevka*, no. 15, 1930. The journal only existed for six months, from February to July 1930. Reproduced from F. Ebin, *Maiakovskii – Detiam* (1961) with permission from the University of British Columbia, Rare Books and Special Collections.

novel (also 1940) by Arkady Gaidar. Set to music by L. Shvarts, the words of "Let Us Take the New Rifles" are sung by the film's heroes, Timur and Zhenya, and a group of Pioneers who are seeing Zhenya's father off to the front.

Arkady Gaidar's novel featured a group of schoolchildren who did good deeds for the community and for neighbourhood families whose fathers were serving in the army. *Timur and His Team* was more than a book; it became the iconic example of the principle of collectivism that the state wished to inspire in Soviet children, and Timur himself became the "nation's heart-throb."[14] Beginning in the fall of 1940 the novel was serialized in the children's newspaper *Pionerskaia Pravda*, broadcast on Central Radio, and made into the blockbuster film directed by Aleksandr Razumnyi.[15] Although *Timur and His Team* was, strictly speaking, a pre-war novel, Gaidar made clear in a *Pravda* interview of 31 December 1940 that Timur's purpose was to "prepare his friends for a future war."[16] When war arrived, Gaidar volunteered for the front and began to work as a war correspondent for *Komsomol'skaia Pravda* in the fall of 1941. Just before the first day of school, on 30 August 1941, Gaidar went on the radio to address the nation's youth, encouraging them to show patriotic loyalty in the face of the Nazi invasion, and asking them to contribute to the war effort by studying hard and doing volunteer work in the rear. Inspired by Gaidar's radio address and promoted by the Central Committee of the Komsomol, *Pionerskaia Pravda*, and Central Radio, a real-life Timurite movement was born, consisting of millions of boys and girls in schools throughout Soviet Russia as well as in other republics like Azerbaijan and Kyrgyzstan.[17]

By 1942 the Timurites had grown to two and a half million members and inspired an all-Union "working Sunday" dedicated to volunteer work for soldiers at the front.[18] By the war's end in 1945, the Timurites numbered three million children, typically between ten and twelve years of age.[19] Timur teams of children did an enormous amount of work to support soldiers at the front, including collecting metals, glass, and coal for factories, gathering medicinal plants, and collecting warm clothes. They supported soldiers' families by looking after pre-schoolers while mothers were at work, and by offering repair and sewing services. In the neighbourhoods they chopped wood, carried water, gathered fallen leaves, cleared snow, and harvested vegetables. In the hospitals they read to the wounded, wrote letters for them, and put on concerts. They took care of other children, walking young ones to school, bringing delinquents back to school, and helping evacuated children.[20] In areas closer to the front, Timur teams collected materials for petrol bombs, sheltered Red Army soldiers, carried out acts of sabotage, provided regular and paramilitary units with intelligence information, and apprehended enemy agents.[21] Through its association with Timur, Mayakovsky's "Let Us Take the New Rifles" fully saturated the culture of war-time children.

Illustrations for Tiny Tots

Many of Mayakovsky's books for children focus on cultivating the qualities, manners, and attitudes of the ideal Soviet child, including cleanliness and a good work ethic, and many model the adult world

Figure 5.4 Two girl nurses carry a wounded boy soldier on a homemade stretcher. Illustration by Alexandra Jakobson, 1941 (see also colour plate 12). Cotsen Children's Library. Reproduced courtesy of the Department of Rare Books and Special Collections, Princeton University.

of labour to child readers. "Let Us Take the New Rifles" distinguishes itself in this body of work as the most overtly militaristic of all Mayakovsky's writing for children. All the illustrated picture books associated with it originate from the period beginning in 1941. The march that had already reached millions of children's ears now became associated with the Great Patriotic War, climbing to prominence in a set of tiny books (*knizhka-malyshka*) published in 1941, 1945, and 1946, with massive combined circulations of one and a half million. The illustrator of this flood of miniature books aimed at a young war-time reader was Aleksandra Jakobson (fig. 5.4). The transformation of "Let Us Take the New Rifles" from aural to visual form, in addition to a new interaction with a war-time cultural context and a new understanding of Mayakovsky as a children's writer worthy of multiple collected editions, resulted in a work of renewed literary weight and significance.

"Let Us Take the New Rifles" had always been dual toned, as a playful poem with a more sombre underlying message. It was about joyful play, but the game was war. It was about dress-up and role-play, but the costumes were army uniforms, and the roles called for snipers and medical orderlies; pretty red flags fluttered in the breeze, but they were attached to bayonets. Jakobson's illustrations tended on the joyful, ludic side of work. The children she depicts are rosy cheeked, well clothed, and energetic. The illustrations are colourful, emphasizing the three-colour (red, blue, and yellow) principle that Jakobson had learned as a student of Kuzma Petrov-Vodkin in Leningrad in the early 1920s. Indeed, the feathery coloured strokes appear as though added by a child's crayon, in the bright colours favoured by a young artist. Jakobson's children look like children rather than little adults, and they are surrounded by natural, grassy, and leafy playgrounds. The innocence and simplicity of these depictions align with Jakobson's principle of children's illustrations, expressed in an undelivered speech on the children's book written in 1946. In the notes for this speech she discussed the importance of rendering the world from a child's perspective and the mistake of producing works for children that overly mature them.[22]

Jakobson's illustrations depict both boys and girls preparing for war; however, there is a gendering of roles in the sense that the boy (in uniform) stands ahead of the girl (in regular clothes but with a red-cross band on her upper arm) on the cover of the 1946 edition. Both boys and girls shoot, but the girls kneel while the boys stand. Although the poem uses the Russian masculine plural word "sanitary" (medical orderlies), only girls are shown as nurses, carrying the boys off the battlefield. This gendering of roles is made even more prominent in A.E. Gubin's illustrations of 1946 and Aleksei Pakhomov's illustrations, which first emerged in the 1949 edition of Mayakovsky's *To Children* and were developed into a full series by the artist for the 1959 edition.

The *knizhka-malyshka* series, at eight centimetres (about 3.25 inches), was no taller than a pencil. It was perfect for little hands to hold, but while its intended pre-school child reader could enjoy Jakobson's illustrations, he or she was likely too young to read the words. "Let Us Take the New Rifles" in its war-time iteration would have been read by a mother or a father who had likely been a first reader of Mayakovsky's words in 1927, who had been told to "be able to aim and shoot!" when the time came, and who was now being called to arms after a decade and a half of drilling and preparation. Though its romping rhythms and cheerful, optimistic war-time illustrations by Jakobson belie its serious message, "Let Us Take the New Rifles," nonetheless delivered that message to its first-generation readers, who were now of the age to enlist for national defence, and their pre-school-aged children, Maya-kovsky's second-generation audience. As Pierre Nora writes of the French children's classic *Tour de la France par deux enfants* (1877), and its use as an elementary school text emphasizing national unity in pre–First World War France, children's books can become important sites of memory (*lieux de mémoire*) that shape a national narrative through the intergenerational circulation of works.[23] As a site of memory, Maya-kovsky's text played the important role of reaching towards a shared, childhood past. And for the first time, that reconstructed past was "our own" Soviet past (rather than a corrected or updated imperial one), calling up a sense of a true historical break in 1917, at which point his-tory started again on Soviet terms: with its own literature, trove of col-lective memories, and iconic cultural personages. Mayakovsky was an ideal figure to connect the child readers of the 1920s to those of the 1940s. War-time forewords to his work for children reminded both generations that Mayakovsky was a "living link" to the values of the revolution. Although the past was only some fifteen years ago, war-time republications of "Let Us Take the New Rifles" created a sense of generational transition. A childhood text associated with the 1920s also made possible a symbolic circumvention of the 1930s, a time of disturb-ing social change and crisis, creating a continuity and purpose between the 1920s and 1940s.

Lev Kassil', in his foreword, "About Mayakovsky," to the 1941 edi-tion of Mayakovsky's *To Children*, reminded readers that "We remem-ber Vladimir Vladimirovich … when we prepare to battle the enemy."[24] Considering that this edition was part of the School Library (Shkol'naia biblioteka) series aimed at children "of the younger age" (five to ten years old), it is likely that the real targets, or at least co-targets, of this foreword were parents who were children during the 1927 Week of Defence of the USSR and had perhaps heeded the call to "with a song / join a shooting circle." Kassil's image of Mayakovsky as a giant man whose "poems were as deadly as bayonets" was one that he revisited in subsequent forewords for young readers.[25] In his foreword to *Maya-kovsky Is with Us*, a collection of Mayakovsky's poems published by the State Children's Publishing House in 1942, Kassil begins by emphasiz-ing the importance that the poet holds for young people. He quotes a letter dated 14 April, the twelfth anniversary of Mayakovsky's death, from a young student nurse serving in besieged Leningrad. The young woman writes to Kassil' because he knew the "live Mayakovsky," with whom she has "become friends" through his poetry.[26] As Kassil' puts it, "Mayakovsky's verses are now experiencing their second life" through republications of his poetry in newspapers for the front and the sense

Figure 5.5 The pen and the
bayonet: cover to *Mayakovsky
Is with Us* by an unknown
artist, published by the State
Children's Publishing House
(1942).

that his words, predicting that "war would come sooner or later," are as
important for "today" as in the 1920s.[27]

The cover image, showing a pen armed with a bayonet (see fig.
5.5), echoes Kassil's assertion that Mayakovsky "armed us" with
his poetry.[28] By 1953, in the foreword to Mayakovsky's *To Children*,
Kassil' had cemented Mayakovsky's image of soldiers defending
Soviet power "not only [with] the ideas of Lenin in their conscience,
not only with guns in their hands, but with the fiery, revolutionary poems of Mayakovsky in their hearts." This post-war foreword
clearly addresses not only its child readers but also their parents,
stating: "When the Great Patriotic War began, we all from the very
first day remembered the many poems of Mayakovsky in which the
poet had already long prepared us for war with the fascists."[29] Building upon the image of the pen and bayonet, Kassil' calls up the hand-
written copies of Mayakovsky's poems that his readers had placed in
their pockets and taken to the front, and that now, with bullet-holes
in them, were displayed in the Mayakovsky museum in Moscow.[30]

These war-time forewords addressed Mayakovsky's first readers, but the illustrations addressed his second ones. An immediate post-war edition of Mayakovsky's *To Children* followed the precedent set by Aleksandra Jakobson in mirroring the age of the intended reader (in this case, "preschool-aged children aged 1–5") in the children depicted. "Let Us Take the New Rifles" was one of three poems illustrated by A.E. Gubin in this 1946 publication in Rostov-on-Don with a modest circulation of fifteen thousand copies. There is a more pastoral feel to Gubin's setting thanks to an uncrowded frame and the presence of a dog and a horse, and the lively rhythm of the poem is mirrored in the jaunty slant of the letters in the title. Only three children are shown in this version, as opposed to the six in Jakobson's and the five in Pakhomov's versions three years later. Although marching is evoked in the first illustration, which shows a procession with a drum, the other illustrations depict the war games of the children: reconnaissance for the boys and nursing for the little girl, a medical intervention that appears to have more to do with modelling maternal care for her pet dog than with any scientific prowess. Despite its modest circulation numbers, taken together with Jakobson's three war-time editions, "Let Us Take the New Rifles" can really be said to have made a belated debut as a war-time picture book fifteen years after its original appearance.

Rifles in Children's Hands

The better-known illustrated version of "Let Us Take the New Rifles" is Aleksei Pakhomov's. He developed this illustrated series in the 1940s and 1950s, the first publication emerging in 1949 and the full series in 1959. Pakhomov illustrated twelve of Mayakovsky's works for children beginning in the late 1930s. As the artist perhaps most associated with children and the war after the emergence of his album from the siege of Leningrad *In Those Days: Leningrad Album* (1946), which included unforgettable renditions of stoic and heroic children and youth, Pakhomov cemented the importance and prestige of Mayakovsky as a "wartime" poet by his association with *To Children*. Pakhomov's illustrations to "Let Us Take the New Rifles" have a curious publication history. His first rendition emerged in the 1949 edition of *To Children*, which exists in two identically titled versions: one with 88 pages and one with 112 pages. "Let Us Take the New Rifles" concludes the longer version. The shorter edition finishes with "Lighting Song" but includes the illustration that would later open "Let Us Take the New Rifles." What is new in these post-war illustrations is the sense of triumph in victory and the heavy gendering of children's roles.

Mayakovsky's picture books for children are generally male oriented: a father gives advice to his son in *What Is Good and What Is Bad*; Mayakovsky's heroes are boy heroes, and villains are boy villains. The professions suggested in *What Should I Be?* (worker, tram driver, chauffeur, doctor, pilot, sailor) use masculine nouns, despite the drive to have women enter the workforce en masse in the 1920s; all the covers of *To Children* illustrated by Pakhomov show exclusively boys. "Let Us Take the New Rifles," however, thanks to its origin as a mixed Pioneer march, had always been addressed to both genders. The poem encourages "us" to join shooting circles and insists that "we" know how to aim and shoot, find the enemy, and carry the wounded. Both Jakobson's and Pakhomov's illustrated versions depict girls and boys as those intended to take up the new rifles, but they show exclusively girl nurses carrying wounded boy soldiers. A significant change took place, however, between Jakobson's cover illustration, which showed both a boy's and a girl's head in side view beneath the title, and Pakhomov's, which showed five boys marching smartly towards the viewer (figs. 5.6 and 5.7). If the message of Jakobson's war-time cover is that it is the duty of both boys and girls to train for war – although the boy, in uniform, is in the front ranks, and the girl, in play clothes, is in the rear – the message of Pakhomov's post-war illustration, with a younger, barefoot boy looking up at an older boy (with a military-style belt) who is leading the march, is that war is a man's business and, with proper drilling and training, will transform a boy into a fully uniformed soldier.

The illustration that initiated Pakhomov's series for "Let Us Take the New Rifles," in fact, originated as the opening illustration to "Lighting Song" (see fig. 5.6), a poem first published in *Pionerskaia Pravda* in August 1929. A mustering call for a Pioneer rally, the "Lighting Song" beckons "millions of brothers" and "millions of sisters" to work and to battle. The poem speaks of patriotic love for the motherland and imagines a giant family with "my republic" as a "big mama," the earth as an "old man," and the "steely working class" as "our big daddy" (*bol'shoi papasha*). Pakhomov at first showed the five boys, empty-handed, as a selection of these "millions of brothers," his execution in spare pencil lines and shading suggesting a sense of representational realism. When he moved the illustration from the "Lighting Song" to "Let Us Take the New Rifles," he used the same figures but armed all the children with rifles that were topped with red flags. This illustration uses a more sombre colour palette than Jakobson's – although the red used for the first letter in each title word is a nod to Mayakovsky's own innovations in typography. After putting rifles in the children's hands, Pakhomov

Figure 5.6 Alexei Pakhomov, illustration to "Lighting-Song," in Vladimir Mayakovsky's *To Children* (1949). Reproduced with permission of the University of British Columbia, Rare Books and Special Collections.

Figure 5.7 Alexei Pakhomov, illustration to "Let Us Take the New Rifles," in Vladimir Mayakovsky's *To Children* (1959). (See also colour plate 13.) Reproduced with permission of the University of British Columbia, Rare Books and Special Collections.

Figure 5.8 Boys aim and shoot in this illustration by Aleksei Pakhomov to
"Let Us Take the New Rifles," 1959. Reproduced with permission of the
University of British Columbia, Rare Books and Special Collections.

added two more illustrations, showing boys aiming and shooting in
drills, a girl wrapping a bandage around a wounded boy soldier (figs.
5.8 and 5.9), and a camouflaged boy doing reconnaissance with binocu-
lars. The title illustration was then repeated as an end-piece in smaller
format, as though the march were fading away.

Mayakovsky, the Soviet Classic for Children

Pakhomov's post-war illustrations express male fellowship and pride.
His use of clean, representational lines and a more muted colour palette
create a more mature, less playful version than did Jakobson's mass-
produced books for tiny tots. They are also the version that was taken
forward into the post-war and post-Stalinist period. They underline
that Mayakovsky had foreseen war, but also victory. V.S. Matafonov
argues that in contrast to the artists who had illustrated Mayakovsky's

Ра-
нят
в лесу,
к сво-
им
сне-
су.
90

Figure 5.9 A girl field nurse bandages a wounded boy soldier in the full
illustrated version of "Let Us Take the New Rifles" by Aleksei Pakhomov,
1959. Reproduced with permission of the University of British
Columbia, Rare Books and Special Collections.

children's books in the 1920s, Pakhomov "read more deeply" into Mayakovsky's works and addressed them to children rather than imitating
Mayakovsky's own posterized, agitational style.[31] It is clear, however,
that Pakhomov's illustrations to works like "Let Us Take the New
Rifles" are also reflections of a childhood that has experienced war.
There is nothing naive and childish about his figures; rather they are
children preparing to be adults, preparing to do adult work, already
sharing in adult cares and responsibilities. In this sense the poem fulfilled the task that Marshak had outlined for children's literature in an
article of 1933. The author and editor had underlined the importance of
"open[ing] the gates of adult life for children" in order to "show them
not only the goals but all the difficulties of our work, all the dangers of
our fight."[32] Jakobson's colourful, patterned world has been replaced

by Pakhomov's solid, serious one. Jakobson's war-time illustrations to Mayakovsky's most militaristic poem were never republished, but Pakhomov's post-war illustrations, forever associating this poem with war-time victory, were readily republished up to and after Stalin's death. Mayakovsky, who had committed suicide in 1930, became something he had never been in the 1920s: a Soviet classic for children. The war-time period was pivotal to this transformation. The publications of his collected works, *To Children*, which began regularly at the end of the 1930s, signalled that he had entered the Soviet children's canon, and the multiple forewords by Lev Kassil' and illustrations by leading artists like Pakhomov bolstered the prestige of his war-time afterlife. "Let Us Take the New Rifles" was transformed via its illustrations, from a marching song to a picture book, and created a "second life" for this poem. As V. Pertsov wrote in 1940, "the impact of Mayakovsky's poems on the masses has, in reality, only just begun." For child readers and their parents serving in the war, "Let Us Take the New Rifles" doubtless had a deeper impact the second time around.

Chapter Six

Pochta: Circulation, Delivery, Return

A Soviet Children's Classic Begins Its Rounds

One of the most popular picture books of the 1920s was Samuil Marshak's *Pochta* (*Mail*), illustrated by Mikhail Tsekhanovsky, a delightful story about a letter that travels around the world just behind its intrepid addressee, finally closing a global circuit to find him where he started, in Leningrad (fig. 6.1). Almost two decades later, Marshak created a sequel illustrated by Adrian Ermolaev, *Pochta voennaia* (*War-Time Mail*), after visiting the front and reconnecting with the first readers of *Mail*, who were now grown up and fighting in defence of the motherland. Whereas the original had celebrated international mail as a marvel of modern technology, *War-Time Mail* honoured the human courage required by the war-time field post, which delivered to mobile fighting units with no fixed address. Reprising Marshak's famous Leningrad postman, who now delivered letters confirming the well-being or loss of loved ones, the sequel connected a multigenerational target audience of child readers and their parents and linked the war-time present to the first post-revolutionary decade. It also reinscribed the sense of the post as a network that reflected the status and strength of the nation, a network that could be damaged by war, downed by enemies, and re-erected through co-operative effort. *Mail* and *War-Time Mail* brought the heroes and priorities of the 1920s and the 1940s together and reminded its grown readers of a shared childhood favourite that encapsulated Soviet values and culture.

Marshak's 1927 *Mail* connected to themes that were important to the Leninist state by highlighting the international solidarity of postal workers, and to the constructivist aesthetic that was dominant at the time, by showcasing the technological wonders of the modern mail system. The arrival of the Leningrad postman and his batch of

Figure 6.1 The cover of Samuil Marshak's 1927 *Mail*, with illustrations by
Mikhail Tsekhanovsky (see also colour plate 14).

international correspondence reminded children of the amazing links
between their home, their neighbourhood, their city, the nation, and
the world. But at the end of the 1920s those links had only recently been
restored. The publication of *Mail* in 1927 corresponded to the moment
when the Soviet postal system finally reached pre-war conditions after
years of impairments caused by the advent of the First World War, the
revolution, and the civil war. This was the system that the first people's
commissar of post and telegraph (Narkompochdel), Vadim Podbel'sky,
called in 1917 "without exaggeration ... the most disorganized branch
of the entire administrative apparatus of the Soviet Republic."[1] The
appearance of this charming and light-hearted story in 1927, then,
doubled as a timely tribute to the complex mechanisms required in
the operation of a modern state. Tsekhanovsky's illustrations to *Mail*
foreground this modernity – the mailmen of the world are the work's
heroes but only in so far as they form part of an efficient international
system that extends from and to the Soviet Union. We do not see the

Figure 6.2 Children crowd around a Leningrad postman during war time, hoping to get word from the front, in Adrian Ermolaev's illustration to Samuil Marshak's 1944 *War-Time Mail*, the sequel to his children's classic *Mail* (1927).

details of the mailmen's faces or expressions, only the purposefulness of their stride. They, like the ship and train on the work's cover, are units in a great universal machine.

Mail skyrocketed to even greater popularity with child audiences when it was adapted as an animated film, directed by its illustrator, Tsekhanovsky, in 1929. Birgit Beumers calls the animated *Mail* "the most important cartoon of early Soviet animation," a work that broke new ground as one of the earliest Soviet films to use sound.[2] Some seventeen years after its first appearance, Marshak reprised his classic story for a new generation of children. His sequel, *War-Time Mail* (*Pochta voennaia*, 1944), illustrated by one of the foremost war-time children's illustrators, Adrian Ermolaev, struck a new, sombre tone and recounted the heroic feats of the Leningrad postman and the postmen for the front, who risked their lives to connect children with their absent soldier fathers (fig. 6.2).[3] *War-Time Mail* pointed to the special significance of mail and

Figure 6.3 The letter that chases Boris Zhitkov from western Europe to the
Amazon until it is safely delivered to its addressee in Leningrad. Illustration
by Mikhail Tsekhanovsky, 1927 (see also colour plate 15). Reproduced with
permission of Rare Books and Special Collections, McGill University Library.

the postal system during the war time, not only for bringing word of
the survival and safety of loved ones but also as a key infrastructure
that signalled the ongoing survival and safety of the state. If a restored
postal system after the civil war symbolized stabilization after years
of insecurity, the recollapse of that system after 1941 became a daily
reminder of the country's upheaval and shattered borders. Marshak's
postmen for the front in *War-Time Mail* were heroes not only because
they braved enemy fire to perform their duties but because their actions
returned functionality to an important but damaged national network.
This final chapter looks at *Mail* and its sequel as an important series that
linked children's literature of the 1920s to war-time children's culture.
Like "Let Us Take the New Rifles," Marshak's sequel harkened back to
a favourite tale of the 1920s and marked that important turning point
when Soviet children's literature began to call upon its own past and
recognize the creation of its own canon of classics, closing the circuit
and bringing children's literature, after its first quarter-century of circulation, back to its first addressees.

Mail was published by the Raduga (Rainbow) Publishing House,
which produced an impressive number of high-quality children's
books in its relatively short existence from 1922 to 1930. The two lions
of Soviet children's literature, Kornei Chukovsky and Samuil Marshak,
headed Raduga and attracted a circle of talented writers and illustrators
to their fold. *Mail* was dedicated to Boris Zhitkov, a fellow children's

Figure 6.4 The back cover of Samuil Marshak's *Mail* (1927), illustrated by Mikhail Tsekhanovsky, which features four postmen from around the world. *Clockwise from top left*: the Leningrad postman leaning forward in rapid motion; the Berlin postman leaning backward due to his considerable girth; the lightly stepping Brazilian postman; and the thin, pipe-smoking English postman. (See also colour plate 16.) Reproduced with permission of Rare Books and Special Collections, McGill University Library.

writer, and tells the story of the certified letter that follows this world traveller from Leningrad to Berlin, London, and Brazil, always arriving just behind its addressee, until finally being forwarded back to Leningrad, covered in fascinating foreign postmarks (fig. 6.3).[4] The story presents the modern modes of transportation upon which a letter could travel swiftly around the world and introduces young readers to the international colleagues of the Leningrad postman – a portly German postman, Mr Smith in London, and Don Bazilio in Brazil (fig. 6.4). Some changes were made to this line-up in republications, with the letter's visit to Berlin excised during the war, and Don Bazilio becoming "gray Bazilio" once Marshak realized that in Portuguese-speaking Brazil men are not titled "Don."[5] *Mail* was a mainstay of the Soviet children's publishing industry, republished at least every year, and often in several editions a year, between 1927 and 1939.

Lenin understood the urgency of controlling Russia's communications network and acknowledged the important role of the postal system when, as one of the first actions of the October Revolution, he ordered the Red Guard to seize the Central Post and Telegraph in Petrograd.[6] Having authority over the postal system, like over the circulation of currency, became a crucial legitimizing factor for a fledgling state. Command of the postal system also offered the Soviets important propaganda gains because post offices handled the subscriptions and circulation of state-issued newspapers, journals, brochures, and books, and the images on postal stamps offered a mass system for propagating the symbols, leaders, and concepts that were important to the state.[7] These symbols reached children in greater numbers than ever before because, under Lenin, stamp collecting was transformed from an elite, mostly adult, specialist activity to a mass educative and literacy initiative for children and youth.[8] Still, despite its great potential in terms of producing images that could encapsulate the priorities of the state and put them into mass circulation for children and adults, in the 1920s the Soviet postal system was still in a period of convalescence and recovery. The end of the civil war saw the re-establishment of the postal link between Soviet Russia and the rest of the world, but inside Soviet Russia itself the postal system struggled to meet its mandate.[9] In response to the appearance of new private courier companies that stepped into the breach, and as part of the effort to promote literacy, the state made the sending of letters and postcards free of charge from 1919 until 1921.[10] The appearance of Marshak's *Mail* in 1927 corresponded to the moment of restored functionality for the postal system. While Tsekhanovsky's cheery illustrations underlined the modernity of new machine systems that could transport objects farther and faster than ever before, the Leningrad postman himself, a dutiful representative of the state who never failed in his appointed responsibilities, emblematized the positive characteristics that the embattled Soviet state urgently needed to project about itself. Intriguingly, the work inspired an American adaptation by the writer William Siegel. *Around the World in a Mailbag* (1932) envisioned Stalin-era Moscow as one of several international mail links, from San Francisco to Peking, Paris, and Egypt, for a rapidly moving letter that pursued the father of Betty and Billy Jackson (fig. 6.5).

Children and War-Time Mail

It was in war time that Marshak's 1927 *Mail* made its most significant impact, when its child readers of the 1920s, many of them now serving

Figure 6.5 Moscow as depicted by the American communist writer William Siegel in *Around the World in a Mailbag* (1932), his adaptation of Marshak's *Mail*.

in the Great Patriotic War, became the models and inspirations for *War-Time Mail*. On Marshak's first visit to the front, in September 1941, he was surprised to be asked by soldiers to recite not his newly prepared war-time poems for adults but the children's classics they remembered and cherished like *Mail*. Marshak recounted: "I began with excitement to read to those people carrying such a heavy burden of daily military labour, and constant danger, the happy and carefree lines which, perhaps, they needed at that moment because they reminded them of home, summer camp, of the childhood and youth that in reality, they had only recently emerged from."[11]

Delivering the mail was an arduous and dangerous, yet vital task during the war. At the front Marshak was asked by the courageous mailmen of the field post, the so-called mailmen for the front, why their contribution to the war had not been recognized, alongside the pilots and tank drivers, by state writers. Marshak decided to honour the feats of these unsung heroes in his *War-Time Mail*, all the while keeping in mind his now-grown readers of *Mail*. Kornei Chukovsky similarly returned to one of his classic children's stories during the war, creating *We'll Defeat Barmalei* (1942) as a war-time sequel to his *Barmalei*, which had been published by Raduga in 1925 with illustrations by Mstislav Dobuzhinsky. Chukovsky's sequel reprises the deeds of the swarthy villain Barmalei and his allies, now imagined as vicious Nazi-style beasts that are ultimately defeated by a land of heroes. The name of the principal hero, pilot Vanya Vasil'chikov, refers to yet another of Chukovsky's stories from the 1920s, *The Crocodile*, in which he first appeared as the boy hero.[12] *War-Time Mail* similarly connected to its cast of the 1920s and introduced new war-time characters. The work had three heroes: the same Leningrad postman, faithfully serving the city some seventeen years later; the children of *Mail*, who had been delighted to hear the Leningrad postman's knock on the door and were now grown up and serving their country at the front; and the mailmen for the front, who had to carry out their duties under enemy fire, delivering to constantly moving addressees who were at last found camped out in forests and trenches (fig. 6.6). Whereas Tsekhanovsky's 1927 illustrations had depicted the anonymous Leningrad postman as an energetic and productive worker, as shown by his lengthy stride and intent, forward-looking gaze, Ermolaev's illustrations of 1944 focused on the humanity of the man behind the uniform (figs. 6.7 and 6.8). The later version shows the postman's dignified, care-worn face in close-up, and his rapid motion stilled, as though in recognition of his sober and serious task. Ermolaev's black-and-white drawings lent a new air of documentality and gravity to the series that addressed the crisis of

Figure 6.6 The mailman for the front must travel long distances to find his moving addressees, in Adrian Ermolaev's 1944 illustration from *War-Time Mail* that shows a mailman emerging from the wilderness, armed with a mailbag and a rifle.

Figure 6.7 Mikhail Tsekhanovsky's Leningrad postman is a rapid and efficient servant of the state, depicted in forward motion, with a wide stride and letter at the ready, 1927. Reproduced with permission of Rare Books and Special Collections, McGill University Library.

Figure 6.8 By 1944, Adrian Ermolaev had stilled the rapid motion
of the Leningrad postman, focusing instead on his care-worn
and compassionate features.

war-time mail. In its second iteration, with the efficient universal postal
machine of the 1920s having been broken by war, the humanity and
courage of the postman comes to the fore, as does his role in *rebuilding*
the modern state at home and re-establishing national boundaries in
the field, step by step.

War-Time Children's Culture and the Mail

The war introduced extreme difficulties for the Soviet postal system in
a number of ways, necessitating the eventual intersection of this hith-
erto adult, state-run domain with war-time children's culture as youth
stepped in to sort and deliver mail from the front. During the war the
mass evacuation of people, state offices, and industries to the east put
a strain on postal routes that were not prepared for such heavy traf-
fic. As a result, post offices and postal outlets became overwhelmed,
and letters, parcels, and telegrams reached their addressees with difficulty.[13] Communications were lost altogether in the Nazi-occupied

territories in Ukraine, Belarus, and Moldova, and postal infrastructure was destroyed when the German army retreated in 1943. Special restoration battalions were required to repair some fifty-eight thousand kilometres of lines and to rebuild one-quarter of all the telephone stations of the Soviet Union, one-third of all the radio signal offices, and some thirteen thousand postal enterprises.[14] Postal workers had the huge and difficult task of maintaining an unbroken and speedy mail-delivery service between soldiers at the front and their loved ones in the rear. For this purpose the military field post (*polevaia pochta*) was created in January 1943.[15] This was a colossal responsibility that included getting seventy million letters to the front every month, as well as thirty million newspapers, which constituted the principal form of political communication between the state and its soldiers.[16] Finally, postal workers had to overcome all these difficulties at a disadvantage because many personnel had been called up for active duty, and, until the end of 1941, postal transportation vehicles were regularly requisitioned for other military duties.[17] As a result of these strains upon the system, mail was not being sorted or reaching its addressees early in the war. In Nazi-occupied centres like Kiev, the postal system collapsed altogether: local populations were denied the right of communication, although this was allowed in other occupied countries.[18] In besieged Leningrad, the domain of the fictional Leningrad postman, postal service never officially halted, but it was drastically handicapped by lack of personnel, by the fact that it had to be delivered entirely by hand or on sleds, and by the fact that postal outlets were explicitly the target of German bombings. The Leningrad central post office was closed for the first two years of the war, 1941–3, because it had been the target of bombing and artillery fire.[19]

In *Mail* the postal system is a complex, adult realm that children learn about and admire. *Mail* is about getting material objects to their destination points quickly through an intricate international system of transport and mail links. We never discover the content of the certified letter for Boris Zhitkov, only that the letter travelled around the world in an organized and timely fashion. But in *War-Time Mail* the emotional content of letters *does* matter a great deal because it brings news of the survival of fathers and the well-being of children at home; a letter from the front meant that "Dad is alive! Dad writes!"[20] In 1944 children were not the onlookers but the active writers and recipients of mail (fig. 6.9). This was a gendered undertaking, with war-time mail being sent principally between a soldier and his son, although the daughter might "add a few lines."[21] Marshak shows that these missives between the defenders of the motherland and the small guardians of the home

Figure 6.9 Children write a letter to their father in *War-Time Mail*. Adrian Ermolaev's 1944 illustration shows the son as the principal author of this important missive from home, although the daughter appears to be older and presumably has more advanced writing skills.

front were paramount to victory because soldiers on the front found that "with such a letter in one's pocket / It's easier to fight."[22]

Letters from the Front

Marshak was not the only artist to acknowledge the significance of war-time mail or to recognize its connection to children's culture. Aleksei Pakhomov dedicated one of his drawings made during the siege, and published in the illustrated album *In Those Days*, to the importance of a war-time letter's arrival (fig. 6.10). The sketch is called simply *The Letter* and shows two children, a boy and a girl, hopefully pulling a letter from

Figure 6.10 Aleksei Pakhomov's drawing entitled *The Letter*, published in his
album of sketches, *In Those Days: Leningrad Album* (1946).

a postbox. The accompanying text by poet Nikolai Tikhonov explains that in the first winter of the siege, 1941–2, the Leningrad city post had almost stopped functioning.[23] A severe lack of personnel and the ubiquitous barrier of snow lay as nearly insurmountable obstacles between the letters that did arrive by airdrop and their delivery to homes. Leningrad's postal outlets had been reduced in war time by more than half, from 203 to 96, and by the spring of 1942 undelivered letters from the front lay unsorted in "piles and piles."[24] Tikhonov writes that this mountainous backlog of correspondence was finally dispatched by "whole brigades of youth," who arrived to sort the mail. An article in *Komsomol'skaia Pravda* of April 1942 called "There's a Letter and Telegram for You" described the important work of Komsomol youth in a Leningrad neighbourhood who, over a period of three weeks, sorted 236 bags of mail and delivered 2,490 letters and 611 telegrams from the front.[25] This sort of contribution came under the war-time rubric of "All for the Front!" and occurred alongside the Union-wide mass volunteer movement of children that was inspired by the children's writer Arkady Gaidar and the boy hero of *Timur and His Team*.

Unlike the Pioneers and within a culture dominated by state-run youth movements, the Timur movement distinguished itself by being a grass-roots organization initiated by children themselves.[26] These children proudly wrote letters to children's journals like *Murzilka*, outlining the chores they had done for the community. A representative letter called "Our Timur Team" from 1942 was signed by four preadolescent girls between the ages of eleven and twelve.[27] During the war years, participation in the Pioneers declined, while volunteer work for the Timur movement soared. One specialist in Soviet children's culture writes that Timur teams also delivered nine hundred letters from the front in Kiev in 1942.[28] While this is unlikely in a city occupied by a brutal regime, the fact remains that the activities of the Timur teams were far reaching and show the incredible impact of children's literature as a mobilizing factor during the war.

Children and youth responded to the war-time value, articulated by Margarita Aliger in a *Pravda* article of 28 June 1941, that "there is no and cannot be any rear in this war."[29] Young postmen like the ones in Leningrad became the hidden, unsung counterparts to the mailmen for the front who were celebrated in Marshak's *War-Time Mail*. The successful delivery of correspondence between the heart of Soviet Russia and the recently occupied borderlands allowed youth to participate in a kind of ongoing redrawing of the map. At the time of the publication of *War-Time Mail* in 1944, the damaged and broken mail network was an emblem of the nation's violation and torn borders, its painful contraction after the Nazi invasion of 1941. As the tide of war began to shift, after 1943, letters and postcards played an important role in marking the passage of victory as the postmen for the front were obliged to travel farther and farther into the territory reclaimed by the Red Army in order to deliver their letters. The more distant the rounds of the mailmen for the front, the closer the Soviet Union was to reclaiming its pre-war boundaries and integrity. As Marshak suggested to his young readers in *War-Time Mail*, soon the field post would extend as far as Berlin, finally sealing victory. In this way, mail was closely connected to the emotion-laden notion of state frontiers and borders, and delivering the mail became an analogue to one of the most popular military tasks taken on by adolescents during the war and celebrated in children's literature and culture – the border guard.[30] *War-Time Mail* made its most significant impact during the war years and the immediate post-war period. It was republished twice yearly and in significant print runs in 1944, 1945, and 1946, but these numbers dropped dramatically after 1949.

Mail, however, remained a perennial favourite with child readers, and the story of this work and its war-time sequel points to an important watershed in Soviet children's culture, namely, the moment when the first readers of post-revolutionary literature could reflect back upon, read to their own children, and hence actualize a new Soviet canon. The children's stories of the 1920s became a cultural trove of narratives and images for a new generation, and illustrated children's literature acted as a crucial tool of validation for the state. Nothing could entrench Soviet culture so effectively as a pool of favourite childhood rhymes, refrains, characters, and images shared by its youngest citizens and transmitted to them by their parents, the older generation of first readers. After 1917, illustrated children's literature had faced two contrasting tasks: to address the future by creating, from scratch, an entirely new bookshelf reflecting the ideology of the state for little comrades; and, at the same time, to address the literature of the past. Sergei Oushakine has recently discussed the problems faced by early Soviet children's literature when it was assigned the monumental task of transmitting Marxist ideas to children.[31] In the 1920s and 1930s all this was happening when the child audience of readers itself was changing rapidly from the elite minority of pre-revolutionary days to a mass and mixed audience of increasingly literate young readers, and the publication industry for children was expanding into an organ of mass communication. Faced at first with a blank slate, illustrated children's literature was often oriented towards the past, to the generation of images that would create an appropriate accompaniment to a carefully selected canon of classics from the imperial era. An important function of illustrations was to nestle into the script of the past, next to the words of Pushkin and Tolstoy, and issue provisos and extensions of meaning. In this sense, illustrations provided a kind of imbedded sequelization: they built an image of the nation *today* built on the text of yesterday.

But *Mail* and *War-Time Mail* signalled a new kind of sequelization process, one that allowed Soviet children's literature to be self-referential, to close its own circle, and address its own past instead of correcting and counteracting the works of the long-distant era that Stalin-era critic Antonina Babushkina called the "encyclopedia of the terrifying past."[32] *Mail* articulates the priorities and aesthetics of children's culture in the 1920s, but *War-Time Mail* marks the moment that the immense and complicated task of canon creation could be recognized by the connection of the first Soviet child readers to their heirs. First promoted alongside the classics of Russian literature in an attempt to controvert the past, the illustrated children's literature of the 1920s became, in war time under Stalin, a classic in its own right.

Conclusion: Yesterday and Today

The twentieth century ushered in new developments in the children's book, which showed ever-increasing attention to the important interaction between word and image. Temple, Martinez, Yokota, and Naylor pinpoint the 1930s as being the time, in the West, when "the concept of the modern picture book" was consolidated and included an understanding of the importance of a unified, overarching book design and the fundamental interdependence of the text and illustrations.[1] In the Soviet Union this innovation had been truly consolidated in the 1920s. Although the pre-revolutionary World of Art movement had introduced the concept of well-crafted book design and beautiful, high-quality illustrations, it was the avant-garde futurist and constructivist groups who took up the importance of graphic design and typography and implemented these ideas within the mass Soviet publishing industry. Book art after the revolution focused on the blending and synthesis of text and image, and with famous author-artist collaborations that extended over multiple book publications, like Marshak and Lebedev, or Chukovsky and Konashevich, many of the iconic early works of Soviet children's literature can properly be considered co-creations featuring side-by-side literary and visual texts.[2] James von Geldern tells us that the Stalin-era state was exceptional in its insistence on the skills of readership, requiring a high degree of hermeneutic mastery from its public. This interpreting experience did not rely solely on reading, however, but also on viewing. The hermeneutic task of readers, even child readers, cannot be fully understood until we recover how literary texts interacted with period illustrations and with the cultural contexts of their production.[3]

One of the points this book has brought to light is that the emergence of a category that could unequivocally be called Soviet illustrated children's literature was far from a clear-cut process. For the first

seven years after the 1917 revolution there was no specifically designated state-run children's publishing industry, but rather a multi-audience state publishing industry and a series of smaller private houses.
While it is easy to discern that a picture book was aimed at the child
reader even if it did not emerge from a children's publishing sector
proper, the boundary between child and adult audiences is much more
blurred when it comes to genres like the fairy tale and Russian classics. Pushkin's fairy tales were appealing to adult *and* child readers,
as was Ershov's *Little Humpbacked Horse*. Therefore, it is reasonable to
assume that before, and even after, the emergence of the State Publishing House in 1924, child and adolescent readers were the consumers of
illustrated literature generally and exposed to the kinds of overarching
cultural themes, such as the anti-religious campaign and the birth of
Soviet aviation, that have been discussed in this book. Although illustrated literature rapidly expanded to new readers after 1917, a mass
illustrated children's literature reached peak operation in the Stalin era,
at about the mid-1930s, when print runs were maximized and cultural
campaigns unified. Still, what we can observe in the Lenin era is the
identification of the child reader as a crucial audience, the birth of a
mass state children's culture (not yet at full strength), and the proliferation of illustrated literature within a rapidly expanding field of publishing. Some of the landmarks in this complex process were the previously
mentioned establishment of the Children's Section of the State Publishing House in 1924, the creation of universal public education in 1930,
the establishment of the vast state-run Children's Literature Publishing
House in 1932, and the regular publication of the public school textbook
called *Russian Literature* after 1936. What happened in and around those
clear-cut landmarks, however, is complicated and sometimes contradictory. Whole categories of children's literature, like the magical fairy
tale, were the subject of long-term, vitriolic public debate. Leading classic authors were either acceptable and then anathema, like Dostoevsky,
or controversial and then adulated, like Pushkin. Illustrations not only
reflect these seismic modulations, but they show how children's culture was centred in, not cordoned off from, the predominant political
culture of the 1920s, 1930s, 1940s, and early 1950s, and how the growth
of illustrated children's literature paralleled and grew out of illustrated
literature generally.

In the West, the 1920s and 1930s were decisive decades for setting
new standards and benchmarks in illustrated children's literature. The
John Newbery Medal was established in 1922 to recognize the most
distinguished contribution to children's literature, followed in 1938 by
the Randolph Caldecott Medal for the most distinguished picture book

for children. Around this time, a growing awareness of child psychology effected a new understanding of the importance of a person's first reading experiences. Alice Dalgliesh, the founding editor of the Children's Book Division of Charles Scribner and Sons, wrote in 1932 that children's stories no longer required an overt moral; rather they should be "ethically sound, to present the true and beautiful and to exclude the wrong or undesirable."[4] The task of children's literature, she said, was to "present right ideals in an attractive light."[5] While Russia and America may have held very different political positions in the 1930s, presenting the "right ideals in an attractive light" was nonetheless exactly what Lenin and Stalin–era Russia held as its mission for children's literature. Soviet children's literature was no less joyful, colourful, or inventive than its Western counterparts in this period, but what did set it apart was a distinctive relationship to the national past.

Negotiations with the Past

Mediating the past emerges as a recurring preoccupation of children's literature and reading from the 1920s to the 1950s, despite the fact that the state held very different attitudes towards the past in the 1920s than it did in the 1930s, 1940s, and early 50s. Lenin-era Russia sought to break away from the forms, the institutions, and the morality of the tsarist era, whereas Stalin-era Russia attempted to bolster its prestige by excavating the past and selecting representative heroes and classics. What both eras held in common, however, was an attitude that treated the national past as vital and powerful, a narrative to be taken command of and brought to submission – in short, one that acknowledged that the past was anything but dead. Under Lenin the literary and historical past was treated as a dangerous cultural category that needed to be vilified and urgently countermanded. This antagonistic stance towards the past emerged not only in the cultural policies of the 1920s towards non-acceptable literary forms, resulting in magical fairy tales being pruned out of collections accessible by the public, but also in newly published works. In Marshak's *Yesterday and Today* (1928), yesterday is represented by a series of outmoded household items, such as the inkpot and the water bucket, which appear hopelessly obsolete in the presence of new technologies like the typewriter and the water tap. Moreover, when the kerosene lamp is called a "foolish peasant woman" (*glupaia baba*) who must step aside for the arrival of the new "citizen," the electric lamp, it is not only household but also human categories that are being judged as antiquated and useless. This wholesale rejection of the past altered under Stalin, when there was a heavily publicized return to the classics and a revival of the national past. This, however, did not imply an unmediated acceptance of the past; rather it involved a painstaking selection process regarding *which* works, which authors, and which historical figures could be brought forward into the present. David Brandenberger has argued that the process of unearthing a "usable past," first introduced in 1918, became characteristic of Stalin-era culture, so that by the war-time period there was a "routine conflation of past and present."[6] The case studies presented in this book show that in fact this process of conflation was entrenched much earlier and that "yesterday and today" became a recurring and revisited theme of the first decades after 1917. What began under Lenin and continued under Stalin was a highly patrolled and policed past, and illustrations had a special role to play in this contentious relationship between yesterday and today. When new illustrations were commissioned for a fairy tale of the past or a tsarist-era classic, they could act as a living voice of the present inserted into the fabric of the past in order to correct, update, and shift meaning.

In her work on representations of the Nazi past in Germany after 1945, Zohar Shavit has pinpointed children's literature as one of the most "effective central socializing agents" of the state. She has examined the tensions between texts that strive to be historically accurate, or at least "historically credible," and the role of children's books as "subjective retellings of national myths" and as important "sources of national pride and identity."[7] Children's literature was particularly consequential in Soviet Russia from the 1920s to the 1950s, when, in contrast to the low cultural status assigned to children's literature in post-war Germany, it was well supported by the state, distributed in mass print runs, and energized by a pool of top writers and artists. Moreover, illustrations in this period allowed for a rich mediation with the past because, as we have seen, they appeared not only in new works *about* the past but also as cues and commentaries inserted *into* the texts of the past themselves, the voice of today mediating the words of yesterday. So while children's literature in post-war Germany may have presented a "wishful image of their history," illustrations allowed Soviet children's literature to have a different focus – a wishful image of the *present* created out of a carefully constructed national past.[8] In war time, children's literature began to reference a new, common Soviet past and create a new canon of classics out of the works of the 1920s.

The Unique Role of Illustrations

Circulation, a theoretical construct adopted from studies of the city and urban culture, suggests an important way of conceptualizing the role of illustrations as uniquely flexible and mobile cultural products. Not only do books circulate through successive audiences of child readers, linking younger generations to older ones through a shared cache of words and images, but new illustrations move fluidly through a fixed piece of work, accruing new meanings and associations for familiar texts as a result of the process. Sequels also recirculate meaning by harkening back to the origin texts and reaching forward to new interpreting communities. As a concept, then, circulation captures the continuous movement and interaction of illustrations with texts, illustrations with cultural contexts, and illustrations with reading audiences, which I have outlined in this book. Circulation allows illustrations, like all cultural artifacts, to "constantly reposition artists and audiences in relationship to each other."[9] The fluid departure and rearrival of circulation allows for targeted patterns of distribution over time. In other words, it is important not just that an illustrated sequel was created but that it was produced in the war years, connecting that time of national reaffirmation to the 1920s and the establishment of Soviet values and reading practices. Moreover, that sequel could target a *certain* public, namely, its own first readers. Thus, as Marc Angenot posits about cultural forms generally, illustrated works in complex ways "absorb, transform and rediffuse bits of textuality" as these artistic products circulate through social spaces.[10]

Illustrations also have an important function in terms of shaping national identity. Benedict Anderson has argued for the significant role played by the proliferation of mass print culture in the process of "stretching the short, tight skin of the nation around the gigantic body of the empire" in Russia in the nineteenth century.[11] This ongoing process of creating an "imagined community" of national identity through the mass spread of printed materials can be usefully extended into the Soviet period.[12] Under Lenin the state-run publishing industry was harnessed as a legitimizing tool for the new regime. It was not only print culture, however, but also visual culture that played a key role in this period in shaping public opinion. Expressing the goals of the state in a visual language was paramount for a nation that was still largely illiterate. For this reason visual propaganda made up such a large proportion of the content of the agit-trains that were sent into the countryside during the civil-war years to persuade the peasantry of the expediency of Soviet power, and for this reason the famous ROSTA window posters that went up in telegraph agencies across Russia could be deciphered in words *or* through pictures. During the 1920s, illustrations had an important role to play in this mass outreach effort, but they played it partly by helping to shape a metaphysical imagined community, namely, the territory of the past, which in turn became instrumental in shaping an image of the Soviet-era Russian nation. Without this special, complex, contentious relationship to the past that was articulated through the media of illustrations, the process of national-identity shaping would not have been so fully expressed in this period.

The process of using mass media like illustrations in a larger national-identity-building project was so pervasive that it resulted in real blunders like the publication of *War-Time Mail* in Estonian translation in 1949. One can only imagine the reaction of Estonian parents reading this story, with its subtext of reclaiming Russian pre-war borders, to their children who would have been born just around the time that Soviet troops reasserted dominion over the Baltic countries, countries that had been ceded to Russian control under the Molotov-Ribbentrop Pact of 1939. Certainly, Estonian readers would have had a very different interpretation of Adrian Ermolaev's illustration showing an armed, uniformed, and advancing Russian mailman emerging from the forest. Still, the relentless project of shaping the imagined community of the Russian nation in this period appears to have taken precedence over considerations of good taste, and the state continued to blithely export russocentric products to non-Russian consumers.

The Legacy of Lenin and Stalin-Era Illustrations

Thanks largely to the high quality and "gaze-appeal" of book art from this period, children's books from the Lenin and Stalin eras, as well as from later in the Soviet period, continue to be the "widely acknowledged classics" of the Putin-era child's library.[13] The works that I have looked at in this book had varying fates after 1953. Marshak's *War-Time Mail* was only rarely republished (in 1961 and 1971), whereas *Mail* continued to be a popular children's picture book and has been republished and reprinted regularly up to today. Collections of Mayakovsky's works titled *To Children* still appeared after the Stalin era (seventy-eight times in book editions), but "Let Us Take the New Rifles" did not always appear in the table of contents. It was, however, republished in 1973 with illustrations by V. Losin, and in 2011 with illustrations by Iu. Korovin. Aleksandra Jakobson's illustrations to "Let Us Take the New Rifles," so widely distributed during the war, were never republished and currently reside in only a few rare book collections worldwide.

Russian classics fared better. Pushkin's *Tale of the Priest and His Worker Balda* was revived in 1971 as a children's opera for puppet theatre, with music by Boris Kravchenko, and entered popular culture more widely as a Soiuzmultfilm cartoon in 1973. Today Balda is even a popular subject for Putin-era children's colouring books. Through the decades

Balda has become steadily younger and blonder and in contemporary renditions, following Stalinist cultural traditions, is unfailingly taller and more vigorous than his opponent, the priest. Since the demise of the Soviet Union in 1991 and the rapprochement between church and state, Balda has had to pay a debt for his years as a poster child for the anti-religious campaign. In 2006 the Russian Orthodox Church banned a jubilee production of Dmitry Shostakovich's long-suppressed *Balda* opera on the basis of the anti-clerical satire contained in the work. Eager to claim prominent cultural figures like Shostakovich and Push- kin for their own purposes, church spokesmen maintained that Shosta- kovich had unwillingly composed his work and that Pushkin himself had regretted ever writing the tale.

From the mid-1950s to the 2010s, *The Little Humpbacked Horse* was republished regularly and in large print runs of several hundred thou- sand. Following the precedent set under Stalin, the target audience for the fairy tale continued to be readers of the youngest age. The appeal of the tale for children was reinforced when *The Little Humpbacked Horse* was made into a popular children's animated cartoon directed by Ivan Ivanov-Vano in 1947, and remade with an additional episode in 1975.

Pushkin's *Bronze Horseman* and Tolstoy's *Anna Karenina* remained mainstays of the public school curriculum. Although other artists were commissioned to illustrate *The Bronze Horseman*, Alexander Benois's illustrated series has been reproduced to accompany the work in pub- lications at least once every decade from the 1960s to today, and fac- simile reprints of Benois's complete and unedited 1923 version of the illustrations began to appear in the 1980s. The work remains an impor- tant touchstone for Russian national identity, especially as that iden- tity shifted after 1991. An intriguing version of *The Bronze Horseman* illustrated by V. Skrodenis in 1995 connects the work to the collapse of the Soviet Union by showing a stumbling and disintegrating Bronze Horseman that has forcefully crashed to the ground (fig. 7.1).

One illustrated version of *Anna Karenina* was never seen by the Rus- sian public in the Stalin era. A luxury edition of the novel, in English translation, was published for the members of the Limited Editions Club of New York by the State Publishing House for Fiction and Poetry in 1933, with a foreword by Anatoly Lunacharsky and illustrations by Nikolai Piskarev. His nineteen woodcut illustrations show a deeply sexualized interpretation of Tolstoy's heroine in erotic poses and trans- lucent dresses. What emerges in Piskarev's illustrations echoes the line taken in Stalin-era textbooks: a commentary on the destructive nature of sexual passion and its effect on the relationship between mother and child. These illustrations were, however, off limits for the Stalin-era

Figure 7.1 V. Skrodenis's 1995 illustration for a German-Russian translation of
The Bronze Horseman, put out by the Russian publishing house Novyi gorod.
The original series is in colour.

schoolchild – although they were directed specifically at the young
reader of the Putin era when they were selected for the Children's Literature republication of *Anna Karenina* in 2006.

This artistic series was not flattering about Anna as a mother. The
illustration titled *Two of Vronsky's Hobbies* shows Vronsky looking
towards his racing horse, Frou-Frou, while Anna stands with her back
turned (fig. 7.2). Outside the frame a small, naked child – presumably
Seriozha – holds his arms out to be picked up but is neither seen nor
heard by his mother. In the final illustration of the edition, *Tailpiece to
Part the Seventh*, which accompanies the text describing Anna's suicide
(fig. 7.3), Anna lies naked under a sheet, eyes closed, neck arched, in a
pose suggestive of both death and consummated passion. Seriozha is
present even in this final illustration – as a tiny portrait on Anna's bed-
side table, once again framed outside his mother's care.

What is striking about this brief review of the post-1953 afterlife, and
particularly the Putin-era afterlife, of these works of Soviet children's

Figure 7.2 *Two of Vronsky's Hobbies* by Nikolai Piskarev, showing Frou-Frou, the racehorse, on the left; Anna on the right; and Anna's son, Seriozha, outside the frame. In *Anna Karenina*, published for the members of the Limited Editions Club of New York by the State Publishing House for Fiction and Poetry, 1933.

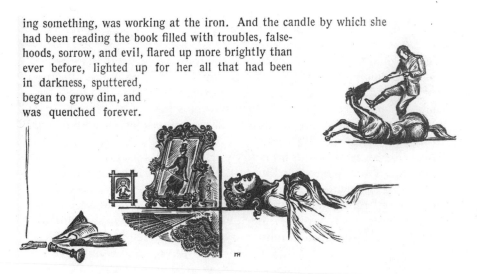

ing something, was working at the iron. And the candle by which she had been reading the book filled with troubles, falsehoods, sorrow, and evil, flared up more brightly than ever before, lighted up for her all that had been in darkness, sputtered, began to grow dim, and was quenched forever.

Figure 7.3 *Tailpiece to Part the Seventh*, Nikolai Piskarev's final illustration of the 1933 edition of *Anna Karenina*, showing Anna's suicide and harking back to the consummation of her affair with Vronsky. The assumption is that he has killed both Frou-Frou and Anna through reckless passion.

literature and reading is how instrumental the Stalinist 1930s was in setting the standards and precedents for children's culture in the long run. The grade levels to which classics were assigned in the public school system have remained largely in place since the 1930s. Balda continues to look like his Stalin-era version (large and blonde) rather than his imperial-era version. The little humpbacked horse, following artists of the Stalin era like N. Kochergin, remains a cute toy pony. Despite the political repudiation of Stalinism, the conventions and visual cues of this era sank deep into the children's culture of ensuing decades and were prolonged even into the post-socialist period.

The illustrated children's books of the 1920s continue to appeal to young readers and their parents. In post-Soviet Russia, reprints of Soviet editions are considered to be both of higher intellectual quality than new works and of higher professional quality than Putin-era editions of the same works. These Soviet classics on today's post-socialist bookshelf are considered "exemplary" and "still the most desired" by today's parents.[14] While "What to Read to Children" lists have now ceded to mommy blogs, the content of the latter's lists remains remarkably similar. Moreover, today's child almost certainly views many of the same illustrations, perhaps even a reprint of the same illustrated edition, that his or her parents, grandparents, or even great-grandparents first received.

Although post-1991 republication of Russian classics from the imperial period has tended to reverse the biases of the Soviet era by bringing forward those works that were censored, banned, or under-published by the Soviets, the children's literature produced by early Soviet writers and illustrators continues to play the role of a "locus for expressing national belonging [and] Russian nationality."[15] In an era of "historical uncertainty" and an "ambiguous position [for Russia] in the international arena," Soviet illustrated children's literature has become a safe haven for expressing a sense of shared cultural values with fellow Russians.[16] Thus, the illustrated children's reading and literature from the 1920s to the 1950s, conceived by its early theorists and practitioners as a revolutionary medium capable of capturing and conveying a new ideology and world-view, has become, under Putin, a vehicle for demonstrating good parenting skills and asserting the seemingly contradictory goals of preserving Soviet cultural ideals while maintaining one's post-socialist identity and economic status. Both Soviet and post-Soviet illustrated children's literature and reading continue to be largely defined by the tension between yesterday and today.

Notes

Introduction

1 P. Dul'skii, *Sovremennaia illiustratsiia v detskoi knige* (Kazan: Typo-lit. Imperatorskago universiteta, 1916), 13 (emphasis mine). All translations from Russian are mine unless otherwise noted. Whenever possible, the transliteration of Russian names and titles complies with the British Standard System, modified to omit hard and soft signs. The only exceptions to this rule pertain to familiar names that have acquired a recognized English spelling, and to material that is quoted from sources using other transliteration systems.

2 Evgeny Steiner, "Mirror Images: On Soviet-Western Reflections in Children's Books of the 1920s and 1930s," in *Children's Literature and the Avant-Garde*, ed. Elina Druker (Amsterdam: John Benjamins, 2015), 190–1.

3 A. Pokrovskaia, *Osnovnye techeniia v sovremennoi detskoi literatura* (Moscow: Rabotnik prosveshcheniia, 1927), 6–7.

4 E. Danko, "Zadachi khudozhestvennogo oformleniia detskoi knigi," in *Detskaia literatura: Kriticheskii sbornik*, ed. Anatoly Lunacharskii (Moscow: Khudozhestvennaia literature, 1931), 210.

5 Lenin died in 1924. Stalin consolidated power in 1928 and remained in power until his death in 1953.

6 As a rule, illustrations appearing in editions published for children and adolescents followed the same cultural trends that we can discern in illustrated literature more broadly in the period 1917–53.

7 This article was published as "The Petersburg Sublime: Alexander Benois and the Bronze Horseman Series (1903–1922)," *Germano-Slavica* 17 (2009–10): 3–24.

8 Chapter 3 first appeared as "The Bronze Horseman Rides Again: The Stalinist Reimaging of Alexander Pushkin's *Mednyi vsadnik*, 1928–53," *Russian Review* 72, no. 1 (January 2013): 24–44.

9 The phrase first emerged in a *Pionerskaia Pravda* article of 1935 that thanked Stalin on behalf of all Soviet youth. It was echoed in the same year in V.M. Gusev's lyrics to the "Song of the Russian Schoolchild," which professed gratitude to "our native land" for producing a shared, happy childhood. See Olga Kucherenko, *Little Soldiers: How Soviet Children Went to War, 1941–1945* (Oxford: Oxford University Press, 2011), 61.

10 The poster was recreated, with a similar iconography, by an artistic collective led by Nina Vatolina in 1950. In the same year, a postage stamp was put into circulation showing elementary school children in a classroom emblazoned with the motto "Thank You for a Happy Childhood!"

11 Sergei Oushakine, "Translating Communism for Children: Fables and Posters of the Revolution," *Boundary 2* 43, no. 3 (August 2016): 170.

12 This is not an exhaustive list of book artists working in the period but represents illustrators whose work is featured in this book.

13 Oushakine, "Translating Communism for Children," 171.

14 Oushakine, 175, 184, 189.

15 Oushakine, 173. The idea is cited from El Lissitzky, "Our Book," in *El Lissitzky: Life, Letters, Texts*, ed. Sophie Lissitzky-Kuppers (New York: Thames & Hudson, 1992), 362.

16 What is understood by "child" is defined later in this introduction.

17 Oushakine, "Translating Communism for Children," 171. Valerii Blinov's *Russkaia detskaia knizhka-kartinka, 1900–41* (Moscow: Iskusstvo XXI vek, 2005) is another excellent treatment of the picture book.

18 See Ben Hellman, *Fairy Tales and True Stories: The History of Russian Literature for Children and Young People (1574–2010)* (Leiden, Netherlands: Brill, 2013), 157.

19 The independent work of the Institute of Children's Reading was short lived, lasting only until 1923, and Pokrovskaia's child-centred concept of children's reading was replaced by a top-down model in which children and parents were instead given recommended reading lists generated by the state. See Irina Arzamastseva, "Podvizhniki detskogo chteniia," *Detskie chteniia* 1 (2012): 18.

20 Maurice Friedberg, *Russian Classics in Soviet Jackets* (New York: Columbia University Press, 1962).

21 Some pre-revolutionary fairy tales, however, were indeed targeted at child readers, for instance Pogorel'skii's "Chernaia kuritsa," Odoevskii's "Gorodok v tabakerke," and Tolstoy's tales for children.

22 See Megan Swift, "The Poet, the Peasant, and the Nation: Aleksandr Puškin's 'Skazka o pope i o rabotnike ego Balde' (1830) in Illustrated Editions, 1917–1953," *Russian Literature* 87–9, no. 1 (Jan.–Apr. 2017).

23 See Swift, "The Poet, the Peasant, and the Nation"; Evgeny Steiner, *Stories for Little Comrades: Revolutionary Artists and the Making of Early Soviet Children's Books* (Seattle: University of Washington Press, 1999).

24 Oushakine, "Translating Communism for Children," 166.

25 Anatoly Lunacharskii, ed., *Detskaia literatura: Kriticheskii sbornik* (Moscow: Khudozhestvennaia Literature, 1931), 4.

26 Pokrovskaia, *Osnovnye techeniia v sovremennoi detskoi literatura*, 7.

27 Viktor Shul'gin, ed., *Deti i Oktiabr'skaia revoliutsiia: Ideologiia sovetskogo shkol'nika* (Moscow: Rabotnik prosvescheniia, 1928), 57. Shul'gin claimed in his foreword that the poll included 1.5 million child responses on questions relating to the revolution, Soviet power, school, religion, the family, and other questions.

28 Julie K. deGraffenried, *Sacrificing Childhood: Children and the Soviet State in the Great Patriotic War* (Lawrence: University Press of Kansas, 2014), 162.

29 Another important source of information was the short-lived periodical *Kniga detiam* [Books for children] (1928–30), which included lists of recommended works.

30 L. Kormchii, "The Forgotten Weapon: About the Children's Book" [Zabytoe oruzhie], *Pravda*, 17 February 1918, no. 28, p. 3. Quoted in Michael Patrick Hearn, *From the Silver Age to Stalin: Russian Children's Book Illustration in the Sasha Lurye Collection* (Amherst, MA: Eric Carle Museum of Picture Book Art, 2003), 8. See also Ben Hellman, "Detskaia literatura kak oruzhie: Tvorcheskii put' L. Kormchego," in *"Ubit' Charskuiu … ": Paradoksy sovet- skoi literatury dlia detei, 1920–1930– e gg.*, ed. Marina Balina and Valerii V'iugin (St Petersburg, Russia: Aleteiia, 2013), 20–45.

31 Samuil Marshak, "Za bol'shuiu detskuiu literaturu," *Komsomol'skaia Pravda*, 22 January 1936.

32 "Ot redaktsii," *Detskie chteniia* 1 (2012): 4, accessed 8 May 2017, http://detskie-chtenia.ru.

33 "Ot redaktsii," 3, 6.

34 Sara Pankenier Weld, *An Ecology of the Russian Avant-Garde Picturebook* (Amsterdam: John Benjamins, 2018), 4.

35 Oushakine, "Translating Communism for Children," 173.

Part I Fairy-Tale Nation

1 *Skazka*, or fairy tale, is defined in Vladimir Dal's 1866 dictionary as "an imagined story, fantastical and unrealizable." In the Soviet period, *skazka* was used broadly to mean a colourful, imaginary children's story.

2 E. Gankina, *Khudozhnik v sovremennoi detskoi knige* (Moscow: Sovetskii khudozhnik, 1977), 24.

3 Pioneer youth group leaders, for instance, put on plays for children from the mid-1920s to the 1930s in which fairy-tale figures were put on trial and found guilty of being "anti-Soviet elements." See Felicity O'Dell, *Socialisation through Children's Literature: The Soviet Example* (Cambridge: Cambridge University Press, 1978), 13. See also Marina Balina, Helena

Goscilo, and M.N. Lipovetsky, *Politicizing Magic: An Anthology of Russian and Soviet Fairy Tales* (Evanston, IL, 2005), 119.

4 Evgeny Dobrenko, *Formovka sovetskogo chitatelia* (St Petersburg, Russia: Akademicheskii proekt, 1997), 173. Krupskaia adhered to the idea of "reader's guidance," which included weeding "morally unacceptable" books out of library collections when readers were deemed unable to properly evaluate ideological content. See Boris Raymond, *Krupskaia and Soviet Russian Librarianship, 1917–1939* (Metuchen, NJ, and London: Scarecrow Press, 1979), 90, 187. The disorganized manner in which Krupskaia's directives were followed in district libraries led to the overzealous removal of both fairy tales and Russian classics such as Pushkin, Gogol, Griboedov, Krylov, Nekrasov, Tolstoy, and Turgenev. The chair of the Central Library Commission complained of these incorrect removals in her article "On the Problem of the Removal of Literature," *Kommunisticheskoe prosveshchenie* no. 4 (1926): 161–3. See Bertram Wolfe, "Krupskaya Purges the People's Libraries," *Survey* no. 72 (1969): 152–3.

5 Frank Miller, *Folklore for Stalin: Russian Folklore and Pseudofolklore of the Stalin Era* (Armonk, NY: M.E. Sharpe, 1990), 6. Other vocal opponents of the fairy tale in the 1920s were Esfir' Yanovskaia and Evgeniia Flerina. This rejection of fairy tales in favour of the "real objects" of this world was happening concurrently in American criticism. Lucy Sprague Mitchell's theory of the "here and now" demanded that children's literature be focused upon the tangible and technological things in the surrounding reality. See Steiner, "Mirror Images," 201, 208.

6 Arzamastseva, "Podvizhniki detskogo chteniia," 25.

7 Russia's most famous literary fairy tales are by Alexander Pushkin. They include the opening fragment from *Ruslan and Liudmila* (1818–20), the satirical *Tale of the Priest and His Worker Balda* (1830), *The Tale of Tsar Saltan* (1831), *The Tale of the Fisherman and the Fish* (1833), *The Tale of The Dead Princess and the Seven Knights* (1833), and *The Tale of the Golden Cockerel* (1834).

8 Kornei Chukovsky, *From Two to Five* (Berkeley: University of California Press, 1963), 124.

9 Nadezhda Krupskaya and N.B. Medvedeva, *N.K. Krupskaia o detskoi literatura i detskom chtenii* (Moscow: Detskaia literatura, 1979), 48.

10 Krupskaya and Medvedeva, 198.

11 David Brandenberger, *National Bolshevism: Stalinist Mass Culture and the Formation of Modern Russian National Identity, 1931–1956* (Cambridge, MA: Harvard University Press, 2002), 78.

12 Marcus C. Levitt, *Russian Literary Politics and the Pushkin Celebration of 1880* (Ithaca, NY: Cornell University Press, 1989), 162.

13 Chukovsky, *From Two to Five*, 118.

14 I. Sokolianskii, A. Popov, and A. Zaluzhnyi, eds., *My protiv skazki* (Kharkov, Ukraine: n.p., 1928). See Balina, Goscilo, and Lipovetsky, *Politicizing Magic*, 106.

15 Felix J. Oinas, "The Political Uses and Themes of Folklore in the Soviet Union," in *Folklore, Nationalism and Politics*, ed. Felix J. Oinas (Columbus, OH: Slavica Publishers, 1978), 77.

16 The poster, which features outmoded fairy-tale characters such as Baba Yaga, Puss in Boots, Chukovsky's Crocodile, and Ivan the Fool from Ershov's *The Little Humpbacked Horse*, can be viewed at www.togdazine.ru /article/1657. See also Hearn, *From the Silver Age to Stalin*, 11.

17 This dividing line is evident in Krupskaia's review of Chukovsky's 1928 book-length study of speech and psychological development in children, titled "*Little Children*: Children's Language, Ekikiki, Senseful Nonsense," in which she opined that children may very well develop their language by speaking nonsense, but this is no reason to give them books full of nonsensical language. See Krupskaya and Medvedeva, *N.K. Krupskaia o detskoi literatura*, 163. Her criticism of Chukovsky's work became even more pointed in a 1928 article published in the leading Soviet newspaper, *Pravda*, in which she attacked fairy tales like his *The Crocodile* as bourgeois nonsense. See N. Krupskaia, "O 'Krokodile' K. Chukovskogo," *Pravda*, 1 February 1928.

18 Arzamastseva, "Podvizhniki detskogo chteniia," 21. The work of the Institute of Children's Reading, weakened by its loss of independence in 1923, was further curtailed in 1928 when all publishing for children was centralized and monopolized by the state. The institute, under its later name as the Institute on Working Methods for Extracurricular Activities, was officially closed in 1930 but unofficially continued its work through the Museum of Children's Literature until 1937. See Arzamastseva, 31–3, and Hellman, *Fairy Tales and True Stories*, 298–9.

19 In 1924 the State Publishing House (Gosizdat) opened a children's section (Detgiz) with Samuil Marshak as editor and Vladimir Lebedev as artistic director. In 1932 all publishing for children was consolidated into one house: Children's Literature (Detskaia literatura).

20 Maksim Gor'kii, "O skazkakh," in *O detskoi literatura: stat'i i vyskazyvania* (Moscow: Detskaia Literatura, 1958), 110–12.

21 Socialist realism, according to the Statute of the Union of Soviet Writers (1934), "demands of the artist the truthful, historically concrete representation of reality in its revolutionary development." The genre demanded positive heroes, the depiction of ideological transformation, and "the education of workers in the spirit of socialism." Katerina Clark argues in *The Soviet Novel: History as Ritual* (Chicago and London: University of Chicago Press, 1981) that the required pairing of the verisimilar (realism) with the utopian (revolutionary romanticism) created a fundamental modal schism in the genre. See Clark for her important study of how the socialist-realist novel encoded the essential "official myths" of the Stalin era, and how its formulaic "master plot" became a

ritualized narrative expressing "the master categories that organize[d] the entire culture." Clark, xii–xiii, 9, 14, 35.

22 Clark, *The Soviet Novel*, 237.

23 See in particular "O skazkakh" (About fairy tales, 1929), republished in Gor'kii, *O detskoi literatura.*

24 The new Soviet fairy tales were no longer set in the distant past, were often explicitly ideological, and were not always intended for child audiences. Mayakovsky's 1922 *Little Red Riding Hood*, illustrated by El Lissitzky, is a good example of an adult fairy tale playing with the conventions of children's literature. While, as Valerii Blinov points out, the "open political irony" of the work is difficult for children, Mayakovsky and Lissitzsky nonetheless appropriate the "naïve spontaneity of the child's perception." See V.V. Maiakovskii, *Dliia golosa* (Berlin: Gos. izd-vo RSFSR, 1923; facsimile reprint, Cologne and New York: Rictman, 1973), 43; and Blinov, *Russkaia detskaia knizhka-kartinka*, 56, 176.

25 Gankina, *Khudozhnik v sovremennoi detskoi knige*, 11.

26 A. Pokrovskaia, "Kak rasskazat' detiam," in *Zhenskii zhurnal*, no. 1 (Moscow: Ogonek, 1929), 15.

27 Lev Tolstoy, who was greatly admired by Krupskaia as a children's author, has a scene in his *Childhood* in which a boy refuses to draw a cow because he has been given a blue crayon.

28 Krupskaya and Medvedeva, *N.K. Krupskaia o detskoi literatura*, 31.

29 Chukovsky was also part of the aesthetic shift towards magic as the by-product of new technologies. Fairy tales like his *Wash to Bits* (1922), featuring a walking, talking sink that chases after dirty children, were set amid the objects of the modern world.

30 Chukovsky, *From Two to Five*, 45.

31 Anne Wilson, *Plots and Powers: Magical Structures in Medieval Narrative* (Gainesville: University Press of Florida, 2001), 3–5, 10. See also Anne Wilson, *Traditional Romance and Tale: How Stories Mean* (Ipswich, UK: Brewer, 1976); Anne Wilson, *Magical Thought in Creative Writing: The Distinctive Roles of Fantasy and Imagination in Fiction* (South Woodchester and Stroud, UK: Thimble Press, 1983); and Anne Wilson, *The Magical Quest: The Use of Magic in Arthurian Romance* (Manchester, UK: Manchester University Press, 1988).

32 Hugh Crago, "What Is a Fairy Tale," in *Considering Children's Literature, a Reader*, ed. Andrea Schwenke Wyile and Teya Rosenberg (Peterborough, ON: Broadview Press, 2008), 168–70.

33 Wilson, *Plots and Powers*, 6–7.

34 Clark, *The Soviet Novel*, 91.

35 Mark Lipovetsky, "Fairy Tales in Critique of Soviet Culture," in *Politicizing Magic: An Anthology of Russian and Soviet Fairy Tales*, ed. Marina Balina, Helen Goscilo, and M.N. Lipovetsky (Evanston, IL: Northwestern University Press, 2005), 233. See also Clark, *The Soviet Novel*.

36 Denis Kozlov, *The Readers of Novyi Mir: Coming to Terms with the Stalinist Past* (Cambridge, MA: Harvard University Press, 2013), 3.

37 Sibelan Forrester, preface to V.Ia. Propp, *The Russian Folktale*, ed. and trans. Sibelan Forrester (Detroit, MI: Wayne State University Press, 2012), xxvi. Of course, magical thinking was not entirely pushed down in the 1920s; it re-emerged in such utopian fictions as "Voyage of the Red Star Pioneer Troop to Wonderland" (1924) by Innokenty Zhukov.

1 The Poet, the Priest, and the Peasant

1 In both the pre-revolutionary and the post-revolutionary periods, *The Tale of the Priest and of His Worker Balda* was published in editions aimed at times at adult audiences and at times at child audiences. Editions designated for children (*dlia detei*) emerged in 1894, 1899, and 1913. See *Skazki russkikh pisatelei dlia detei: Sbornik redaktsii gazety Kievskoe slovo* (Kiev and Kharkov, 1894); *Skazka o kuptse Kuz'me Ostolope i rabotnike ego Balde* (Kiev, 1899); and A.S. Pushkin, *Sobranie sochinenii dlia detei: Besplatnoe prilozhenie k zhurnalu "Zhavoronok"* (St Petersburg: T-vo khudozh. pechati, 1913). In 1912 *Balda* was published in a textbook for students (*posobie dlia uchachikhsia*) in Odessa, Kiev, and St Petersburg. It would be oversimplifying matters, however, to claim that child readers accessed this tale and its illustrations exclusively through editions designated for children, in particular in the period before 1924, when state-run children's publishing had not yet been established. My study therefore encompasses illustrated versions of *Balda* more broadly from the 1920s to the 1950s.

2 Friedberg, *Russian Classics in Soviet Jackets*, 19.

3 A.A. Kaiev, *Russkaia literatura: Uchebnik dlia uchitel'skikh institutov; Chast' pervaia; Fol'klor, Drevnerusskaia literatura, Literatura XVIII veka* (Moscow, 1949), 15.

4 Both the names Balda and Ostolop mean "blockhead."

5 The work appeared in the journal *Son of the Fatherland*, no. 5 (1840). Pushkin himself had been killed in a duel in 1837.

6 Clergy in the Russian Orthodox Church were divided between "black" and "white," with the distinction that "black clergy" remained celibate and were eligible for preferment.

7 Sheila Fitzpatrick, *Stalin's Peasants: Resistance and Survival in the Russian Village after Collectivization* (New York: Oxford University Press, 1994), 33.

8 Daniel Peris, "The 1929 Congress of the Godless," in *The Stalin Years: A Reader*, ed. Christopher Read (Basingstoke, UK: Palgrave Macmillan, 2003), 39.
9 Fitzpatrick, *Stalin's Peasants*, 33, 35.
10 Annie Gérin, *Godless at the Workbench: Soviet Illustrated Humoristic Antireligious Propaganda* (Regina, SK: Dunlop Art Gallery, 2003), 38.
11 This ardently atheist writer was lampooned by Mikhail Bulgakov in his novel *Master and Margarita* (written in 1928–40, partially published in 1966–7, and fully published in 1973) as the talentless anti-religious poet Homeless.
12 Fitzpatrick, *Stalin's Peasants*, 30.
13 Fitzpatrick, 13, 24. In 1921 as part of the end of War Communism and the beginning of the New Economic Policy, the Bolsheviks temporarily abandoned their alliance with the *bedniaks* and announced a new policy of alliance with the entire "toiling peasantry," except for *kulaks*. These policies lasted until 1928.
14 Vladimir N. Brovkin, *Russia after Lenin: Politics, Culture and Society, 1921–1929* (New York: Routledge, 1998), 57.
15 A. Zhelanskii, *Skazki Pushkina v narodnom stile: Balda; Medvedikha; O rybake i rybke; Opyt issledovaniia po rukopisiam poeta s dvumia fotosnimkami* (Moscow: Gosudarstvennoe izdatel'stvo "Khudozhestvennaia literatura," 1936), 11–15. Zhelanskii links Balda to the Ivanko-Medvedko figure recorded in folk tales by Afanasiev, a half-man, half-bear of incredible strength but incredible stupidity.
16 Brovkin, *Russia after Lenin*, 96. The League of Godless emerged from the group Society of Friends of the Newspaper *Godless* in 1925, adding a bellicose epithet to become the League of Militant Godless in 1929. See Peris, "The 1929 Congress of the Godless," 43, 62.
17 Brovkin, *Russia after Lenin*, 96.
18 Peris, "The 1929 Congress of the Godless," 43.
19 Fitzpatrick, *Stalin's Peasants*, 75.
20 Fitzpatrick, 262.
21 Fitzpatrick, 274–7.
22 Fitzpatrick, 10.
23 Fitzpatrick, 25.
24 Karen Petrone, *Life Has Become More Joyous, Comrades: Celebrations in the Time of Stalin* (Bloomington: Indiana University Press, 2000), 113–14.
25 Petrone, 120.
26 Petrone, 124.
27 Fitzpatrick, *Stalin's Peasants*, 38, 59.
28 Fitzpatrick, 59–60, 204.

29 Gérin, *Godless at the Workbench*, 42. *Bezbozhnik* (Godless) and *Bezbozhnik u stanka* (Godless at the workbench) were two separate publications, both dedicated to anti-religious propaganda.

30 Until 1928 the Commissariat of Enlightenment pursued a policy of areligious education in the schools. This was replaced by an anti-religious policy and later by the official inclusion of atheism in the school curriculum. See Peris, "The 1929 Congress of the Godless," 63n2; and Gérin, *Godless at the Workbench*, 42–3.

31 Gérin, 44.

32 Svetlana Boym, *Common Places: Mythologies of Everyday Life in Russia* (Cambridge, MA: Harvard University Press, 1994), 130.

33 In 1936, Palekh artists created huge murals for "The Fairy Tale Room" and "The A.M. Gorky Room" at the Leningrad Palace of Pioneers. Appropriately, the border between fairy tale and reality is indistinguishable in these murals, where the figure of Gorky appears as a folk character in a depiction of Russia's fairy-tale past. See N.M. Zinoviev, *Iskusstvo Palekha* (Leningrad: Khudozhnik RSFSR, 1975), 220.

34 Butorin's artistic style derives from the seventeenth-century Stroganov style of icon painting, which emphasized the complexity of a many-sided narrative, as opposed to the Novgorod style, which highlighted simplicity and effect. See Zinoviev, *Iskusstvo Palekha*, 80.

35 Iu.A. Vainkop, "M.I. Chulaki i ego balet 'Skazka o pope i rabotnike ego Balde,'" in *Skazka o pope i o rabotnike ego Balde: Balet v 4 aktakh; Musika M. Chulaki*, ed. Aleksandr Sergeevich Pushkin (Leningrad: Leningradskii gos. Akademicheskii Malyi opernyi teatr, 1940), 33–43.

2 Up, Up, and Away on the Little Humpbacked Horse

1 Kendall E. Bailes, "Technology and Legitimacy: Soviet Aviation and Stalinism in the 1930s," *Technology and Culture* 17, no. 2 (April 1976): 60. Bailes goes on to say that while some of these claims were not validated by the International Aeronautical Federation, the records themselves were "not really so important as the political uses that were made of them."

2 Some representative titles include *Tvoi mashinnye druz'ia* [Your machine friends], by Nikolai Agnivtsev (Moscow and Leningrad: Raduga, 1926); *Krylia sovetov* [Wings of the Soviets], by I. Stuchinskaia (Moscow: GIZ, 1930); *V oblakakh* [In the clouds], by Aleksandr Deineka (Leningrad: Gos. Izd-vo, 1930); and *Cherez Polius v Ameriku* [Through the Pole to America], by Georgii Baidukov (Moscow: Izd-vo Detskoi literatury, 1938).

3 See, for instance, Galina Vladychina, *Neobychnaia istoriia ob izobretenii vozdushnogo shara o velikom uchenom Mongol'f'e, o shelkovoi iubke i*

goriiaschchei zharovne [The unusual story about the invention of an air
balloon by the great scientist Montgolfier, about a silk skirt and the hot
brazier (Moscow: Molodaia gvardiia, 1927); Nina Sakonskaia, *Pesn' o
dirizhable* [The song of the dirigible] (Moscow: OGIZ, 1931); and Lev
Kassil', *Tseppelin* [The Zeppelin] (Moscow: OGIZ, 1931).

4 Roman Karmen's *Aerosani* [Aerosleds] (Moscow: Molodaia gvardiia,
1931) is about a journey in a vehicle that is part car, part sleigh, and part
airplane.

5 Kucherenko, *Little Soldiers*, 55.

6 The characters and themes used by Ershov, including Ivan the Fool and
a magical horse, and boiling in a vat, winning the hand of a princess,
and ousting the tsar, appear as motifs in numerous oral tales recorded by
Afanasiev in the nineteenth century, including "The Firebird and Princess
Vasilisa," "Sivka-burka" or "Sivko-burko," and "The Pig with the Golden
Bristles, the Duck with the Golden Feathers, a Golden-Horned Deer, and a
Golden-Maned Stallion." In the tale "Baba Yaga and the Midget Zamorishek"
it is the hero, not the magical horse, who is a "runt." See Jack V. Haney, *An
Introduction to the Russian Folktale* (Armonk, NY: M.E. Sharpe, 1999), 78–80.

7 The Stalin-era critic Mark Azadovsky links the ruff to a "squabbler-bully"
appearing in folklore, named Ersh Shchetinnikov. See Azadovsky's
"Konek-Gorbunok," in *O Konke Gorbunke: Sbornik statei* by M.K.
Azadovskii, P.P. Gorlov, S.S. Danilov, and A.A.Briantsev (Leningrad:
Leningradskii teatr iunykh zritelei imeni A.A. Briantseva, 1937), 34.

8 In contrast, the first reviewer of the tale, the famous critic Vissarion
Belinsky, protested that the folk language of the work was not convincing,
saying, "Under the homespun peasant coat, your frock coat can always be
seen." This review appeared in the journal *Molva* in 1835.

9 Apparently the same problem existed during the author's lifetime.
Ershov's only contemporary memoirist, A.K. Yaroslavtsev, began his work
by saying that when Ershov's obituary appeared in St Petersburg, even
those who recognized his name remarked that they thought he had died
long ago. See A.K. Yaroslavtsev, *P.P Ershov, Avtor skazki Konek-gorbunok:
Biograficheskie vospominaniia universitetskogo tovarishcha ego A.K. Iaroslavtsova*
(St Petersburg, Russia: Tip. V. Demakova, 1872), 1.

10 In 1946 a notebook containing Ershov's poetry was discovered in the
Central Literary Archive. See Viktor Utkov, "Tvorchestvo Petra Pavlovicha
Ershova, vstupitel'noe slovo i kommentarii," in P.P. Ershov, *Sochineniia*
(Omsk, Russia: Omskoe oblastnoe gosudarstvennoe izd-vo, 1950), 26–7.

11 See A.G. Gornfeld, "P.P. Ershov i ego skazka," in *Konek-gorbunok*, ed.
P.P. Ershov (Moscow-Leningrad: Gosizdat, 1929), 6; M.K. Azadovskii,
Predislovie [Introduction] to P.P. Ershov, *Konek-gorbunok* (Moscow:
Academia, 1934), 10; and M.K. Azadovskii, "Konek-Gorbunok," in *O Konke
Gorbunke: Sbornik statei* (Leningrad, 1937), 24.

12 Azadovskii, "Konek-Gorbunok," 1937, 27.

13 Antonina P. Babushkina, "Skazka Ershova Konek-Gorbunok," in *Istoriia russkoi literatury* (Moscow: Gosuchpedizd, 1948), 181.

14 Babushkina, 181.

15 See A.M. Putintsev, "Skazka P.P. Ershova 'Konek-Gorbunok' i ee istochniki," *Trudy Voronezhskogo universiteta*, 1925, 341; and N.V. Kolokolt'sev and V.V. Litvinov, *Russkaia literatura, uchebnik dlia 2 klassa pedagogicheskikh uchilishch* (Moscow: Gosudarstvennoe uchebno-pedagogicheskoe izdatel'stvo Ministerstva RSFSR, 1946), 70.

16 See S. Basov-Verkhoiantsev, *Konek-skakunok, russkaia skazka* (Berlin: Henrich Caspari, 1918).

17 A.A. Briantsev, "Iz zapisnoi knizhki rezhissera," in *O Konke Gorbunke: Sbornik statei*, ed. Mark Azadovskii et al (Leningrad: Leningradskii teatr iunykh zritelei imeni A.A. Briantseva, 1937), 73–6.

18 Military aviation came under a separate department, the Chief Directorate of the Workers and Peasants Red Air Fleet, beginning in May 1918.

19 David Baker, *Flight and Flying: A Chronology* (New York: Facts on File, 1994), 147.

20 Baker, 147.

21 Andrei Kruchina, *Konek-letunok, Aero-skazka* (Nikolaevsk, Russia: Izd. O.D.V.F., 1925), 15.

22 Lennart Andersson, *Soviet Aircraft and Aviation, 1917–1941* (Annapolis, MD: Naval Institute Press, 1994), 138–69.

23 Andersson, 43.

24 Andersson, 350.

25 The little humpbacked horse was portrayed on stamps in 1961 and 1988.

26 Other notable feats included a daring aerial rescue of passengers stranded on an ice floe in the Chukchi Sea in 1934. See John McCannon, *Red Arctic: Polar Exploration and the Myth of the North in the Soviet Union, 1932–1939* (New York: Oxford University Press, 1998), 5.

27 McCannon, 69, 116.

28 Bailes, "Technology and Legitimacy," 54.

29 McCannon, *Red Arctic*, 56.

30   Risunki E. Safonovoi, "Kto oni," *Chizh*, no. 3 (1937): 10.

31 See *Chizh*, no. 7 (1938): 7–9, and no. 11 (1938) (back cover).

32 McCannon, *Red Arctic*, 135.

33 McCannon, 125; and Miller, *Folklore for Stalin*, 11.

34 Kucherenko, *Little Soldiers*, 48.

35 A *Pravda* article of 16 May 1934 announced the rehabilitation of "erstwhile marginalized history and geography" in the classroom. See Kucherenko, *Little Soldiers*, 48.

36 The emphasis on building patriotism was revealed by the term used synonymously with *stranovedenie*: *rodinovedenie* (motherland studies).

Emily Johnson explains that *stranovedenie, rodinovedenie,* and *kraevedenie* (area studies) all originated as translations of the German *Heimatkunde* (homeland studies). See Emily D. Johnson, *How St. Petersburg Learned to Study Itself: The Russian Idea of Kraevedenie* (University Park: Pennsylvania State University Press, 2006), 4.

37 Johnson, 55–6.

38 *We Are from Igarka* was a series of children's letters from the Soviet-built city of Igarka, edited by Maxim Gorky until 1936 and afterwards by Samuil Marshak. See McCannon, *Red Arctic,* 89. "Wide Is My Motherland," known as "Song of the Motherland," was composed by Isaac Dunaevsky, with lyrics by Vasily Lebedev-Kumach, for the Stalinist blockbuster film *Circus* in 1936.

39 McCannon, *Red Arctic,* 76.

40 The Trans-Siberian Railway was inaugurated in 1890 by Tsar Nicholas II, but only connected Vladivostok, Russia's largest port on the Pacific Ocean, to Moscow in 1916.

41 McCannon, *Red Arctic,* 7–9.

42 Jack Zipes, "Fairy Tale Discourse: Towards a Social History of the Genre," in *Fairy Tales and the Art of Subversion: The Classical Genre for Children and the Process of Civilization* (London: Heinemann, 1983), 3, 8.

Part II The Afterlife of Russian Classics

1 For the purposes of this book, "classics" is used in the very narrow sense of the great Russian writers of the nineteenth century.

2 "O gosudarstvennom izdatel'stve," in *Vtoroi vserossiiskii s"ezd Sovetov rabochikh i soldatskikh deputatov: Sbornik dokumentov* (Second All-Russian Congress of the Soviets of Workers' and Soldiers' Deputies: A collection of documents.), ed. D.A. Chugaev, L.I. Terent'eva, P.I. Anisimova, and A.F. Butenko (Moscow: Gos. izd-vo polit. lit-ry, 1957), 243–4. The English-language translation of the Decree on the State Publishing House appears in *The Bolshevik Revolution, 1917–1918: Documents and Materials,* ed. James Bunyan and H.H. Fisher (Stanford and London: Stanford University Press, 1934), 595–6; or http://soviethistory.msu.edu, accessed 24 July 2018.

3 Friedberg, *Russian Classics in Soviet Jackets,* 22.

4 Decree on the State Publishing House, accessed 24 July 2018, http://soviethistory.msu.edu.

5 Decree on the State Publishing House.

6 Friedberg, *Russian Classics in Soviet Jackets,* 68.

7 These statistics, which include only single-authored works, are based on the data available through the catalogue of the Russian National Library (St Petersburg). Its electronic catalogue provides information on the

number of books published in Russian within a given date range and can be sorted by publishing house. My list of classics is not exhaustive and does not include figures such as Leskov and Nekrasov.

8 The pre-eminence of Tolstoy as the author of a classic was cemented in this period by the marking of the one-hundredth anniversary of his birth in 1928 and a republication of his complete artistic works, including those censored in the imperial era. In the journal *Ogonek*, early subscribers to this full collection were also promised a poster of the famed writer for their walls, while in the satirical anti-religious journal *Godless at the Workbench*, God himself was pictured as a mixture of Tolstoy, the anarchist communist Pyotr Kirpotkin, and Jesus. See Gérin, *Godless at the Workbench*, 38–9.

9 By the 1960s, *Crime and Punishment* was deemed the most appropriate Dostoevsky text for public school students, who read it at age sixteen, in grade nine.

10 The editions of *Brothers Karamazov* included F.M. Dostoevskii, *Brat'ia Karamazovy, dliia srednego vozrasta* (Riga, Latvia: N. Gudkov, 1928); and *Malchiki: Iz romana "Brat'ia Karamazovy,"* Bibliotechka shkol'nika (Moscow-Leningrad: Gosudarstvennoe izdatel'stvo detskoi literatury, 1947), illustrated by V. Ladyagina. Editions of *Crime and Punishment* included F.M. Dostoevskii, *Prestuplenie i nakazanie: Klassiki sredne shkole* (Petrograd, Russia: Izdatel'stvo "Blago," 1923); F.M. Dostoevskii, *Prestuplenie i nakazanie: Roman v 6 chastiakh s epilogom; Shkol'naia seriia klassikov* (Moscow: Gosudarstvennoe izdatel'stvo detskoi literatury, 1934). The edition of *Notes from the House of the Dead* was F.M. Dostoevskii, *Zapiski iz mertvogo doma: Shkol'naia seriia klassikov* (Leningrad: Izdatel'stvo Detskoi literatury, 1935).

11 Anatoly Lunacharsky, cited in F.M. Dostoevskii, *Zapiski iz mertvogo doma: Shkol'naia seriia klassikov* (Leningrad: Izdatel'stvo Detskoi literatury, 1935), 404.

12 See D.L. Sorkina, *Dostoevskii v shkole* (Tomsk, Russia: Izd-vo Tomskogo universiteta, 1969), 4.

13 See Kevin M.F. Platt and David Brandenberger, eds., *Epic Revisionism: Russian History and Literature as Stalinist Propaganda* (Madison: University of Wisconsin Press, 2006), 4.

14 A photo of the "Arctic room" is featured in *L'URSS en construction*, no. 6, 1937, a journal destined for foreign consumption.

15 Levitt, *Russian Literary Politics*, 154.

16 Petrone, *Life Has Become More Joyous*, 113; O.S. Murav'eva, "Obraz Pushkina: Istoricheskie metamorfozy," in *Legendy i mify o Pushkine*, ed. M.N. Virolainen (St Petersburg, Russia: Gumanitarnoe agentstvo "Akademicheskii Proekt," 1994), 123

17 Levitt, *Russian Literary Politics*, 154.

18 G. Abramovich, B. Brainina, and A. Egolin, *Russkaia literatura, uchebnik dlia 9-go klassov srednei shkoly: Chast' 2* (Moscow: Gos. Uchebno-pedagogicheskikh izdatel'stvo, 1938-9), 3.

19 A.A. Zerchaninov, D.Ia Raikhin, and V.I. Strazhev, *Russkaia literatura, uchebnik dlia IX klassa srednei shkoly* (Moscow: Gosudarstvennoe uchebno-pedagogicheskoe izdatel'stvo Narkomprosa RSFSR, 1940), 440.

20 A.A. Zerchaninov and N.G. Porfiridov, *Russkaia literatura: Uchebnik dlia 1 klassa pedagogicheskikh uchilishch* (Moscow: Gosudarstvennoe uchebno-pedagogicheskoe izdatel'stvo, 1946), 4–5.

21 N. Pospelov, P. Shabliovsky, and A. Zerchaninov, *Russkaia literatura, uchebnik dlia VIII klassa srednei shkoly. Izdanie sed'moe* (Moscow: Gosudarstvennoe uchebno-pedagogicheskoe izdatel'stvo Ministerstva prosveshcheniia RSFSR, 1947), 4.

22 V.V. Ermilov, "Velikii russkii pisatel' F.M. Dostoevskii," *Literatura i iskusstvo*, no. 36 (5 September 1942).

23 Friedberg, *Russian Classics in Soviet Jackets*, 157.

3 The Bronze Horseman Rides Again

1 The six editions of A.S. Pushkin, *Mednyi vsadnik*, discussed in this chapter are the two Stalin-era versions illustrated by Alexander Benois (Moscow-Leningrad, 1936, and Moscow-Leningrad, 1945); and four other editions, by Aleksei Kravchenko (Moscow, 1936), Igor' Ershov (Leningrad, 1949), Mikhail Grigor'ev (Leningrad, 1949), and Mikhail Rodionov (Leningrad, 1949).

2 Chegodaev, *Puti razvitiia russkoi sovetskoi knizhnoi grafiki*, 34.

3 Chegodaev, 65. Since the exhibition departed from tradition and displayed works according to the author they illustrated – rather than the artist who had created them – the dearth of socialist-realist depictions of Pushkin's work meant that the "father of new Russian literature" presided over a virtual blank space.

4 E.Z. Gankina, *Russkie khudozhniki detskoi knigi* (Moscow, 1963), 7. There was a strong interest in book illustration among the *miriskusstniki* (members of the World of Art group) in general, from Konstantin Somov's illustrations in Alexander Blok's *Balagan* in 1909 to Ivan Bilibin's illustrations in Pushkin's *Tale of Tsar-Saltan* in 1910. After the revolution, former World of Art members such as Mstislav Dobuzhinsky became well known as book illustrators and were commissioned for works like Dostoevsky's *White Nights* (1923).

5 If we compare Benois's eerie *Bronze Horseman* series to his set of children's book illustrations, the highly praised *Alphabet* (*Azbuka*) of 1904, it becomes all the more evident that the former series was conceived for the adult

reader. The *Azbuka*, which Catriona Kelly has described as "shot through with nostalgia for the world of pre-Emancipation Russian country life," was not republished until 1990. See Kelly, *Children's World*, 49.

6 Editions of *The Bronze Horseman* for the juvenile reader were aimed at the middle and senior student (*srednego i starshego vozrasta*), in other words, twelve- to seventeen-year-olds.

7 Benois's reputation as a retrospectivist was supported not only by the period details portrayed in his 1904 illustrations but also by their format in the polytype style of the 1830s. The small size of the original drawings was intended to reproduce the pocket-size effect of the almanacs of the 1820s. See Aleksandr Benua, N.I. Aleksandrova, and D.S. Likhachev *Moi vospominaniia v piati knigakh*, books 4 and 5 (Moscow: Nauka, 1980), 396.

8 The intriguing publication history of Benois's illustrations to *The Bronze Horseman* is treated at length by A.L. Ospovat and R.D. Timenchik, "Istoriia odnogo izdaniia," in *Pechal'nu povest' sokhranit'* (Moscow: Kniga, 1987), 215–55.

9 The Bronze Horseman monument was erected by Catherine the Great as a tribute to Peter the Great and unveiled in 1782. It was designed by Etienne-Maurice Falconet and stands on Senate Square, known as Decembrist Square in Stalinist times, in central St Petersburg.

10 Alison Rowley, *Open Letters: Russian Popular Culture and the Picture Postcard, 1880–1922* (Toronto: University of Toronto Press, 2013), 14.

11 Rowley, 14.

12 Chegodaev, *Puti razvitiia*, 61.

13 The connection between poet and tsar is emphasized by the mirror imaging of hand gestures (see fig. 3.5).

14 Murav'eva, "Obraz Pushkina," 118, 123.

15 Megan Swift, "The Petersburg Sublime: Alexander Benois and the Bronze Horseman Series (1903–1922)," *Germano-Slavica* 17 (2009): 5.

16 Petrone, *Life Has Become More Joyous*, 79, 123.

17 Stephanie Sandler, *Commemorating Pushkin: Russia's Myth of a National Poet* (Stanford: Stanford University Press, 2004), 87. Pushkin anniversaries were celebrated in 1880, 1889, 1921, 1924, 1937, 1949, 1987, and 1999.

18 Chegodaev, *Puti razvitii*, 33.

19 Gankina, *Russkie khudozhniki*, 27.

20 Chegodaev, *Puti razvitii*, 64.

21 Petrone, *Life Has Become More Joyous*, 119.

22 As Benois had created the first full-length illustrated edition of *The Bronze Horseman*, pre-1936 readers of the illustrated work would have associated images of the work with him, and hence the intellectual journal *World of Art*, where he was co-editor along with Sergei Diaghilev. After many years as a leading editor, writer, artist, and curator, Benois emigrated from the

Soviet Union in 1924. Kravchenko exhibited with the World of Art group in 1911, although he had a more acceptable biography by virtue of his birth in a peasant family.

23 Lisa A. Kirschenbaum, *The Legacy of the Siege of Leningrad, 1941–1995: Myth, Memories, and Monuments* (New York: Cambridge University Press, 2006), 141–2.

24 Steven Maddox, "Healing the Wounds: Commemorations, Myths, and the Restoration of Leningrad's Imperial Heritage, 1941–50" (PhD. diss., University of Toronto, 2008), 216–17.

25 Kirschenbaum, *Legacy of the Siege*, 143–5.

26 See O.A. Kudriavtseva, *Zhizn' i tvorchestvo A.S. Pushkina: Materialy dlia vystavki v shkole i detskoi biblioteke k 150-letiiu so dnia rozhdeniia poeta* (Moscow: Gos izd-vo Detskoi lit-ry, 1949), 30; and Sandler, *Commemorating Pushkin*, 16.

27 Further evasions of the ban on Leningrad exceptionalism can be cited, such as the children's book *Sovietskaia byl'* by G. Fish, published by Detgiz in 1950. This collection includes a story about the heroism of the Leningrad scholars and scientists who guarded the seed bank and who, despite starvation conditions (and contrary to American rumours), managed not to consume the seeds.

28 Kirschenbaum, *Legacy of the Siege*, 146.

29 In the late 1950s Ershov went on to establish himself as a children's illustrator.

30 In fact, Benois did show one post-flood moment in the third and final version of his series, published in 1923, but it is an eerie moment in which passersby notice that the Bronze Horseman is missing from its pedestal.

31 L. Kon, "Novinki Detgiza (Rekomendatel'nyi obzor)," in *Nedelia detskoi knigi*, ed. S. Liubimov (Moscow: Gos. Izd-vo Detskoi lit-ry, 1950), 143.

32 In the Stalinist era Russian classics accounted for an increasingly large percentage of the output of Detizdat, from 9 per cent in 1933 to 15 per cent in 1940. See Friedberg, *Russian Classics in Soviet Jackets*, 72.

33 The publication data available in Maurice Friedberg's work on the Soviet publishing industry focuses on 1955–8, when the average print run for a book was seventeen thousand. See Friedberg, *Russian Classics in Soviet Jackets*, 155.

34 Brandenberger, *National Bolshevism*, 79. Brandenberger cites an entry in Kornei Chukovsky's diary, in which the well-known children's author refers to the 1936 demand of party functionary V.I. Mezhlauk for "Pushkin for the masses."

35 Friedberg, *Russian Classics in Soviet Jackets*, 68.

36 Dora Shturman, *The Soviet Secondary School*, trans. Phillipa Shimrat (London: Routledge, 1988), 55. Seven years of public school education became the mandate as of 1930. See Shturman, 55.

37 Gankina, *Russkie khudozhniki*, 54.

38 G.L. Abramovich and F.M. Golovenchenko, *Russkaia literatura: Uchebnik dlia 8-ogo klassa srednei shkoly* (Moscow: Gos. uchebno-pedagogicheskoe izd-vo, 1936), 88.

39 See G.L. Abramovich and F.M. Golovenchenko, *Russkaia literatura: Uchebnik dlia 8-go i 9-go klassa srednei shkoly* (Moscow: Gos. uchebno-pedagogicheskoe izd-vo, 1938–9), 120; A. Zerchaninov, N.G. Porfiridov, and N.L. Brodskii, *Russkaia literatura, uchebnik dlia I klassa pedagogicheskikh uchilishch* (Moscow: Gosudarstvennoe uchebno-pedagogicheskoe izdatel'stvo Ministerstva prosveshcheniia RSFSR, 1946), 397; and Pospelov, Shabliovskii, and Zerchaninov, *Russkaia literatura*, 263.

40 Pospelov, Shabliovskii, and Zerchaninov, *Russkaia literatura*, 265.

41 Zerchaninov and Porfiridov, *Russkaia literatura*, 347.

42 S.M. Florinskii, *Russkaia literatura: Uchebnik dlia VIII-ogo klassa srednei shkoly* (Moscow: Gosudarstvennoe uchebno-pedagogicheskoe izdatel'stvo, 1959), 153.

43 Zerchaninov and Porfiridov, *Russkaia literatura*, 397.

44 Pospelov, Shabliovskii, and Zerchaninov, *Russkaia literatura*, 262.

45 My translation from the French original, in "Un grand fils du people russe," *L'URSS en construction* no. 6 (1949): 18.

46 I wish to thank Dr Terence Marner for his insights on the eschatological imagery imbedded in this illustration.

47 Benedict Anderson, *Imagined Communities: Reflections on the Origin and Spread of Nationalism* (London: Verso, 2006), 22.

48 N.M. Barsova-Shestakova, "Aleksandr Sergeevich Pushkin: Zhizn' i tvorchestvo," in *Pushkinskie dni 1949*, ed. A.A. Zhokov (Moscow: Izd. Moskovskogo gorodskogo instituta u sovershenstvovaniia uchitelei, 1949), 130–2.

49 S.A. Smirnov, "O podgotovke i provedenii v shkolakh g. Moskvy 150-letiia so dnia rozhdeniia A.S. Pushkina," in *Pushkinskie dni 1949*, ed. A.A. Zhokov, E.I. Velichkovskii, and M.I. Voronkov (Moscow: Izd. Moskovskogo gorodskogo instituta u sovershenstvovaniia uchitelei, 1949), 134.

50 Kudriavtseva, *Zhizn' i tvorchestvo A.S. Pushkina*, 3, 23.

51 Levitt, *Russian Literary Politics*, 158.

52 Barsova-Shestakova, "Aleksandr Sergeevich Pushkin," 11.

53 Benois's original 1904 series were republished by Khudozhestvennaia literatura in 1964.

54 Aleksandr Benua, A.N. Savinov, and I.S. Zil'bershtein, *Aleksandr Benua razmyshliaet: Stat'i, pis'ma, vyskazivaniia* (Moscow: Sovetskii khudozhnik, 1968), 712.

4 Anna Karenina and the Mother-and-Child Reunion

1 Lenin's articles on Tolstoy included "Lev Tolstoy as a Mirror of the Russian Revolution" (1908), "L.N. Tolstoy and the Contemporary Workers'

Movement" (1910), "L.N. Tolstoy" (1910), "Tolstoy and the Proletarian Fight," (1910) and "L.N. Tolstoy and His Epoch" (1911), in V.I. Lenin, *Stat'i o Tolstom* (Moscow: Gos. izd.-vo "Khudozhestvennaia literatura," 1939); translated as Vladimir Il'ich Lenin, *Articles on Tolstoy* (Amsterdam: Fredonia Books, 1951).

2 Sarah Ashwin, "Gender, State and Society in Soviet and Post-Soviet Russia," in *Gender, State and Society in Soviet and Post-Soviet Russia*, ed. Sarah Ashwin (London: Routledge, 2000), 11.

3 Tatiana Pletneva, "Razgovory s chitateliami o materinstve" [Conversations with readers about motherhood], *Zhenskii zhurnal*, no. 6 (1927): 11.

4 V.G. Sakhnovsky, "Rabota nad spektaklem 'Anna Karenina,'" in *Anna Karenina v postanovke Moskovskogo Ordena Lenina Khudozhestvennogo Akademicheskogo Teatra Soiuza SSR im. M. Gorkogo*, ed. Vladimir Ivanovich Nemirovich-Danchenko (Moscow: Izdanie MKhaT, 1938), 40–1.

5 Vrubel's illustration even appeared on the inside cover when another artist, V. Milashevsky, was commissioned to create new illustrations to the work in 1936.

6 S. Tret'iakov, "Novyi Lev Tolstoy," in *Literatura fakta, pervyi sbornik materialov rabotnikov LEFa*, ed. N.F. Chuzhak (Moscow: Zakharov, 2000), 29.

7 Elizabeth Waters, "The Modernization of Russian Motherhood, 1917–37," in *The Stalin Years: A Reader*, ed. Christopher Read (Houndmills, UK: Palgrave Macmillan, 2003), 31.

8 Quoted in Olga Issoupova, "From Duty to Pleasure? Motherhood in Soviet and Post-Soviet Russia," in *Gender, State and Society in Soviet and Post-Soviet Russia*, ed. Sarah Ashwin (London: Routledge, 2000), 31.

9 Issoupova, 31.

10 Ashwin, "Gender, State and Society," 10.

11 Ashwin, 7.

12 Loralee MacPike, "The Fallen Woman's Sexuality," in *Sexuality and Victorian Literature*, ed. Don Richard Cox (Knoxville: University of Tennessee Press, 1984), 57. See also Bill Overton, "Children and Childlessness in the Novel of Female Adultery," *Modern Language Review*, no. 2 (1999): 318. My thanks to Martina Winkler for pointing me to these sources.

13 MacPike, "The Fallen Woman's Sexuality," 57.

14 A.G. Gusakova, A.N. Dubovnikov, and A.A. Ozerova, *Russkaia literatura XIX veka, uchebnik dliia pedagogicheskikh uchilishch* (Moscow: Gos. Uchebno-pedagogicheskoe izdatel'stvo Narkomprosa RSFSR, 1938), 426.

15 Gusakova, Dubovnikov, and Ozerova, 426.

16 Abramovich, Brainina, and Egolin, *Russkaia literatura*, 99.

17 Abramovich, Brainina, and Egolin, 100.

18 Abramovich, Brainina, and Egolin, 100.

19 A.A. Zerchaninov, D.Ia. Raikhin, and V.I. Strazhev, *Russkaia literatura, uchebnik dlia IX klassa srednei shkoly* (Moscow: Gosudarstvennoe uchebno-pedagogicheskoe izdatel'stvo Narkomprosa RSFSR, 1940), 386.

20 Zerchaninov, Riakhin, and Strazhev, 391.

21 Pletneva, "Razgovory s chitateliami o materinstve," 11.

22 Pletneva, 11.

23 A.A. Zerchaninov, D.Ia. Raikhin, and V.I. Strazhev, *Russkaia literatura, uchebnik dliia IX klassa srednei shkoly* (1940), 390.

24 That line remained consistent throughout the Stalinist era: the textbooks of 1948, 1949, and 1950 all treat Anna Karenina in the same way.

25 Quoted in D. Kogan, *M.A. Vrubel'* (Moscow: Iskusstvo, 1980), 72.

26 Waters, "The Modernization of Russian Motherhood," 34.

27 Waters, 34. Russian political posters had used images of women as *rodina* (the motherland) during the Russo-Japanese war of 1904–5, but Lenin's internationalist (as opposed to nationalist) stance meant that women did not appear as the motherland on posters in the 1920s. See Victoria E. Bonnell, *Iconography of Power: Soviet Political Posters under Lenin and Stalin* (Berkeley: University of California Press, 1997), 71.

28 *For the Motherland!* replaced Toidze's 1941 *The Motherland Calls*, which featured a similarly matronly woman in red, but – perhaps less poignantly – no child.

29 Vladimir Ivanovich Nemirovich-Danchenko, *Anna Karenina v postanovke Moskovskogo Ordena Lenina Khudozhestvennogo Akademicheskogo Teatra Soiuza SSR im. M. Gorkogo* (Moscow: Izdanie MKhaT, 1938), 202.

30 T. Dashkova, "Vizual'naia representatsiia zhenskogo tela v sovetskoi massovoi kul'ture 30-h godov," *Logos* 11/12, 1999, accessed 28 November 2014, http://www.ruthenia.ru.

31 Issoupova, "From Duty to Pleasure?," 32.

32 Issoupova, 38.

33 Issoupova, 38.

34 Susan E. Reid, "All Stalin's Women: Gender and Power in Soviet Art of the 1930s," *Slavic Review* 57, no. 1 (1998): 135. In the 1930s a new state-sponsored role for wives, the *obshchestvennitsa* (activist wife), was created. The *obshchestvennitsa* did volunteer service to help her husband's profession or elevated the cultural level of the family and the masses in general. This was a consolidation of the call at the end of the 1920s for wives to take on more volunteer work in order to strengthen the state. See Mary Buckley, "The Untold Story of the Obshchestvennitsa of the 1930s," *Europe-Asia Studies* 48, no. 4 (June 1996): 569–86.

35 My thanks to Martina Winkler for her insightful comments at our shared conference panel in fall 2015.

36 Abramovich, Brainina, and Egolin, *Russkaia literatura*, 100.

37 A.A. Zerchaninov, D.Ia. Raikhin, and V.I. Strazhev, *Russkaia literatura,* *.
uchebnik dliia IX klassa srednei shkoly, 384.

38 E.N. Kupreianova, *Roman L.N. Tolstogo "Anna Karenina"* (Tula, Russia:
Oblastnoe knizhnoe izdatel'stvo, 1953), 11.

39 Kupreianova, 6.

40 Kupreianova, 10.

41 Kupreianova, 10–11.

42 Kupreianova, 11.

43 Kupreianova, 19–21.

Part III War-Time Picture Books

1 Nikolai Smirnov, *What Is the Red Army For* [*Dlia chego Krasnaia Armiia*],
illustrated by Olga and Galina Chichagova (Moscow: Molodaia gvardiia,
1926).

2 Kucherenko, *Little Soldiers*, 46, 75.

3 I. Startsev, *Detskaia literatura za gody Velikoi Otechestvennoi voiny, 1941–45*
(Moscow: Gos. Izd.-vo detskoi literatury, 1947), 128.

4 O'Dell, *Socialisation through Children's Literature*, 54.

5 Gankina, *Khudozhnik v sovremennoi detskoi literatura*, 166.

6 John Dunstan, *Soviet Schooling in the Second World War* (New York: St
Martin's Press, 1997), 79.

7 Dunstan, 98.

8 Dunstan, 81.

9 Arkady Gaidar, "V Dobryi put'!" in *Sobranie sochinenii v cheterekh tomakh*,
vol. 3 (Moscow, 1964), 303.

10 Dunstan, *Soviet Schooling in the Second World War*, 89–91.

11 Dunstan, 101–4.

12 Dunstan, 113, 138.

13 Dunstan, 120.

14 Gaidar, "Voina i deti," in *Sobranie sochinenii v cheterekh tomakh*, vol. 3
(Moscow: Izdatel'stvo "Detskaia literatura," 1964), 310.

15 Dunstan, *Soviet Schooling in the Second World War*, 127, 135.

16 Ann Livschiz, "Children's Lives after Zoia's Death: Order, Emotions and
Heroism in Children's Lives and Literature in the Post-War Soviet Union,"
in *Late Stalinist Russia: Society between Reconstruction and Reinvention*, ed.
Juliane Fürst (Abingdon, UK: Routledge, 2006), 193.

17 deGraffenried, *Sacrificing Childhood*, 235.

18 O. Alekseeva, "Sovetskaia kniga – Moguchee sredstvo
kommunisticheskogo vospitaniia detei," in *Nedelia detskoi knigi*, ed. S.
Liubimov (Moscow-Leningrad: Gos. Izd. Det. Lit, 1950), 103. Zoia reached
legendary status after the picture of her frozen, naked corpse, printed in

Pravda in January 1942, inspired retellings and commemorations of her sacrificial death in articles, textbook entries, drawings, posters, postage stamps, a bestselling novel by Sofia Zarechnaia (1942), and an eponymous feature-length film directed by Lev Arnshtam (1944). Illustrated postcards depicting Zoia's seizure by fascist soldiers were printed in mass quantities beginning in 1942 so that even in private correspondence to and from the front, Zoia reminded soldiers and their families of what was at stake in the war. For an example of a "Zoia letter," see A.A. Vinokurov and S.B. Tkachenko, *Voennaia tsenzura v SSSR 1941–53: 2-e izdanie, ispravlennoe i dopolnenoe* (Moscow: Izdatel'stvo "Ulei," 2012), 53.

5 Mayakovsky Is Marching with Us

1 These works include *What Is Good and What Is Bad* [*Chto takoe khorosho i chto takoe plokho*] (illustrated by N. Denisovskii, 1925); *Let's Stroll* [*Guliaem*] (illustrated by I. Sunderland, 1926); *This Little Book of Mine about the Sea and about the Lighthouse* [*Eta knizhechka moia pro moria i pro maiak*] (illustrated by B. Pokrovskii, 1927); *The Fire-Horse* [*Kon'-ogon'*] (illustrated by L. Popova, 1927); *No Page without an Elephant or a Lioness* [*Chto ni stranitsa, – to slon, to l'vitsa*] (illustrated by K. Zdanevich, 1928); *Read and Go to Paris and China* [*Prochti i katai, v Parizh i v Kitai*] (illustrated by P. Aliakrinskii, 1929); and *What Should I Be?* [*Kem byt'?*] (illustrated by N. Shifrin 1929).

2 These were "Let Us Take the New Rifles" ["Voz'mem vintovki novye"] (first published with musical score by K. Pokrasa in *Pionerskaia Pravda*, 1927); and "Little May Song" ["Maiskaia pesenka"] (published with musical score by G. Gnesina in *Ezh*, 1928).

3 In Pokrovskaia, *Osnovnye techeniia v detskoi literatura* (1927). See F. Ebin, *Maiakovskii – Detiam*, 2nd ed. (Moscow: Detgiz, 1989), 26.

4 The review appeared in a December 1925 issue of *Pechat' i revoliutsiia*. See Ebin, *Maiakovskii*, 25.

5 In 1926 these included *The Tale of Petia, Who Is Fat, and of Sima, Who Is Skinny*; *What Is Good and What Is Bad*; and *Let's Stroll*. See Ebin, *Maiakovskii*, 24.

6 Ebin, *Maiakovskii*, 24.

7 The first Mayakovsky book, *Detiam*, was published by Molodaia gvardiia in 1931 and illustrated by David Shterenberg, but as the previous list shows, publishing Mayakovsky *To Children* became a regular phenomenon from 1937.

8 Other Soviet authors published in collections for children included Aleksei Tolstoy, Samuil Marshak, and Arkady Gaidar in *Sovetskim detiam* (Moscow: Detgiz, 1942); and Kornei Chukovsky, *Detiam*, 2nd. ed. (Moscow: Iskusstvo, 1945). In other words, Mayakovsky was published for children

alongside, and in even greater frequency, than leading war-time authors and the most significant writers of children's literature from the 1920s.

9 Stephen Lovell, *Shadow of War: Russia and the USSR, 1941 to the Present* (Chichester, UK: Wiley-Blackwell, 2010), 4.

10 Lovell, 4.

11 M.A. Kornil'eva-Radina and E.P. Radin, *Novym detiam novye igry: Podvizhnye igry shkol'nogo i vneshkol'nogo vozrastov ot 7 do 18 let v refleksologicheskom i pedologicheskom osveshchenii* (Moscow: Izd-vo Narkomzdrava RSFSR, 1927), 151.

12 See for instance L. Gerkan, *Bud' gotov k trudu i oborone: Kak sdat' normy na znachok "BGTO"* (Moscow: Molodaia gvardiia, 1935).

13 "Let Us Take the New Rifles" was published in *Pionerskaia Pravda* on 4 February 1928 with a new score by K. Korchmarev; in *Pioner* on 12 June 1927; in *Bol'shevistkii molodniak* on 10 July 1927; in Mayakovsky *No. S [Novye Stiki]*, in 1928; in *Pionerskaia Pravda* on 6 July 1929 with the original music score by Pokrasa; and in the collection *Flazhki na shtykakh: Sbornik k oktiabriu* in 1930, with music score by E. Tarakhovskaia.

14 Kucherenko, *Little Soldiers*, 26, 75.

15 A.N. Balakirev, "Timurovtsy: Malen'kye volontery velikoi voiny," *Vestnik Buratskogo universiteta* 7 (2015): 19, accessed 10 June 2016, http://cyberleninka.ru.

16 See Kucherenko, *Little Soldiers*, 75.

17 Evgeny Dobrenko, "'The Entire Real World of Children': The School Tale and 'Our Happy Childhood,'" *Slavic and East European Literature* 49, no. 2 (Summer 2005): 232; and Balakirev, "Timurovtsy," 22.

18 O'Dell, *Socialisation through Children's Literature*, 195.

19 Balakirev, "Timurovtsy," 20, 22.

20 Balakirev, 20.

21 Kucherenko, *Little Soldiers*, 122–3.

22 Aleksandra Jakobson, "Konspekt vystuplenie A. Iakobson na obsuzhdenii vystavki detskoi knigi," quoted in G. Leont'eva, *Aleksandra Nikolaevna Iakobson* (Leningrad: Khudozhnik RSFSR, 1988), 48–9.

23 Pierre Nora, *Realms of Memory: Rethinking the French Past*, vol. 1, *Conflicts and Divisions*, trans. Arthur Goldhammer (New York: Columbia University Press, 1996), 15–16.

24 Lev Kassil, "Pro Maiakovskogo," in *Detiam*, ed. V. Maiakovskii (Moscow-Leningrad: Detgiz, 1941), 3.

25 Kassil, 4.

26 Lev Kassil, "Zhizn' stikha," in *Maiakovskii s nami*, by Vladimir Mayakovsky (Moscow: Detgiz, 1942), 4.

27 Kassil, "Zhizn' stikha," 5–6.

28　Kassil, "Zhizn' stikha," 5–6.

29　Kassil, "Pro Maiakovskogo," 6.

30　Kassil, "Pro Maiakovskogo," 6–7.

31　V.S. Matafonov, *Aleksei Fedorovich Matafonov* (Moscow: Izobrazitel'noe iskusstvo, 1981), 180–1.

32　S. Marshak, "Literatura detiam: O nasledstve i nasledstvennosti v detskoi literature," *Literaturnyi sovremennik*, no. 12 (1933): 196.

6 *Pochta*: Circulation, Delivery, Return

1　N. Purtsev, *Razvitie sviazi v SSSR* (Moscow: Izdatel'stvo "Sviaz'," 1967), 55.

2　Birgit Beumers, "Comforting Creatures in Children's Cartoons," in *Russian Children's Literature and Culture*, ed. Marina Balina and Larissa Rudova (New York: Routledge, 2008), 158.

3　The title has also been translated as *Military Mail* by Ben Hellman, in "Samuil Marshak, Yesterday and Today," which appears in Balina and Rudova, *Russian Children's Literature*.

4　In 1928 Zhitkov, known for his adventure stories, published a picture book called *Devchonki* (*Little Girls*), illustrated by Vera Ermolaeva, Zhitkov's own tribute to international co-operation, in which the little girls of the world decide to trade clothes and national costumes.

5　S. Marshak, *Sobranie sochinenii v 8-kh tomakh.* vol. 6. (Moscow: Khudozhestvennaia literatura, 1971), 330–1. Sara Pankenier Weld deals with illustrations in successive republications of *Mail* from the 1920s to the 1930s in her *Ecology of the Russian Avant-Garde Picturebook*.

6　Purtsev, *Razvitie sviazi v SSSR*, 46.

7　Purtsev, 74.

8　I.Ia. Levitas, *Filateliia shkol'nikam* (Moscow: Radio i sviaz', 1988), 71.

9　Levitas, 120.

10　Levitas, 65, 66.

11　Marshak, *Sobranie sochinenii v 8 tomakh*, 330–1.

12　This war-time sequel appeared serially in *Pionerskaia Pravda* in 1942 and in three separate book editions in 1943 before becoming the object of a scathing article by P. Iudin, "The Vulgar and Dangerous Concoction of K. Chukovsky," published on 1 March 1944 in *Pravda*. The story was not republished in its entirety until 2001. See Kornei Chukovsky, "Odoleem Barmaleia," in *Sobranie sochinenii v piatnadtsati tomakh*, vol. 1 (Moscow: Terra-Knizhnyi Klub, 2001), 454–90, 589.

13　Purtsev, *Razvitie sviazi v SSSR*, 230.

14　Purtsev, 232–4.

15　Purtsev, 239.

16 Purtsev, 241.

17 The Central Committee responded to these problems by disallowing the cancellation of mail transport for military or agricultural reasons, and also by allowing mail cars to be attached to military trains. See Purtsev, *Razvitie sviazi v SSSR*, 241.

18 G.G. Werbizky, *Ostarbeiter Mail in World War II: Documents and Correspondence* (Tenafly, NJ: Hermitage Publishers, 1996), 13.

19 Purtsev, *Razvitie sviazi v SSSR*, 241, 243.

20 S. Marshak, *Pochta voennaia* (Moscow: Gos. izd-vo detskoi literatury, 1944), 91.

21 Marshak, 95.

22 Marshak, 101.

23 Nikolai Tikhonov, *V te dni. Leningradskii al'bom*, ed. Risunki A. Pakhomova (Moscow-Leningrad: Detgiz, 1946), 26.

24 Tikhonov, 26; and Purtsev, *Razvitie sviazi v SSSR*, 243.

25 K. Filatova, "Vam pis'mo i telegramma," *Komsomol'skaia Pravda*, 23 April 1942, 2.

26 Balakirev, "Timurovtsy," 19. Timurite activity was absorbed by the state under Komsomol as of 1943.

27 "Our Timur Team," *Murzilka* 1–2 (1942): 17.

28 O'Dell, *Socialisation through Children's Literature*, 195.

29 Olga Kucherenko quotes the Aliger article and discusses the "ideological fusion of the front and the rear, exalted in children's literature," in *Little Soldiers*, 123.

30 Kucherenko, 97.

31 Oushakine, "Translating Communism for Children," 166.

32 A. Babushkina, "Vospitatel'noe znachenie klassicheskoi literatury," *Sredniaia Shkola* 5 (1939): 49.

Conclusion

1 Charles Temple, Evelyn Freeman, and Joy Moss, *Children's Books in Children's Hands: An Introduction to Their Literature* (Boston: Allyn & Bacon, 1998), 172.

2 Such author-artist collaborations include Marshak and Lebedev in *Ice Cream* (1925), *Circus* (1925), *Yesterday and Today* (1925), *The Poodle* (1925), *The Silly Little Mouse* (1925), and *Baggage* (1926); and Chukovsky and Konashevich in *Buzzing Fly* (1927), *Barabek* (1929), *What a Muddle* (1929), and *Telephone* (1934). For more on this see D.F. Fomin, "V.M. Konashevich i K.I. Chukovsky: K istorii tvorcheskikh vzaimootnoshenii," in *Russkoe iskusstvo XX vek, Issledovaniia i publikatsii*, ed. G.F. Kovalenko (Moscow: Nauka, 2009), 228–94.

3 James von Geldern, "Conclusion: Epic Revisionism and the Craft of a Soviet Public," in *Epic Revisionism: Russian History and Literature as Stalinist Propaganda*, ed. Kevin M.F. Platt and David Brandenberger (Madison: University of Wisconsin Press, 2006), 328.

4 Alice Dalgliesh, *First Experiences with Literature* (New York: Charles Scribner and Sons, 1932), 8–9.

5 Dalgliesh, 8–9.

6 Brandenberger, *National Bolshevism*, 5, 143.

7 Zohar Shavit, "On the Use of Books for Children in Creating the German National Myth," in *The Presence of the Past in Children's Literature*, ed. Ann Lawson Lucas (Westport, CT: Praeger, 2003), 124.

8 Shavit, 124.

9 Alexandra Boutros and Will Straw, eds., *Circulation and the City: Essays on Urban Culture* (Montreal and Kingston, ON: McGill-Queen's University Press, 2010), 3.

10 Marc Angenot, "Social Discourse Analysis: Outlines of a Research Project," *Yale Journal of Criticism* 17, no. 2 (Fall 2004): 212.

11 Benedict Anderson, *Imagined Communities: Reflections on the Origin and Spread of Nationalism*, rev. ed. (ACLS E-Book, 2006), 86, http://quod.lib .umich.edu.

12 Anderson, 6.

13 Anastasia Rogova, "How to Make Good Kids with Books: Post-Soviet Parenting and the Commodification of Children's Literature," *Soviet and Post-Soviet Review* 43 (2016): 257.

14 Rogova, 249, 258–9.

15 Rogova, 249, 258–9.

16 Rogova, 249, 258–9.

Bibliography

Abramovich, G.L., B. Brainina, and A. Egolin. *Russkaia literatura, uchebnik dliia 9-go klassa srednei shkoly: Chast' 2*. Moscow: Gos. Uchebno-pedagogicheskikh izdatel'stvo, 1938–9.

Abramovich, G.L., and F.M. Golovenchenko. *Russkaia literatura: Uchebnik dlia 8-go i 9-go klassa srednei shkoly*. Moscow: Gos. uchebno-pedagogicheskoe izd-vo, 1938–9.

– *Russkaia literatura: Uchebnik dlia 8-go klassa srednei shkoly*. Moscow: Gos. uchebno-pedagogicheskoe izd-vo, 1936.

Alekseeva, O. "Sovetskaia kniga – Moguchee sredstvo kommunisticheskogo vospitaniia detei." In *Nedelia detskoi knigi*, edited by S. Liubimov, 102–15. Moscow-Leningrad: Gos. Izd. Det. Lit, 1950.

Anderson, Benedict. *Imagined Communities: Reflections on the Origin and Spread of Nationalism*. Rev. ed. ACLS E-Book, 2006. http://quod.lib.umich.edu.

Andersson, Lennart. *Soviet Aircraft and Aviation, 1917–1941*. Annapolis, MD: Naval Institute Press, 1994.

Angenot, Marc. "Social Discourse Analysis: Outlines of a Research Project." *Yale Journal of Criticism* 17, no. 2 (Fall 2004): 199–215.

Arzamastseva, Irina. "Podvizhniki detskogo chteniia." *Detskie chteniia* 1 (2012): 12–42. Accessed 8 May 2017. http://detskie-chtenia.ru.

Ashwin, Sarah. "Gender, State and Society in Soviet and Post-Soviet Russia." In *Gender, State and Society in Soviet and Post-Soviet Russia*, edited by Sarah Ashwin, 1–29. London: Routledge, 2000.

Azadovskii, M.K. Predislovie [Introduction] to P.P. Ershov, *Konek-gorbunok*. Moscow: Academia, 1934.

– "Konek-Gorbunok." In *O Konke Gorbunke: Sbornik statei*. Leningrad, 1937.

Azadovskii, M.K., P.P. Gorlov, S.S. Danilov, and A.A. Briantsev. *O Konke Gorbunke: Sbornik statei*. Leningrad: Leningradskii teatr iunykh zritelei imeni A.A. Briantseva, 1937.

Babushkina, Antonina P. *Istoriia russkoi detskoi literatury*. Moscow: Gosuchpedizd, 1948.
– "Vospitatel'noe znachenie klassicheskoi literatury." *Sredniaia Shkola* 5 (1939): 49.
Bailes, Kendall E. "Technology and Legitimacy: Soviet Aviation and Stalinism in the 1930s." *Technology and Culture* 17, no. 2 (1976): 55–81.
Baker, David. *Flight and Flying: A Chronology*. New York: Facts on File, 1994.
Balakirev, A.N. "Timurovtsy: Malen'kye volontery velikoi voiny." *Vestnik Buratskogo universiteta* 7 (2015): 19–23. Accessed 10 June 2016. http://cyberleninka.ru.
Balina, Marina, Helena Goscilo, and M.N. Lipovetsky. *Politicizing Magic: An Anthology of Russian and Soviet Fairy Tales*. Evanston, IL: Northwestern University Press, 2005.
Balina, Marina, and Larissa Rudova, eds. *Russian Children's Literature and Culture*. New York: Routledge, 2008.
Barsova-Shestakova, N.M. "Aleksandr Sergeevich Pushkin: Zhizn' i tvorchestvo." In *Pushkinskie dni 1949*, edited by A.A. Zhokov. Moscow: Izd. Moskovskogo gorodskogo instituta u sovershenstvovaniia uchitelei, 1949.
Basov-Verkhoiantsev, S. *Konek-skakunok, russkaia skazka*. Berlin: Henrich Caspari, 1918.
Benua, Aleksandr, N.I. Aleksandrova, and D.S. Likhachev. *Moi vospominaniia v piati knigakh* [My memoirs in five books]. Moscow: Nauka, 1980.
Benua, Aleksandr, A.N. Savinov, and I.S. Zil'bershtein. *Aleksandr Benua razmyshliaet: Stat'i, pis'ma, vyskazivaniia*. Moscow: Sovetskii khudozhnik, 1968.
Beumers, Birgit. "Comforting Creatures in Children's Cartoons." In *Russian Children's Literature and Culture*, edited by Marina Balina and Larissa Rudova, 158–89. New York: Routledge, 2008.
Bird, Robert, ed. *Adventures in the Soviet Imaginary: Children's Books and Graphic Art*. Chicago: University of Chicago Library, 2011.
Blinov, Valerii. *Russkaia detskaia knizhka-kartinka, 1900–41*. Moscow: Iskusstvo XXI vek, 2005.
Bonnell, Victoria E. *Iconography of Power: Soviet Political Posters under Lenin and Stalin*. Berkeley: University of California Press, 1997.
Boutros, Alexandra, and Will Straw, eds. *Circulation and the City: Essays on Urban Culture*. Montreal and Kingston, ON: McGill-Queen's University Press, 2010.
Boym, Svetlana. *Common Places: Mythologies of Everyday Life in Russia*. Cambridge, MA: Harvard University Press, 1994.
Brandenberger, David. *National Bolshevism: Stalinist Mass Culture and the Formation of Modern Russian National Identity, 1931–1956*. Cambridge, MA: Harvard University Press, 2002.

Briantsev, A.A. "Iz zapisnoi knizhki rezhissera." In *O Konke Gorbunke: Sbornik statei*, edited by M.K. Azadovskii, P.P. Gorlov, S.S. Danilov, and A.A. Briantsev. Leningrad: Leningradskii teatr iunykh zritelei imeni A.A. Briantseva, 1937.

Brovkin, Vladimir N. *Russia after Lenin: Politics, Culture and Society, 1921–1929*. New York: Routledge, 1998.

Buckley, Mary. "The Untold Story of the Obshchestvennitsa of the 1930s." *Europe-Asia Studies* 48, no. 4 (June 1996): 569–86.

– *Puti razvitiia russkoi sovetskoi knizhnoi grafiki*. Moscow: Iskusstvo, 1955.

Carroll, Lewis. *Alice's Adventures in Wonderland*. London: Macmillan, 1865.

Central Committee of the CPSU. "Decree on the State Publishing House." In *The Bolshevik Revolution, 1917–1918: Documents and Materials*, edited by James Bunyan and H.H. Fisher, 595–6. Stanford and London: Stanford University Press, 1934.

Chukovsky, Kornei. *Barmalei*. Drawings by M. Dobuzhinskogo. Moscow: Raduga, 1925.

– *Diary, 1901–1969*. Edited by Victor Erlich. Translated by Michael Henry Heim. New Haven, CT: Yale University Press, 2005.

– *From Two to Five*. Berkeley: University of California Press, 1963.

– "Odoleem Barmaleia." In *Sobranie sochinenii v piatnadtsati tomakh*, vol. 1, 454–90. Moscow: Terra-Knizhnyi Klub, 2001.

Clark, Katerina. *The Soviet Novel: History as Ritual*. Chicago and London: University of Chicago Press, 1981.

Crago, Hugh. "What Is a Fairy Tale." In *Considering Children's Literature: A Reader*, edited by Teya Rosenberg and Wyile A. Schwenke, 162–78. Peterborough, ON: Broadview Press, 2008.

Dalgliesh, Alice. *First Experiences with Literature*. New York: Charles Scribner and Sons, 1932.

Danko, E. "Zadachi khudozhestvennogo oformleniia detskoi knigi." In *Detskaia literatura: Kriticheskii sbornik*, edited by Anatoly Lunacharskii, 196–219. Moscow: Khudozhestvennaia literature, 1931.

Dashkova, T. "Vizual'naia representatsiia zhenskogo tela v sovetskoi massovoi kul'ture 30-h godov." *Logos* 11/12, 1999. Accessed 28 November 2014. http://www.ruthenia.ru.

deGraffenried, Julie K. *Sacrificing Childhood: Children and the Soviet State in the Great Patriotic War*. Lawrence, KS: University Press of Kansas, 2014.

Dobrenko, Evgeny. "'The Entire Real World of Children': The School Tale and 'Our Happy Childhood.'" *Slavic and East European Literature* 49, no. 2 (Summer 2005): 225–48.

– *Formovka sovetskogo chitatelia*. St Petersburg, Russia: Akademicheskii proekt, 1997.

Dolinin, A.S., ed. *Dostoevsky, Stat'i i materialy*. St Petersburg, Russia: Mysl', 1922.

Dostoevskii, F.M. *Brat'ia Karamazovy, dliia srednego vozrast*. Riga, Latvia: N. Gudkov, 1928.

– *Malchiki. Iz romana "Brat'ia Karamazovy."* Bibliotechka shkol'nika. Moscow and Leningrad: Gosudarstvennoe izdatel'stvo detskoi literatury, 1947.

– *Povesti*. Leningrad: Khudozhestvennaia literatura, 1940.

– *Prestuplenie i nakazanie: Klassiki sredne shkole*. Petrograd, Russia: Izdatel'stvo "Blago," 1923.

– *Prestuplenie i nakazanie: Roman v 6 chastiakh s epilogom; Shkol'naia seriia klassikov*. Moscow: Gosudarstvennoe izdatel'stvo detskoi literatury, 1934.

– *Russkim detiam iz sochinenii F.M. Dostoevskogo*. St Petersburg, Russia: Tipografiia Oresta Millera, 1883.

– *Zapiski iz mertvogo doma: Shkol'naia seriia klassikov*. Leningrad: Izdatel'stvo detskoi literatury, 1935.

Dul'skii, P. *Sovremennaia illiustratsiia v detskoi knige*. Kazan, Russia: Tipo-lit. Imperatorskago universiteta, 1916.

Dunstan, John. *Soviet Schooling in the Second World War*. New York: St Martin's Press, 1997.

Ebin, F. *Maiakovskii – Detiam*. Moscow: Detgiz, 1961. 2nd ed., Moscow: Detgiz, 1989.

Ermilov, V.V. *Protiv reaktsionnykh idei v tvorchestve F.M. Dostoevskogo*. Moscow: Izdatel'stvo "Pravda," 1948.

Ershov, P.P., A.N. Tikhonov, M.K. Azadovskii, and N. Rozenfel'd. *Konek-gorbunok*. Moscow: Academia, 1934.

Fitzpatrick, Sheila. *Stalin's Peasants: Resistance and Survival in the Russian Village after Collectivization*. New York: Oxford University Press, 1994.

Florinskii, S.M. *Russkaia literatura: Uchebnik dlia VIII-go klassa srednei shkoly*. Moscow: Gosudarstvennoe uchebno-pedagogicheskoe izdatel'stvo, 1959.

Fomin, D.F. "V.M. Konashevich i K.I. Chukovsky: K istorii tvorcheskikh vzaimootnoshenii." In *Russkoe iskusstvo XX vek, Issledovaniia i publikatsii*, edited by G.F. Kovalenko, 228–94. Moscow: Nauka, 2009.

Friedberg, Maurice. *Russian Classics in Soviet Jackets*. New York: Columbia University Press, 1962.

Gaidar, Arkady. "Frontovye zapisi." In *Sobranie sochinenii v cheterekh tomakh*, vol. 3, 285–319. Moscow: Izdatetl'stvo "Detskaia literatura," 1964.

– *Timur and His Gang*. Translated by Zina Voynow. Illustrated by Zhenya Gay. New York: Charles Scribner's Sons, 1943.

–"V Dobryi put'!" In *Sobranie sochinenii v cheterekh tomakh*, vol. 3, 302–4. Moscow: Izdatetl'stvo "Detskaia literatura," 1964.

– *Voennaia taina*. Drawings by D. Shmarinova. Moscow-Leningrad: Izdatel'stvo detskoi literatury, 1936.

- "Voina i deti." In *Sobranie sochinenii v cheterekh tomakh*, vol. 3, 305–12. Moscow: Izdatetl'stvo "Detskaia literatura," 1964.

Gankina, E. *Khudozhnik v sovremennoi detskoi knige.* Moscow: Sovetskii khudozhnik, 1977.

- *Russkie khudozhniki detskoi knigi.* Moscow: Sovetskii khudozhnik, 1963.

Gérin, Annie. *Godless at the Workbench: Soviet Illustrated Humoristic Antireligious Propaganda.* Regina, SK: Dunlop Art Gallery, 2003.

Gerkan, L. *Bud' gotov k trudu i oborone: Kak sdat' normy na znachok "BGTO."* Moscow: Molodaia gvardiia, 1935.

Gor'kii, Maksim. *M. Gor'kii i sovetskaia pechat'.* Moscow: izd-vo "Nauka," 1964.

- *O detskoi literatura: Stat'i i vyskazyvaniia.* Moscow: Detskaia Literatura, 1958.

Gorky, Maxim. "Address Delivered to the First All-Union Congress of Soviet Writers." In *On Literature, Selected Articles,* translated by V. Dober. Moscow: Foreign Languages Publishing House, 1950.

Gornfeld, A.G. "P.P. Ershov i ego skazka." In *Konek-gorbunok,* edited by P.P. Ershov, 6–14. Moscow-Leningrad: Gosizdat, 1929.

Gusakova, A.G., A.N. Dubovnikov, and A.A. Ozerova. *Russkaia literatura XIX veka, uchebnik dliia pedagogicheskikh uchilishch.* Moscow: Gos. Uchebno-pedagogicheskoe izdatel'stvo Narkomprosa RSFSR, 1938.

Haney, Jack V. *An Introduction to the Russian Folktale.* Armonk, NY: M.E. Sharpe, 1999.

Hearn, Michael P. *From the Silver Age to Stalin: Russian Children's Book Illustration in the Sasha Lurye Collection; The Picture Book Revolution.* Amherst, MA: Eric Carle Museum of Picture Book Art, 2003.

Hellman, Ben. "Detskaia literatura kak oruzhie: Tvorcheskii put' L. Kormchego." In *"Ubit' Charskuiu …": Paradoksy sovet- skoi literatury dlia detei, 1920–1930– e gg.,* edited by Marina Balina and Valerii V'iugin, 20–45. St Petersburg, Russia: Aleteiia, 2013.

- *Fairy Tales and True Stories. The History of Russian Literature for Children and Young People (1574–2010).* Leiden, Netherlands: Brill, 2013.

Iakobson [Jakobson], Aleksandra. "Konspekt vystuplenie A. Iakobson na obsuzhdenii vystavki detskoi knigi." In *Aleksandra Nikolaevna Iakobson,* by G. Leont'eva, 48–9. Leningrad: Khudozhnik RSFSR, 1988.

Issoupova, Olga. "From Duty to Pleasure? Motherhood in Soviet and Post-Soviet Russia." In *Gender, State and Society in Soviet and Post-Soviet Russia,* edited by Sarah Ashwin, 30–54. London: Routledge, 2000.

Johnson, Emily D. *How St. Petersburg Learned to Study Itself: The Russian Idea of Kraevedenie.* University Park, PA: Pennsylvania State University Press, 2006.

Kaiev, A.A. *Russkaia literatura: Uchebnik dlia uchitel'skikh institutov; Chast' pervaia; Fol'klor, Drevnerusskaia literatura, Literatura XVIII veka.* Moscow: Gos. Uchebno-pedagog. izd-vo, 1949.

Kassil', Lev. "Gaidar. Vstupitel'naia stat'ia." In *Sobranie sochinenii v cheterekh tomakh*, edited by Arkady Gaidar, 5–35. Moscow: Izdatetl'stvo "Detskaia literatura," 1964.

– "Pro Maiakovskogo." In *Detiam*, edited by V. Maiakovskii, 3–6. Moscow-Leningrad: Detgiz, 1941.

– "Zhizn' stikha." In *Maiakovskii s nami, 4*, by V. Mayakovsky. Moscow-Leningrad: Detgiz, 1942.

Kelly, Catriona. *Children's World: Growing Up in Russia, 1890–1991*. New Haven, CT: Yale University Press, 2007.

Kirschenbaum, Lisa A. "Innocent Victims and Heroic Defenders: Children and the Siege of Leningrad." In *Children and War*, edited by James Marten, 279–90. New York: New York University Press, 2002.

– *The Legacy of the Siege of Leningrad, 1941–1995: Myth, Memories, and Monuments*. New York: Cambridge University Press, 2006.

– *Small Comrades: Revolutionizing Childhood in Soviet Russia, 1917–32*. New York: Routledge Falmer, 2000.

Kogan, D. *M.A. Vrubel'*. Moscow: Iskusstvo, 1980.

Kolokolt'sev, N.V., and V.V. Litvinov. *Russkaia literatura, uchebnik dlia 2 klassa pedagogicheskikh uchilishch*. Moscow: Gosudarstvennoe uchebno-pedagogicheskoe izdatel'stvo Ministerstva RSFSR, 1946.

– *Russkaia literatura, uchebnik dlia 3 kursa pedagogicheskikh uchilishch*. Moscow: Gosudarstvennoe uchebno-pedagogicheskoe izdatel'stvo Ministerstva Prosveshcheniia RSFSR, 1959.

Kon, L. "Novinki Detgiza (Rekomendatel'nyi obzor)." In *Nedelia detskoi knigi*, edited by S. Liubimov, 143–56. Moscow: Gos. Izd-vo Detskoi lit-ry, 1950.

Kornil'eva-Radina, M.A., and E.P. Radin. *Novym detiam novye igry: Podvizhnye igry shkol'nogo i vneshkol'nogo vozrastov ot 7 do 18 let v refleksologicheskom i pedologicheskom osveshchenii*. Moscow: Izd-vo Narkomzdrava RSFSR, 1927.

Kozlov, Denis. *The Readers of Novyi Mir: Coming to Terms with the Stalinist Past*. Cambridge, MA: Harvard University Press, 2013.

Kraevskii, P.D., V.V. Litvinov, V.I. Mashtakov, and A.K. Kazanskaia. *Russkaia literatura, chast' vtoraia, uchebnik-khrestomatiia dliia IX klassov nerusskikh shkol*. Moscow: Gosudarstvennoe uchebno-pedagogicheskoe izdatel'stvo ministerstva prosveshcheniia RSFSR, 1950.

Kruchina, Andrei. *Konek-letunok, Aero-skazka*. Nikolaevsk, Russia: Izd. O.D.V.F., 1925.

Krupskaia, N.K. *O kommunisticheskom vospitanii*. Moscow: Molodaia gvardiia, 1956.

– *On Education, Selected Articles and Speeches*. Moscow: Foreign Languages Publishing House, 1957.

Krupskaya, Nadezhda K., and N.B. Medvedeva. *N.K. Krupskaia o detskoi literatura i detskom chtenii: Izbrannoe*. Moscow: Detskaia literatura, 1979.

Kucherenko, Olga. *Little Soldiers: How Soviet Children Went to War, 1941–1945.* Oxford: Oxford University Press, 2011.

Kudriavtseva, O.A. *Zhizn' i tvorchestvo A.S. Pushkina: Materialy dlia vystavki v shkole i detskoi biblioteke k 150- letiiu so dnia rozhdeniia poeta.* Moscow: Gos izd-vo Detskoi lit-ry, 1949.

Kuleshov, E., and I. Antipova, eds. *Detskii sbornik: Stat'ii po detskoi literatura i antropologii detstva.* Moscow: Ob'edinennoe gumanitarnoe izdatel'stvo, 2003.

Kupreianova, E.N. *Roman L.N. Tolstogo "Anna Karenina."* Tula, Russia: Oblastnoe knizhnoe izdatel'stvo, 1953.

Lenin, V.I. *Articles on Tolstoy.* Amsterdam: Fredonia Books, 1951.

– *Stat'i o Tolstom.* Moscow: Gos. izd.-vo "Khudozhestvennaia literatura," 1939.

Levitas, I. *Filateliia shkol'nikam.* Moscow: Radio i sviaz', 1988.

Levitt, Marcus C. *Russian Literary Politics and the Pushkin Celebration of 1880.* Ithaca, NY: Cornell University Press, 1989.

Lipovetsky, Mark. "Fairy Tales in Critique of Soviet Culture." In *Politicizing Magic: An Anthology of Russian and Soviet Fairy Tales,* edited by Marina Balina, Helen Goscilo, and M.N. Lipovetsky, 233–50. Evanston, IL: Northwestern University Press, 2005.

Livschiz, Ann. "Children's Lives after Zoia's Death: Order, Emotions and Heroism in Children's Lives and Literature in the Post-War Soviet Union." In *Late Stalinist Russia: Society between Reconstruction and Reinvention,* edited by Juliane Fürst, 192–208. Abingdon, UK: Routledge, 2006.

– "Growing Up Soviet: Childhood in the Soviet Union, 1918–1958." PhD diss., Stanford University, 2007.

Lovell, Stephen. *The Shadow of War: Russia and the USSR, 1941 to the Present.* Chichester, UK: Wiley-Blackwell, 2010.

Lunacharskii, A.V., ed. *Detskaia literatura: Kriticheskii sbornik.* Moscow: Khudozhestvennaia literature, 1931.

– "Dostoevskii kak khodozhnik i myslitel'." In *Biblioteka pisatelei dlia shkoly i iunoshestva,* edited by E.F. Nikitina and F.M. Dostoevskii. Moscow: Kooperativnoe izdatel'stvo pisatelei "Nikitinskoe subbotniki," 1928 (repub. 1929).

– Introduction to *Anna Karenina,* by Leo Tolstoy. Translated by Constance Garnett. Edited by Leo Tolstoy, Bernard Guilbert Guerney, and Gustavus Spett. Moscow: State Publishing House for Fiction and Poetry, 1933.

MacPike, Loralee. "The Fallen Woman's Sexuality." In *Sexuality and Victorian Literature,* edited by Don Richard Cox, 54–71. Knoxville: University of Tennessee Press, 1984.

Maddox, Steven. "Healing the Wounds: Commemorations, Myths, and the Restoration of Leningrad's Imperial Heritage, 1941–50." PhD diss., University of Toronto, 2008.

Maiakovskii, V.V. *Detiam*. Drawings by A.E. Gubin. Rostov-on-Don, Russia: Rostizdat, 1946.

– *Detiam*. Drawings by A. Pakhomov. Moscow and Leningrad: Gos. Izd-vo detskoi literatury, 1949.

– *Dliia golosa*. Berlin: Gos. izd-vo RSFSR, 1923.

– *Voz'mem vintovki novye*. Illustrations by A. Jakobson. Moscow: Detizdat, 1941.

– *Voz'mem vintovki novye*. Illustrations by A. Jakobson. Moscow and Leningrad: Izd-vo i 2-ia f-ka det. knigi Detgiza, 1945, 1946.

Marshak, Samuil. "Literatura detiam: O nasledstve i nasledstvennosti v detskoi literature." *Literaturnyi sovremennik*, no. 12 (1933): 196.

– *Pochta* [Mail]. Leningrad and Moscow: Raduga, 1927.

– *Pochta voennaia* [War-Time Mail]. Moscow: Gos. izd-vo detskoi literatury, 1944.

– *Sobranie sochinenii v 8-kh tomakh*. Vol. 6. Moscow: Khudozhestvennaia literatura, 1971.

– "Za bol'shuiu detskuiu literature." *Komsomol'skaia Pravda*, 22 January 1936.

Matafonov, V.S. *Aleksei Fedorovich Pakhomov*. Moscow: Izobrazitel'noe iskusstvo, 1981.

Mayakovsky, Vladimir. *Polnoe sobranie sochinenii*. Moscow: Gosudarstvennoe izdatel'stvo khudozhestvennoi literatury, 1955.

McCannon, John. *Red Arctic: Polar Exploration and the Myth of the North in the Soviet Union, 1932–1939*. New York: Oxford University Press, 1998.

Miller, Frank J. *Folklore for Stalin: Russian Folklore and Pseudofolklore of the Stalin Era*. Armonk, NY: M.E. Sharpe, 1990.

Murav'eva, O.S. "Obraz Pushkina: Istoricheskie metamorfozy." In *Legendy i mify o Pushkine*, edited by M.N. Virolainen. St Petersburg, Russia: Gumanitarnoe agentstvo "Akademicheskii Proekt," 1994.

Nemirovich-Danchenko, Vladimir Ivanovich. *Anna Karenina v postanovke Moskovskogo Ordena Lenina Khudozhestvennogo Akademicheskogo Teatra Soiuza SSR im. M. Gorkogo*. Moscow: Izdanie MKhaT, 1938.

Noever, Peter, ed. *Schili-byli=shili-byli: Russische Kinderbücher, 1920–1940*. Vienna: Schlebrügge, 2004.

Nora, Pierre. *Realms of Memory: Rethinking the French Past*. Translated by Arthur Goldhammer. Vol. 1, *Conflicts and Divisions*. New York: Columbia University Press, 1996.

Norris, Stephen M. *A War of Images: Russian Popular Prints, Wartime Culture, and National Identity*. DeKalb, IL: Northern Illinois University Press, 2006.

O'Dell, Felicity Ann. *Socialisation through Children's Literature: The Soviet Example*. Cambridge: Cambridge University Press, 1978.

"O gosudarstvennom izdatel'stve." In *Vtoroi vserossiiskii s"ezd Sovetov rabochikh i soldatskikh deputatov: Sbornik dokumentov* [Second All-Russian Congress of

the Soviets of Workers' and Soldiers' Deputees: A collection of documents],
ed. D.A. Chugaev, L.I. Terent'eva, P.I. Anisimova, and A.F. Butenko, 243–4.
Moscow: Gos. izd-vo polit. lit-ry, 1957.

Oinas, Felix J. "The Political Uses and Themes of Folklore in the Soviet
Union." In *Folklore, Nationalism, and Politics*, edited by Felix J. Oinas, 157–75.
Columbus, OH: Slavica Publishers, 1978.

Olich, Jacqueline M. "Competing Ideologies and Children's Books: The
Making of a Soviet Children's Literature, 1918–1935." PhD diss., University
of North Carolina, Chapel Hill, 1999.

Ospovat, A.L., and R.D. Timenchik. "Istoriia odnogo izdaniia." In *Pechal'nu
povest' sokhranit'*, 215–55. Moscow: Kniga, 1987.

Oushakine, Sergei. "Translating Communism for Children: Fables and
Posters of the Revolution." *Boundary 2* 43, no. 3 (August 2016): 159–219.

Overton, Bill. "Children and Childlessness in the Novel of Female Adultery."
Modern Language Review, no. 2 (1999): 314–27.

Peris, Daniel. "The 1929 Congress of the Godless." In *The Stalin Years: A
Reader*, edited by Christopher Read. Basingstoke, UK: Palgrave Macmillan,
2003.

Petrone, Karen. *Life Has Become More Joyous, Comrades: Celebrations in the Time
of Stalin*. Bloomington: Indiana University Press, 2000.

Platt, Kevin M.F., and David Brandenberger, eds. *Epic Revisionism: Russian
History and Literature as Stalinist Propaganda*. Madison: University of
Wisconsin Press, 2006.

Pletneva, Tatiana. "Razgovory s chitateliami o materinstve." *Zhenskii zhurnal*,
no. 6 (1927): 11–12.

Pokrovskaia, A. "Kak rasskazat' detiam." *Zhenskii zhurnal*, no. 1 (1929): 5.

– *Osnovnye techeniia v sovremennoi detskoi literatura*. Moscow: Rabotnik
prosveshcheniia, 1927.

Pospelov, N., and P. Shabliovskii. *Russkaia literatura: Uchebnik dlia VIII klassa
sredenei shkoly*. Moscow: Gosudarstvennoe uchebno-pedagogicheskoe
izdatel'stvo Narkomprosa RSFSR, 1940.

Pospelov, N., P. Shabliovskii, and A. Zerchaninov. *Russkaia literatura, uchebnik
dlia VIII klassa srednei shkoly*. Moscow: Gosudarstvennoe uchebno-
pedagogicheskoe izdatel'stvo Ministerstva prosveshcheniia RSFSR, 1948.

– *Russkaia literatura, uchebnik dlia VIII klassa srednei shkoly. Izdanie sed'moe*.
Moscow: Gosuchpedizdat, 1947.

Propp, V. *The Russian Folktale by Vladimir Yakovlevich Propp*. Edited and translated
by Sibelan Forrester. Detroit, MI: Wayne State University Press, 2012.

Purtsev, N. *Razvitie sviazi v SSSR*. Moscow: Izdatel'stvo "Sviaz'," 1967.

Pushkin, A.S. *Mednyi vsadnik* [The Bronze Horseman]. Illustrated by
Aleksandra Benua. Engraving on wood in colour by A.P. Ostoumovoi. *Mir
iskusstva* 11 (1904): 1–40.

– Skazka o kuptse Kuz'me Ostolope i rabotnike ego Balde. Kiev: T.A. Gubanov, 1899.

– *Skazka o pope Ostolope i rabotnike ego Balde: Dem'ian Bednyi, Skazka o Batrake Balde i o strashnom sude.* Moscow: Gosudarstvennoe izdatel'stvo, 1919.

– *Sobranie sochinenii dlia detei: Besplatnoe prilozhenie k zhurnalu "Zhavoronok."* St Petersburg: T-vo khudozh. pechati, 1913.

Pushkin, A.S., ed. *Skazka o pope i o rabotnike ego Balde: Balet v 4 aktakh. Musika M. Chulaki.* Leningrad: Leningradskii gos. Akademicheskii Malyi opernyi teatr, 1940.

Pushkin, A., M. Lermontov, and V. Zhukovskii. *Skazki russkikh pisatelei dlia detei: Sbornik redaktsii gazety Kievskoe slovo.* Kiev and Kharkov, Ukraine: F.A. Ioganson, 1894.

Putintsev, A.M. "Skazka P.P. Ershova 'Konek-Gorbunok' i ee istochniki." *Trudy Voronezhskogo universiteta,* 1925, 341. Voronezh, Russia: Izd-vo Voronezhskogo universiteta, 1925.

Raymond, Boris. *Krupskaia and Soviet Russian Librarianship, 1917–1939.* Metuchen, NJ, and London: Scarecrow Press, 1979.

Reid, Susan E. "All Stalin's Women: Gender and Power in Soviet Art of the 1930s." *Slavic Review* 57, no. 1 (Spring 1998): 133–73.

Riordan, James. *Soviet Sport: Background to the Olympics.* London: Basil Blackwell, 1980.

– "Sport in Soviet Society: Fetish or Free Play." In *Home, School and Leisure in the Soviet Union,* edited by Jenny Brine, Maureen Perrie, and Andrew Sutton, 215–38. London: George Allen & Unwin, 1980.

Rogova, Anastasia. "How to Make Good Kids with Books: Post-Soviet Parenting and the Commodification of Children's Literature." *Soviet and Post-Soviet Review* 43 (2016): 243–61.

Rothenstein, Julian, and Olga Budashevskaya, eds. *Inside the Rainbow: Russian Children's Literature, 1920–1935; Beautiful Books, Terrible Times.* London: Redstone Press, 2013.

Rowley, Alison. *Open Letters: Russian Popular Culture and the Picture Postcard, 1880–1922.* Toronto: University of Toronto Press, 2013.

Sakhnovsky, V.G. "Rabota nad spektaklem 'Anna Karenina.'" In *Anna Karenina v postanovke Moskovskogo Ordena Lenina Khudozhestvennogo Akademicheskogo Teatra Soiuza SSR im. M. Gorkogo,* edited by Vladimir Ivanovich Nemirovich-Danchenko, 35–176. Moscow: Izdanie MKhaT, 1938.

Sandler, Stephanie. *Commemorating Pushkin: Russia's Myth of a National Poet.* Stanford, CA: Stanford University Press, 2004.

Semenikhin, Vladimir. *Kniga dlia detei 1881–1939: Detskaia illiustrirovannaia kniga v istorii Rossii 1881–1939: Iz kollektsii Aleksandra Lur'e.* Moscow: Ulei, 2009.

Shavit, Zohar. "On the Use of Books for Children in Creating the German National Myth." In *The Presence of the Past in Children's Literature*, edited by Ann Lawson Lucas, 123–32. Westport, CT: Praeger, 2003.

Shturman, Dora. *The Soviet Secondary School*. Translated by Philippa Shimrat. London: Routledge, 1988.

Shul'gin, V., ed. *Deti i Oktiabr'skaia revoliutsiia: Ideologiia sovetskogo shkol'nika*. Moscow: Rabotnik prosvescheniia, 1928.

Smirnov, Nikolai. *Dlia chego Krasnaia Armiia* [What is the Red Army for]. Illustrated by Olga and Galina Chichagova. Moscow: Molodaia gvardiia, 1926.

Smirnov, S.A. "O podgotovke i provedenii v shkolakh g. Moskvy 150-letiia so dnia rozhdeniia A.S. Pushkina." In *Pushkinskie dni 1949*, edited by A.A. Zhokov, E.I. Velichkovskii, and M.I. Voronkov, 133–5. Moscow: Izd. Moskovskogo gorodskogo instituta usovershenstvovaniia uchitelei, 1949.

Sokol, Elena. *Russian Poetry for Children*. Knoxville: University of Tennessee Press, 1984.

Sokolianskii, I., A. Popov, and A. Zaluzhnyi, eds. *My protiv skazki*. Kharkov, Ukraine: n.p., 1928.

Sorkina, D.L. *Dostoevskii v shkole*. Tomsk, Russia: Izd-vo Tomskogo univ., 1969.

Stachakov, A. Predislovie [Introduction] to L.N. Tolstoy, *Anna Karenina*, iii–xx. Moscow-Leningrad: Gosizdat, 1928.

Startsev, I. *Detskaia literatura za gody Velikoi Otechestvennoi voiny, 1941–45*. Moscow: Gos. Izd.-vo detskoi literatury, 1947.

Steiner, Evgeny. "Mirror Images: On Soviet-Western Reflections in Children's Books of the 1920s and 1930s." In *Children's Literature and the Avant-Garde*, edited by Elina Druker, 189–213. Amsterdam: John Benjamins, 2015.

– *Stories for Little Comrades: Revolutionary Artists and the Making of Early Soviet Children's Books*. Seattle: University of Washington Press, 1999.

Swift, Megan. "The Bronze Horseman Rides Again: The Stalinist Reimaging of Alexander Pushkin's *Mednyi vsadnik*, 1928–53." *Russian Review* 72, no. 1 (January 2013): 24–44.

– "The Petersburg Sublime: Alexander Benois and the Bronze Horseman Series (1903–22)." *Germano-Slavica* 17 (2009): 3–24.

– "The Poet, the Peasant, and the Nation: Aleksandr Pushkin's 'Skazka o pope i o rabotnike ego Balde' (1830) in Illustrated Editions, 1917–1953." *Russian Literature* 87–9 (Jan.–Apr. 2017): 123–46.

Temple, Charles, Evelyn Freeman, and Joy Moss. *Children's Books in Children's Hands: An Introduction to Their Literature*. Boston: Allyn & Bacon, 1998.

Tikhonov, Nikolai. *V te dni: Leningradskii al'bom*. Edited by Risunki A. Pakhomova. Moscow-Leningrad: Detgiz, 1946.

Tret'iakov, S. "Novyi Lev Tolstoy." In *Literatura fakta, pervyi sbornik materialov rabotnikov LEFa*, edited by N.F. Chuzhak, 29–33. Moscow: Zakharov, 2000.

Trifonov, Nikolai, and N.I. Kudriashev. *Russkaia sovietskaia literatura: Uchebnik dlia X klassa nerusskoi srednei shkoly.* Moscow: Gos. Uchebno-pedagog. Izd-vo, 1956.

Tseitlin, A.G. *Russkaia literatura pervoi polovini XIX veka: Uchebnik dlia vysshchikh uchebnikh zavedenii.* Moscow: Gos. Ucheb-ped. Idz-vo Narkomprosa RSFSR, 1940.

Utkov, Viktor. "Tvorchestvo Petra Pavlovicha Ershova, vstupitel'noe slovo i kommentarii." In P. P. Ershov, *Sochineniia.* Omsk, Russia: Omskoe oblastnoe gosudarstvennoe izd-vo, 1950.

Uziel, Daniel. "Wehrmacht Propaganda Troops and the Jews." *Yad Vashem Studies* 29 (2001): 27–65. William Templer Shoah Resource Centre, the International School for Holocaust Studies. Accessed 8 January 2013. http://www1.yadvashem.org.

Vainkop, Iu.A. "M.I. Chulaki i ego balet 'Skazka o pope i rabotnike ego Balde.'" In *Skuzka o pope i o rabotnike ego Balde: Balet v 4 aktakh; Musika M. Chulaki,* edited by Aleksandr Sergeevich Pushkin, 33–43. Leningrad: Leningradskii gos. Akademicheskii Malyi opernyi teatr, 1940.

Vinokurov, A.A., and S.B. Tkachenko. *Voennaia tsenzura v SSSR 1941–53: 2-e izdanie, ispravlennoe i dopolnenoe.* Moscow: Izdatel'stvo "Ulei," 2012.

Waters, Elizabeth. "The Modernization of Russian Motherhood, 1917–37." In *The Stalin Years: A Reader,* edited by Christopher Read. Houndmills, UK: Palgrave Macmillan, 2003.

Weld, Sara Pankenier. *An Ecology of the Russian Avant-Garde Picturebook.* Amsterdam: John Benjamins Publishing, 2018.

– *Voiceless Vanguard: The Infantilist Aesthetic of the Russian Avant-Garde.* Evanston, IL: Northwestern University Press, 2014.

Werbizky, G.G. *Ostarbeiter Mail in World War II: Documents and Correspondence.* Tenafly, NJ: Hermitage Publishers, 1996.

Wilson, Anne. *The Magical Quest: The Use of Magic in Arthurian Romance.* Manchester, UK: Manchester University Press, 1988.

– *Magical Thought in Creative Writing: The Distinctive Roles of Fantasy and Imagination in Fiction.* South Woodchester and Stroud, UK: Thimble Press, 1983.

– *Plots and Powers: Magical Structures in Medieval Narrative.* Gainesville: University Press of Florida, 2001.

– *Traditional Romance and Tale: How Stories Mean.* Ipswich, UK: Brewer, 1976.

Wolfe, Bertram. "Krupskaya Purges the People's Libraries." *Survey* no. 72 (1969): 152–3.

Yaroslavtsev, A.K. *P.P. Ershov, Avtor skazki Konek-gorbunok: Biograficheskie vospominaniia universitetskogo tovarishcha ego A.K. Iaroslavtsova.* St Petersburg, Russia: Tip. V. Demakova, 1872.

Zerchaninov, A., and N.G. Porfiridov. *Russkaia literatura: Uchebnik dlia I klassa pedagogicheskikh uchilishch*. Moscow: Gosudarstvennoe uchebno-pedagogicheskoe izdatel'stvo ministersvtva prosveshchenii RSFSR, 1946.

– *Russkaia literatura, uchebnik dlia 1 kursa pedagogicheskikh uchilishch*. Moscow: Gosudarstvennoe uchebno-pedagogicheskoe izdatel'stvo, 1953.

Zerchaninov, A., N.G. Porfirdov, and N.L. Brodskii. *Russkaia literatura, uchebnik dlia 1 klassa pedagogicheskikh uchilishch*. Moscow: Gosudarstvennoe uchebno-pedagogicheskoe izdatel'stvo Ministerstva prosveshcheniia RSFSR, 1946.

Zerchaninov, A., D.Ia. Raikhin, and V.I. Strazhev. *Russkaia literatura, uchebnik dliia IX klassa srednei shkoly*. Moscow: Gosudarstvennoe uchebno-pedagogicheskoe izdatel'stvo Narkomprosa RSFSR, 1940; 1947; 1948.

– *Russkaia literatura, uchebnik dliia IX klassa srednei shkoly*. Moscow: Gosudarstvennoe uchebno-pedagogicheskoe izdatel'stvo Ministerstva Prosveshcheniia RSFSR, 1948.

– *Russkaia literatura, uchebnik dliia IX klassa srednei shkoly*. Moscow: Gos. Uch-ped Izd. Ministerstva RSFSR, 1949.

– *Russkaia literatura, uchebnik dliia IX klassa srednei shkoly*. Moscow: Gos. Uchebno-pedagogicheskoe izdatel'stvo Ministerstva Prosveshcheniia RSFSR, 1950.

Zhelanskii, A. *Skazki Pushkina v narodnom stile: Balda; Medvedikha; O rybake i rybke; Opyt issledovaniia po rukopisiam poeta s dvumia fotosnimkami*. Moscow: Gosudarstvennoe izdatel'stvo "Khudozhestvennaia literatura," 1936.

Zinoviev, N.M. *Iskusstvo Palekha*. Leningrad: Khudozhnik RSFSR, 1975.

Zipes, Jack. *Fairy Tales and the Art of Subversion: The Classical Genre for Children and the Process of Civilization*. London: Heinemann, 1983.

Index